YOUR DOWN'S
SYNDROME CHILD

YOUR DOWN'S SYNDROME CHILD

Everything Today's Parents Need to Know About Raising Their Special Child

Eunice McClurg

DOUBLEDAY & COMPANY, INC.
GARDEN CITY, NEW YORK   1986

Library of Congress Cataloging-in-Publication Data

McClurg, Eunice, 1923–
    Your Down's syndrome child.

    Includes index.
    1. Down's syndrome—Popular works. 2. Mentally handicapped children—Care and
hygiene. 3. Child rearing. I. Title. [DNLM: 1. Down's Syndrome—popular works. WS
107 M478y]
RJ506.D68M39 1986   649'.1528   85-31098
ISBN 0-385-23023-0

This book is dedicated to my daughter, Peggy,
and my son-in-law, Bill, for their encouragement
and especially to my granddaughter, Cindy,
for her consistent enthusiasm and support.

Acknowledgments

The material in this book stems from twenty years of working with parents of Down's syndrome children. During this time, these extraordinary people allowed me to learn firsthand how they coped with a trying situation and survived. From them I learned and received much more than I could give. Without their encouragement, support, and assistance, this book never would have been written.

Over the years I have met and worked with so many of these courageous parents that it is impossible to personally acknowledge all of them. Yet there are families to whom I am especially grateful for sharing their triumphs, their trials, their fears, and their hopes. To these families I extend my heartfelt thanks: John Adams, Arnell Beckman, Richard Boje, Scott Bronson, Pat Colbert, Tony DeLuca, John Hinz, Steve Hudak, Bob Johnson, Ron Johnson, Dan Koch, Jeff Levy, Merlyn Mellem, Pat O'Donnell, Ken Ottum, Dan Rittle, Carolyn Wilk, and Gwen Williard.

In addition, I would like to express my appreciation to Dr. Don Bartlett and Mary Zagaros for their special friendship and encouragement.

I am likewise indebted to Mrs. Muriel Humphrey Brown, Dr. Allen Abeson, Representative Gerry Sikorski, Dr. Elizabeth Boggs, Dave Powell, and Senator Gene Merriam for their support and suggestions.

My sincere thanks go also to Anne Sweeney, my editor, and Scott Edelstein, my agent, who believed in and understood the need for this book.

Contents

Introduction

If you are like most parents, you have looked forward to having a perfect, healthy baby. Now the long wait is over. The miracle of birth is done. Yet your world is not radiating with pride and joy. Something has gone wrong. Something has happened over which you had no control. You've been told that your baby has a chromosome mixup known as Down's syndrome, or mongolism. Suddenly, without warning and for no apparent reason, something that supposedly happens only to other people has happened to you.

As an expectant mother you took care of yourself, you ate properly and avoided anything you thought might harm the baby. The pregnancy probably wasn't complicated and neither was the delivery. Now, as a parent of a newborn Down's child, you can only think, "Why? Why us?"

At this point you are likely to suffer much pain, uncertainty, and confusion. Suddenly you are confronted with a situation for which you have no information, experience, or training. You can appeal to friends and family for emotional support, but until now there has not been a place for you to turn for practical, down-to-earth information and advice about your new Down's baby. What kind of special care will your baby need? What are your options as a parent? How will your child grow and mature—physically, emotionally, and psychologically? What effects will a Down's child have on the rest of your family? How can you and your child best cope with this condition? What can you do to help your child's life be as full and happy as possible?

Your Down's Syndrome Child is a handbook of practical information and advice for parents who have a child with this condition, whether it be a new baby, an infant, a young child, or an adolescent. It is written in everyday language and speaks directly to you, the parents. A guide for coping and successfully dealing with the problems of having and raising a Down's child, this book examines situations—both problems and joys

—that you and your child are likely to encounter as he or she grows older.

   Much of the information and advice presented here is illustrated by actual anecdotes and stories from other parents of Down's syndrome children. Over the years I have gathered this information and these stories during parent counseling sessions. From these sessions I have gained firsthand knowledge of the joys, the sorrows, the problems, and the triumphs they've encountered.

Eunice McClurg

YOUR DOWN'S
SYNDROME CHILD

CHAPTER 1

The Birth of Your Down's Syndrome Baby

Few words are more terrifying to parents of newborn babies than "Your child has Down's syndrome." After months of waiting, these words have turned your world upside down. All your plans, dreams, and preparations for this baby have been abruptly shattered in a matter of seconds. Now, like thousands of other parents, you are faced with the stark reality of knowing your baby is a Down's child.

When you heard those words, did you know what they meant? Probably not. But most parents don't either. Most parents, however, have learned how to cope, and so can you.

WHAT IS DOWN'S SYNDROME?

Down's syndrome (also called Down syndrome) is a developmental disorder associated with mental retardation. For many years it was better known as *mongolism*, a term coined by British physician Langdon Down. He was the first to recognize and describe certain physical characteristics which Down's babies have in common. Among them are slanted eyes and flat nasal bridges, which give an appearance like that of Asiatic people. Because of this resemblance, the descriptive words "mongoloid" and "mongolism" were used. Such words, however, are now considered inappropriate and discriminatory by parents and professionals alike.

You probably wondered why your baby was born with this disorder. "Why?" you asked. "Why us? Is God punishing us for some misdeed? Is there some mysterious unknown condition in our family tree that is at fault? Why do we have to bear this terrible burden?"

Down's syndrome has been studied and researched by geneticists, educators, statisticians, and other scientists for years. Because of this research, some of these questions can now be answered.

Down's syndrome occurs at the moment of conception. Ordinarily each cell in our bodies contains forty-six chromosomes, arranged in pairs of twenty-three. These chromosomes determine our sex and physical features. A human sperm and a human egg each contain twenty-three chromosomes so that there will be a normal complement of forty-six when the two unite in fertilization.

During fertilization, each chromosome in the sperm and egg splits into two. But sometimes, if this splitting does not occur in the usual way, an extra chromosome is carried into the fertilized egg, making a total of forty-seven instead of the normal forty-six. The faulty separation can originate in either the egg or the sperm.

Through research we know that 95 percent of all Down's syndrome births are caused by the presence of this extra chromosome. In these cases, since the twenty-first pair of chromosomes is always the one affected, the condition is called *trisomy 21*. Trisomy 21 is not hereditary in any way.

Two other types of imperfect chromosome separation account for the remaining Down's births. One, known as *translocation,* occurs when the extra chromosome breaks up and part of it fastens onto another. This is the cause of 3 to 4 percent of all Down's births. However, translocation does not automatically cause Down's syndrome. In fact, in many cases translocation can happen without it having any noticeable effect on the child at all. Many normal people have this cellular condition which is, to them, totally benign. People with this condition do not usually even know they have it.

Translocation is hereditary, however, and parents who have this condition will often (but not necessarily) pass it on to their children. These children may have the correct number of chromosomes; they may be Down's babies; or they may be normal but carry the translocation condition.

Your physician can perform a test soon after your baby's birth to determine whether he or she has the translocation type of Down's syndrome. If your child does have it, then both parents should have a chromosome examination to determine who is the carrier of this condition.

The third type of Down's syndrome, *mosaicism,* is extremely rare and occurs in only about 1 percent of all Down's syndrome births. While people with trisomy 21 have forty-seven chromosomes in each of their cells, people with mosaicism have forty-six chromosomes in some of their cells and forty-seven in others. Mosaicism is not hereditary.

In all three types of Down's syndrome the cause is the same: the faulty chromosome separation during conception. We do not yet know exactly how or why the faulty separation occurs, or how or why it disrupts the orderly development of a baby's body and brain.

People want to know what causes Down's syndrome, which can occur in offspring of parents of varying races, intellects, and backgrounds. There does appear to be a link between parental age and the incidence of Down's births. For years scientific studies indicated that the mother's age was the major influencing factor: older mothers were more likely to have Down's children, especially those aged thirty-five or older at the time of conception.

Although scientists aren't sure why maternal age is associated with Down's syndrome births, they do have some theories to explain the increased risk. The most common theory is that since a woman is born with all the eggs necessary for having children, at thirty-five her eggs are also thirty-five years old, which may mean that they are past their prime and less likely to function normally. Other scientists believe that chemicals and radiation might be responsible for damaging the genetic material in the eggs and causing Down's syndrome. And since the eggs of older women have been exposed to chemicals and radiation for a longer period of time, the chances for genetic damage are thus increased.

Studies conducted from 1965 to 1977 clearly show that paternal age is also related to the occurrence of Down's births. The evidence suggests that faulty chromosome separation in the sperm is more likely to occur in men aged forty-nine and older. The studies also suggest that in one fourth of all cases the chromosome error originates in the sperm rather than in the egg, and the error is related to paternal age. Further, Danish and Japanese research conducted in 1977 and 1978 found a significantly higher number of Down's children fathered by men aged fifty-five years or older, as compared to fathers under the age of forty-nine.

However, age is not the only contributing factor to Down's syndrome. The Danish and Japanese research also revealed a remarkable increase in the number of Down's babies being born to mothers and fathers in their early twenties or younger. This phenomenon has not been adequately explained, although research is beginning to turn up clues that there may be a hormonal cause for both younger and older women.

Another common theory about the cause of Down's syndrome links the passage of time between ovulation and fertilization with the number of Down's births. According to this theory, eggs fertilized within twenty-four hours of ovulation have the best chance of developing normally.

Researchers are also looking into whether drugs or diet are possible causes of Down's syndrome.

If you think there is any possibility at all that your unborn child may have Down's syndrome or some other defect, you should consider having an amniocentesis test. In this medical process, amniotic fluid is drawn from the womb, and chromosome abnormalities can be detected early on from studies done on the fetal cells in the fluid.

WHAT ARE THE SIGNS OF DOWN'S SYNDROME?

When a newborn is examined, there are certain telltale signs of Down's syndrome that a doctor can spot. The most obvious are slanted eyes, small ears, a protruding tongue, short stubby fingers, broad hands with an unusual crease extending across the entire palm, flexible joints, and weak muscle tone. Because of the last two characteristics, Down's children are often described as "floppy." Recurring respiratory problems are also very common among these children. A list of physical characteristics most common to people with Down's syndrome appears in Appendix I.

It is important for you to know that although more than fifty characteristics are common among Down's children, no child has all of them. However, if five or more of these signs are detected, the baby's chromosomes will be analyzed to see what kind of chromosomal damage, if any, is present. (Very often one or two of the characteristics common to

Down's children will be found in other people who are otherwise totally normal. The straight crease across the palm is one such common characteristic.)

Prior to the 1970s, physicians weren't sure what their role should be once a baby was diagnosed as having Down's syndrome. In those early days there was little a doctor could do to help the family. Amniocentesis and chromosome analysis hadn't been developed, so the physician couldn't tell the parents whether or not the disorder was hereditary.

Although Down's syndrome is one of the few disorders that can be accurately diagnosed at birth, the doctor who recognizes these symptoms is faced with a difficult task. How does he or she tell the parents?

Until rather recently the treatment for mentally retarded people was to keep them out of sight and out of mind. Consequently, huge state institutions with the capacity to house thousands of people were built in remote areas. And the care that Down's syndrome people received at these institutions was, at best, only slightly higher than that given to animals. The lack of medical and educational techniques, coupled with society's apprehension toward mentally retarded people, posed a real dilemma for the doctor. How, and how soon, should parents be told that their child was a Down's baby? Some doctors preferred to say nothing until parents suspected something was wrong with their child.

Take the case of Bruce, who was born in the mid-1950s. At age three months, he had pneumonia. Medication prescribed by the family doctor seemed to cure the disease, except for a deep hoarse cough that persisted. Finally, three months later, his parents sought the advice of a pediatrician.

"My husband didn't go with me to keep the appointment," says the mother. "As the doctor began examining Bruce, I was told to leave the room. I knew something was terribly wrong, but I was too frightened to ask questions, so I went out to the waiting room."

She spent an agony-filled hour pacing the floor before she was called back to the examining room. She entered quietly and saw two doctors huddled over her tiny son. As she approached them, she heard one say, "This baby is mongolian."

The other man nodded his head in agreement.

"What does that mean?" interrupted the mother.

"It means he's severely retarded," the doctor answered. "The best thing you can do is put him in an institution."

The mother clearly remembers going to the nearest window and wanting to jump out.

"Then I looked at my baby," she says. "I grabbed him, held him tight, and left."

The parents next decided to consult their family doctor, and to their utter amazement, he also insisted that Bruce be sent to an institution. "It's the best place for him," explained the doctor. "As he gets older you won't be able to handle him."

The parents chose to ignore that advice and kept their son at home, treating him just as they did his older sister. And other doctors chose to ignore or deny the condition altogether.

I know of several cases in which the parents suspected Down's syndrome because the babies either had some of the characteristic features or developed much more slowly than other children in the family. And yet when these parents shared their concern with their doctors, they were put off with "I don't think so" replies.

Then there were situations like David's. His parents worried about his constant respiratory problems and wondered about his flat nose, stubby fingers, and smooth palms. After a year of changing doctors and looking for help, one physician finally said, "There isn't much I can do because this type of child always has severe lung ailments."

"What do you mean? This type of child?" the parents asked.

"Don't you know he's a mongoloid?" replied the doctor. "It's written on his record." Up until that point no doctor had been brave enough to break the news to David's parents.

These parents, too, decided to raise their child at home rather than entrust him to a state institution.

Today Bruce and David are visible testimony of their parents' love and tutoring. They are perfectly groomed, well mannered young men, living in their communities and working in sheltered employment programs.

In a way, Bruce and David's parents were more fortunate than others in the same situation during that era. Some doctors broke the news to families in a most dehumanizing way. "You have a mongoloid. Don't take it home and get attached to it" was a fairly common warning. "It'll be nothing more than a vegetable. Put it into an institution immediately."

Parents who heeded such thoughtless and inaccurate advice later regretted their hasty actions. The remorse they first experienced after learning their children had Down's syndrome was intensified as they helplessly watched them mature into mute, vacant-eyed, completely dependent adults. And so the doctors' predictions were fulfilled because of the inadequate love and care provided at the massive and impersonal institutions.

The doctor who delivered Kerri, a child with Down's syndrome living in Minneapolis, used a different approach, not at all uncommon in the 1970s. He felt obligated to immediately tell the parents the worst that could happen.

"It was a grim prediction," says Kerri's father, "of heart problems, respiratory ailments, poor muscle tone that would prevent Kerri from ever learning to walk, talk, eat, or dress herself." But today these parents believe that the litany of problems their doctor recited was one way to justify his suggestion that Kerri be placed in an institution.

Fortunately, things are different now. No longer is institutionalization the norm, and no longer is it automatically recommended by doctors without a second thought. More and more people are raising their Down's children at home, providing them with the love and care that they would give normal children. These parents have not regretted their decisions, and unless there are unusual circumstances this home care will result in Down's children (and later Down's adults) who are happier, better adjusted, and better able to live as functioning members of society.

Nowadays parents are usually given more of a choice when they learn that they have produced a Down's baby. Of course, the choice is not an easy one to make, and you will need a good deal of information to make it wisely—usually more information than your doctor will give you. Chapter 2 of this book examines your options and choices in detail and provides you with all the important information you will need to consider the situation carefully.

Since the early seventies, new and exciting advances have been taking place in the medical and educational treatment of Down's syndrome children. These include open-heart surgery, infant stimulation programs, and mandatory special education. At the same time, organizations like the Association for Retarded Citizens and the Down Syndrome National Congress have begun sponsoring ongoing parent support programs and other services to help parents cope with and raise their Down's syndrome children.

Of course not all of these options will be available in your community. Appendix II of this book includes a list of organizations that may be of help to you.

In the past decade, changes have taken place in our institutions as well. Many of these facilities have become considerably more humane and are providing more personal care, as well as some educational and vocational training for retarded residents. The most dramatic changes have taken place within the institutions' physical environment. Huge wards containing as many as a hundred beds have been converted to smaller units accommodating four or fewer people in each unit. These units are decorated in bright cheery colors and residents' possessions help to personalize the decor. The mammoth and infamous dayrooms to which residents were herded and then locked inside have been remodeled into smaller, attractive recreation or living rooms. A greater effort is now made to integrate residents into the community life outside of the institution.

There are signs that positive changes will continue to occur. However, they are not occurring in every institution, and it is still not uncommon, even today, for some doctors to recommend immediate institutionalization for Down's syndrome babies. No matter what your doctor suggests, and no matter how he or she treats you, the decision is yours and yours alone—and it should be made carefully and wisely.

INITIAL REACTIONS

Once you learn that your child has Down's syndrome, do *not* make any immediate decisions about foster care, adoption, or institutional placement—even if your doctor urges you to. Give yourself a chance to get control of your emotions first. You'll probably go through some dishearteningly weird times, possibly so weird that you may wonder if you are losing your mind. You'll likely experience emotional reactions of extraordinary intensity—fear, bitterness, guilt, anger, self-hatred. And these emotions may change so rapidly that you may feel as if you are on a roller coaster. At first you may have a great deal of pain, or you may feel that your situation is terribly unfair.

After nine months of preparing for this baby, it is hard to believe your child isn't perfect. Your hopes may soar if you were told there's "a chance" the baby is Down's. You think the doctor may be mistaken, or he or she may be acting only on a suspicion. Yet the baby must have some symptoms that aroused the doctor's concern. Chromosome tests will confirm the doctor's suspicions, or prove them unwarranted. If these tests do show that your baby has Down's syndrome, the sooner you can accept this reality, the better.

The shock of learning that your child is disabled probably won't come all at once. It's usually more of a gradual process that takes a long time before complete realization and acceptance set in. But the sooner you realize that the child of your dreams will never be, the sooner you'll learn to accept and love this baby who happens to have some limitations. With this acceptance, you and your baby will have a brighter future.

COPING

First you must learn to cope with the "Why us?" which has a way of cropping up just when you thought you had it conquered. The emotional shock you first felt when you learned your baby had Down's syndrome will surface from time to time. And probably no parent escapes the terror of an occasional thought that perhaps their child's life could (or even should) come to a premature end.

One of the best ways to get through these emotional crises is to talk with other parents of Down's children. If you don't know of any, call your local chapter of the Association for Retarded Citizens, the National Down Syndrome Congress, the United Way or your city, county, or state social services office. Many of these agencies provide a service that helps parents of Down's children contact one another. Just knowing that someone else has had the same experience is therapeutic. You'll also get all kinds of hints from these other parents on how they coped. Best of all, you'll get the encouragement and hope that you need.

This book, of course, will also supply you with encouragement, hope, and useful hints on coping and child raising. But even the best books are no substitute for personal contact. So seek out that contact and, once you have made it through your own emotional crises, I recommend that you talk with other parents of Down's children so you can pass on what you have learned and lend your support.

There will be times when you will feel sorry for your innocent baby and wonder why he or she has to suffer at the hands of a suspicious, rejecting society. Feeling sorry and wondering are unavoidable, but don't spend too much time on it. Society's attitude toward disabled people is becoming more and more accepting and receptive. And later on, if you so desire, you can play an important part in making that attitude even more positive.

MYTHS ABOUT DOWN'S SYNDROME CHILDREN

What were your first thoughts after you learned about your child? Did images of short, squat, obese people with tongues protruding and dull eyes staring into the distance float up from your subconscious mind?

This image is, of course, totally inaccurate. Such misleading ideas have existed among the general population since the 1800s, when Langdon Down unflatteringly described people with this syndrome as imitative, humorous idiots.

Not only has this stereotyped opinion prevailed over the years, it has also fostered the development of other misconceptions about Down's people. Some of the more popular ones are:

All these children are alike. This notion is simply not true. The only things Down's children have in common are the physical characteristics that make them easily recognizable. Down's people are not all placid, cheerful, given to mimicry, obstinate, or congenial. Each displays the same wide range of personality traits common to any human being, and they differ from one another as much and in the same ways as do any other people.

All Down's children are severely mentally retarded. False. Their intellectual ability is no more identical than are their physical or personality characteristics.

The World Health Organization classifies retarded children into three major groups: mildly, moderately, and severely retarded. Mildly retarded people are considered educable, which means their intellectual functioning ranges from one half to three fourths that of a normal person of the same age. Academic achievement for educable mentally retarded children varies from the second to seventh grade level.

Moderately retarded children are deemed to be trainable. These children will function at a level of one third to one half their normal peers, and they rarely progress beyond second grade level in academic subjects.

Although these two groups, the mildly and moderately retarded children, are low academic achievers, they are capable of acquiring good social and occupational skills.

Severely retarded people need lifelong custodial care.

Most Down's children are moderately retarded. Some will function within the mildly retarded range, and only a few are severely retarded. *These children mature differently from other children.* Every child is unique and has his or her own built-in road map for growth and development. For a Down's child this development follows the same general progressive pattern as that of other children. The only differences are in the pace of development and the level of achievement.

Demonstration projects have proven that early intervention programs like infant stimulation and preschool education can make a difference in a Down's child's rate of performance and learning. As in non-Down's children, this rate of performance will vary and show individual differences. Some Down's babies learn to walk at about twelve to eighteen months of age, while others may not do so until they are two, three, or even four years old. Such variations can be found in all areas of general functioning.

TELLING OTHERS ABOUT YOUR DOWN'S BABY

Chances are your friends and relatives have some of the misconceptions about Down's syndrome people which I have just dispelled, and very likely you are wondering what they'll think or how they'll react when you tell them about your baby. And knowing that you must tell them probably creates more fear and tension for you.

It won't be easy, but try to explain your baby's condition in a simple and candid manner. Tell them that he or she has Down's syndrome, that it's caused by an extra chromosome, and that your baby is likely to be mentally retarded. Some parents told me they couldn't use the words "mentally retarded," so they substituted "brain-damaged." Other parents said they explained that the baby would be slow to develop and would need more care than other babies.

Sometimes grandparents go through a difficult time after learning about the new baby. They may not want to believe the diagnosis, or they may hope that it can be outgrown. Others may feel so sorry for the baby that they'll become overprotective or show favoritism over other grandchildren. You will need patience and persistence to help grandparents accept the facts and treat your child appropriately.

If you have other children, they too must be told. Just how much you tell them depends on their ages. Tell them what you feel they should know; later, when they ask questions—and they will—you should answer them as honestly, clearly, simply, and directly as possible. Most parents agree that a gently factual explanation is the easiest way to inform siblings about the new baby's condition.

Children three years old or younger may not be able to understand, however, so for children this young it may be best at first to simply say that a new baby brother or sister has arrived. Be willing, though, to honestly answer any questions a child of any age asks.

Then there are friends and neighbors who must be told. This, too, can be difficult. If you wait for them to come to you, they might not, simply because they don't know what to say or ask. So it is usually best for you to reach out to them and explain your baby's condition. In most cases, you can use the same explanation that you use for your relatives.

Probably the most frustrating and agonizing situation occurs when friends offer their sympathy and condolences, acting as if your child were something of a living curse on you. How can you deal with such a situation? Some parents suggest countering their remarks by describing your baby as having lots of hair, or huge blue eyes—anything that will help people feeling this way to understand that there is more to your baby than his or her disabling condition. The parents I know who have had these experiences later realized that their friends were really trying to be kind in the only way they knew how.

Perhaps the best way to help others understand that a Down's child is every bit a human being is to simply let them watch your interactions with your child. Your love and acceptance of your baby will be communicated to them, and they in turn will follow your example.

THE YEARS AHEAD

Most parents of Down's children wonder at first if they will have the parenting skills to care for their babies. The answer in most cases is yes. Conventional child-raising techniques work very well with Down's children. Just remember that it is going to take your baby longer than most children to learn and to understand what you are trying to teach. You'll have to be very patient, and there will likely be times when you are convinced your child will never learn anything. But don't give up; your child can learn, but at a slower pace than that of normal children. As parents of a Down's child, you must realize that the changes you make, now and in the years to come, will be different from those you would have made had you given birth to the healthy baby of your dreams.

It is possible that your baby may have more health problems than other babies. Heart defects, respiratory ailments, and ear infections are the most common of these problems. Not all Down's babies have these problems, however, and it may well be that your child will enjoy generally good health.

Remember, too, that your baby is first of all a baby. In spite of Down's syndrome, he or she has the same basic needs as other babies and requires tender loving care. Your child's physical and emotional needs will always be comparable to those of other children his or her age. The only difference between your child and other children will be in intellectual development.

Finally, remember that with your love and caring, and with the help of special programs, your child can achieve a life that is rewarding and fulfilling. This love and caring, and these special programs, will be discussed in the chapters that follow.

CHAPTER 2

Bringing Baby Home

Once you have accepted the fact that your baby has Down's syndrome, you will be confronted with some soul-searching questions. Can you accept this baby into your family? If you do, what kind of life will you have? What effects will this child have on you, your spouse, your other children, your friends and relatives, and your family in general? If you don't take your baby home, what will life be like for him or her in an institution, group home, or foster home? How will that affect the rest of your family?

The choice to bring your baby home into your family may be a difficult one to make, but it is one that you *can* make. It is important, though, that you make this choice carefully and wisely. Do not make it on the spur of the moment or on a whim. Consider all the issues and options thoroughly, and take however much time you may need.

Wrestling with these questions (and perhaps even agonizing over them) is normal. If you were warned by your pediatrician, or anyone else, not to take your new baby home, the wrestling can be even more difficult. Still, only you and your spouse should make the final decision.

Talking to others may help you make your decision. At the very least, it can provide comfort and support. You should feel free to talk with friends, relatives, your doctor, another doctor, your religious counselor, or anyone else you wish before making your decision. You may also want to discuss the situation with the parents of other Down's syndrome children. You and your spouse as well will want to talk closely with each other about your feelings, reactions, worries, fears, hopes, doubts, and ideas.

Probably the greatest sense of isolation can occur when you see other parents bubbly with joy over their normal newborn babies. And you can't help feeling envious because those parents don't have to grapple with the decisions confronting you.

"You may even feel as though that differentness has transferred to you, because normal people don't give birth to abnormal babies," some parents have said.

Given time, however, these feelings generally pass.

MAKING YOUR DECISION

The decision you must make, of course, is whether or not you can provide the care your child needs. Today most parents decide to raise their Down's children in their own homes; and, in general, babies with Down's syndrome thrive better when raised by their own parents. However, not all parents can shoulder the responsibilities of raising a child with this disorder, especially if that child has severe or recurring medical problems. And, again, the decision to raise your baby yourself, or to place him or her in a group home, foster home, or institution is entirely yours and your spouse's.

Here are some important things you should consider to help you reach your decision.

If you have been given a grim picture of how little your baby will be able to accomplish, do not be swayed by this information. *No one* can predict what your newborn baby can or cannot accomplish. Each child with Down's syndrome is unique, and so are his or her abilities, talents, and limitations. The only thing you know for certain is that your child will be slower to learn and develop than normal babies. Had your baby not been born with Down's syndrome, chances are that no one would even think of predicting what your child would or would not be capable of doing.

What you should do now is exchange your original dreams and hopes for this baby for new dreams and hopes that are more realistic. Of course, this isn't easily accomplished. You will have to ask yourself if you can really love and help this infant who is limited and imperfect. You may be reluctant to answer that question because you are not quite ready to accept the unknown future this baby offers you. However, you must also ask yourself these questions: Would the future be any more certain if the baby of your dreams had been born? Isn't everyone limited and imperfect? Is there ever any guarantee that *any* child will grow up happy, healthy, and free of problems?

Other parents who have faced the same situation tell me they took time to pray, to grieve, to cry, to talk, and to think. You and your spouse should feel free to do the same. In fact, allowing yourself this time to feel, react, and consider the issues is one of the best and most important things you can do for yourself, for your spouse, and for your new baby.

Physical contact with your baby—touching, holding, cuddling, and caressing—often helps parents make their decision. One set of parents told me, "It was during physical contact with our baby that we began to realize we could love and care for her." These parents decided to keep their baby with them rather than entrust her to a foster home, group home, or institution.

Occasionally extensive physical contact is not possible. Kerri, the child mentioned in the first chapter, was born with a severe case of jaundice. "She was in an isolette, swathed in bandages, and hooked up to what seemed like hundreds of wires and tubes," remembers her father. Still, for Kerri's parents it was physical contact with Kerri that made them decide to raise her at home. Says her father, "The moment we touched our baby we knew we could not part with her."

If touching, holding, and examining your baby does not help you to make a decision, you will have to do some self-examining. Perhaps the first question you will ask yourself is whether or not you have the parenting skills necessary to care for this baby. Most (though not all) parents do. Remember, most people become parents with few well-developed skills and even fewer guidelines. There are no qualifying examinations for entering into parenthood. You and your spouse must judge for yourselves whether you are able to handle the responsibilities of your child.

As you search within yourself to decide what to do, there are three other items to consider. First, remember that because your child has Down's syndrome it does not mean that he or she is helpless. It does mean, however, that there are some limitations.

Second, society is beginning to apply a new philosophy toward people who are retarded. It is called the Normalization Principle, and slowly but surely it is becoming the guiding light for developing appropriate treatment and education programs needed by people who have Down's syndrome. *"People who are retarded,"* say the proponents of this principle, *"have the right to patterns and conditions of everyday life that are as close as possible to the norms and standards of mainstream society."* This concept is supported by a United Nations declaration published in the early seventies. (This document, which clearly outlines the rights of retarded people, is discussed in detail in Appendix III.)

What all of this means to you is that if you decide to raise your child at home, there will be organizations and programs available to help your child adjust to society, and to help you help him or her make those adjustments. It also means that you will probably not have to care for your child all of his or her life. A great many programs based on the normalization concept are devoted to helping people with Down's syndrome become as independent as possible when they reach the age of adulthood. These programs enable adults with Down's syndrome to live on their own, either alone or with other adults who are disabled, with supervision provided by counselors or social service agencies as is necessary.

Third, although many children who have Down's syndrome are born in good physical health, some have moderate to severe medical problems at birth, and others may develop certain health problems as they grow older. These are discussed in detail in Chapter 3.

For some children these health problems may be chronic, for others they may not. If your child does have such a health problem, you will need to carefully consider your ability to handle this responsibility.

In making your decision, take time also to consider your own moral and religious beliefs, and your faith in human endeavor and survival. These are important, and they should not be passed over, ignored, or given a backseat to more "practical" considerations. Remember, whatever decision you and your spouse make, you will want to be able to live comfortably with it.

Some parents find themselves questioning or even changing some of their own beliefs when they learn that their child has Down's syndrome. There is nothing wrong with these questions or changes, and they can even be signs of personal growth of the parents.

The important thing is to be sincere in your beliefs and decisions— that is, to believe in something because you *feel* that way, not because you would *like to* feel that way, or because others want or expect you to feel that way. If you will honestly and sincerely accept your own feelings, then you will be able to make a wise decision about your child.

Social service agencies and city, county, and state agencies can help provide information and support. Many hospitals also have programs that can provide these same kinds of help. Check with your hospital's social worker. In most cases, the services of all these organizations are free, and you shouldn't hesitate to make use of them as you need to.

If you believe you have made the right decision, you will find hidden resources of strength to help you carry out and live with that decision.

SEEKING ALTERNATIVE CARE

What options are available if you decide on out-of-home care for your child?

In most communities there are three choices: adoption, foster care, and institutional placement. Of the three, adoption is probably the least likely, simply because few families are willing to adopt handicapped children. So until recently the only real choice you would have had was institutional placement. Now, however, foster care is becoming a pleasanter option for parents who cannot keep their disabled babies.

Traditionally foster care has been provided by a family not related to a child's natural family. In the early seventies, though, a new version of foster care was introduced—group homes. There are some basic differences and similarities between foster and group home care. Both are limited in the number of children they may serve; however, a group home usually serves more children than does a foster home. In foster homes, families accept children into their homes and provide round-the-clock care. Group homes also provide round-the-clock care, but the care is divided among employed staff members—professionals or paraprofessionals with backgrounds in social work or related fields—each of whom works eight-hour shifts. The family atmosphere for child rearing provided by foster homes is therefore difficult to achieve in group homes.

Although both types of programs must be licensed to operate, group homes must also adhere to rules determined and enforced by the state government. These rules are intended to protect the human and civil rights of the residents and to ensure they experience a lifestyle that is as close to normal as possible.

If foster or group home care is not available in your locale, then you may have to consider an institution. Since the early seventies, a powerful movement by advocacy agencies like the Association for Retarded Citizens has been effective in upgrading the care and treatment of people living in institutions. This movement continues across the nation, with the ultimate goal of phasing out these facilities altogether and replacing them with foster homes and group homes. In the meantime, the impersonal, institutional appearance of these facilities is gradually diminishing due to class action lawsuits filed against them by parents of children living there.

Before you decide on any of these alternatives, you should investigate them carefully and allow adequate time for your investigation. You should visit these facilities and feel free to make more than one visit. While there, speak with the foster parents or the staff members; observe how they interact with the children; inquire about the daily schedule and the care given; notice the physical environment and the location. Is it pleasant and cheerful? Is it located in an area that is safe, and where children have access to a community and the activities in that community? Ask any other questions that will help you choose the facility that most ensures that your child will receive the best of care. Such assurance will help ease the difficult task of seeking alternative care.

Finding the right facility is one difficulty you will face, but coping with the effect your decision will have on your family is still another. If your child has been brought home, the immediate result of sending him or her elsewhere will be a disruption in your family's life because everyone—you, your spouse, and your other children—will have to adjust to your child's absence. No doubt all of you will worry about the care and treatment he or she is receiving, and surely other close family relatives will want to know why this child must live away from home.

Once your decision is made, explain to your other children, the grandparents, relatives, and friends that you are seeking alternative care. Tell them why you believe this kind of care is necessary for your child. Let them know that you are not abandoning your baby, that he or she will always be a part of your family, but the care that the child needs is more than you can provide. Explain that you intend to keep family ties intact by visiting your child as often as possible and that he or she will come home for visits on weekends or holidays. An open, frank explanation should help your family and your friends take a positive and accepting attitude toward your decision.

See Appendix IV for a checklist of items that can help you make a wise choice about out-of-home care for your child.

PICKING UP THE PIECES

Once you have made your decision, either to bring your baby home or seek alternative care, you will want to establish order in your own life, and in the lives of other family members, once again.

Many parents do this by converting their pain into energy. Now may be the time to complete some long-forgotten project or to start a new one. Take up an activity that has always interested you but that, for one reason or another, you have never gotten around to. Give in to an overwhelming desire to cook, or to take long walks, or to keep everything meticulously clean and neat. This burst of energy may last days, weeks, or even months, when suddenly you will realize there are no more projects, no reason to reclean something that already shimmers. And by this time you will notice the pain is not so intense anymore, and gradually you'll begin to slow down.

On the other hand, you may find yourself spending the first few weeks in slow motion, performing only the most necessary tasks. You may feel exhausted and weak. For a while, you should allow yourself to accept these feelings as ways of dealing with your grief. But as the weeks and months pass, try to *gradually* return to your normal way of life. You can do it, just as thousands of parents have done in the past. Encourage your spouse and other family members to do the same. And be willing to call on the support or help of any of the people and organizations that know how to deal with this to assist you in putting your life back together.

You may find solace and comfort by learning as much as you can about Down's syndrome. A desire to read everything available is not unusual, but look for material that is up to date. This means books, pamphlets, and articles that have been published in the last ten years. Information published prior to the early seventies is obsolete because continued research on Down's syndrome reveals new and more accurate facts on what causes faulty chromosome separation.

For many parents, the most effective help comes from parent outreach and parent support programs. "These programs will help ease your fears, shock, and pain," say many parents who took advantage of them, "because you will realize that you are not alone." Parent outreach arranges contact between parents of newborn Down's syndrome babies and other parents who have gone through what you as new

parents are just now experiencing. Those who have weathered the storm are sometimes called "veteran parents." These outreach programs are available in many parts of the country through a cooperative agreement between hospitals and social service agencies. When a baby with Down's syndrome is born, the hospital social worker informs the parents about the program. If parents are receptive, arrangements are made for them to be visited either at the hospital or at home.

It is a good idea to take advantage of this kind of opportunity if you can. There is a sharing of ideas and information, and very often long-term friendships develop. You will discover that having someone you can talk to will be especially helpful when you are having a particularly bad day.

Many communities offer a follow-up program to parent outreach known as parent support. In this program, parents meet regularly with a group leader or counselor. They share ideas, learn parenting skills, and provide moral support for each other.

If you are reluctant to join such a group, that's not unusual. Several parents told me they were hesitant because they expected to meet older parents who would be lamenting their fates. But instead they found warmhearted, compassionate moms and dads of all ages, willing to share their successes, offer comfort, and answer questions.

Social service agencies now recognize the need for, and are providing, support groups for siblings. These groups give brothers and sisters of children with Down's syndrome the opportunity to share concerns or ask questions that they may be reluctant to ask their parents. If siblings are teased or ridiculed by their friends and classmates because of the baby, a support group can help them learn to deal with the problem.

Information about all these programs should be available from your hospital's social workers. If not, find out if your community has a Health and Social Service Department, and ask it for help.

HOW RETARDED IS YOUR BABY?

First of all, you must understand that your baby is a unique person, different from his or her parents and siblings, and different from other babies with Down's syndrome. *The old stereotyped image of a short, heavy, unattractive person is simply not true.* Your baby's social, emotional, and physical growth will take place at his or her own individual rate.

But it is true that your baby will develop at a slower rate than most babies. For example, the average baby smiles at the age of one month. Your little one may not smile until he or she is two or three months old. Many babies roll over at five months, yet it could take your baby eight or more months to learn this skill. Most babies can sit up by themselves at seven months, but your child may be more than ten months old before this happens.

Until the sixties, no one believed that anything could be done to stimulate the development of these children—so nothing was done. But now we know that with early stimulation, and with appropriate education later on, children with Down's syndrome can achieve many remarkable things.

Your own child's accomplishment will depend in part on your efforts as parents, and in part on the kind of programs available in your community. Your baby was born with strengths and weaknesses, just like other human beings. If you can learn to recognize and understand those strengths and weaknesses, your baby is likely to achieve high levels of development.

THE DEVELOPMENT OF DOWN'S SYNDROME CHILDREN

Your baby will go through all the same stages of growth and development as do nonhandicapped babies, and he or she will do so in the same meaningful, organized way. The only difference will be in the rate and level of development.

There are five basic areas of development common to all children: language, muscular, social, emotional, and cognitive. Development in most of these areas is simultaneous.

LANGUAGE DEVELOPMENT

Language development consists of two important parts—receptive and expressive. Receptive language refers to your child's ability to understand what he or she hears. When the baby begins to follow verbal instructions, you'll know that receptive language is developing.

Expressive language is your child's speech development. Those first babbling sounds he or she makes are the forerunners of speech. Your baby's language development depends on the verbal interaction he or she has with you, the parents, and with other children in the family. This interaction should start at the earliest possible moment.

MUSCULAR DEVELOPMENT

Two sets of muscles are involved in muscle development—the large ones that control head, leg, and trunk movement, and the small ones controlling hand and finger movement. Professionals refer to head and trunk movement as *gross motor development,* which determines how well your child holds up his or her head, learns to roll over, sits up, crawls, stands, walks, and runs. Hand and finger movement are known as *fine motor development,* which controls how well your baby uses his or her hands and fingers.

SOCIAL DEVELOPMENT

One of the greatest challenges for all parents is helping their children become socially accepted. But to parents of a child with Down's syndrome this challenge may prove even greater. Society is hesitant to accept a person with visible defects. Since a Down's child often looks "different," he or she will sometimes encounter stares, whispers, or quick side glances. This problem can increase if the child displays inappropriate or immature behavior. It is therefore important for you to start teaching your child at a very early age the difference between acceptable and unacceptable social behavior.

EMOTIONAL DEVELOPMENT

The emotional development of all babies is vital to their general functioning. Their smiles, laughter, tears, and gurgling sounds are signals of happiness or unhappiness. Since babies with Down's syndrome are slower to respond emotionally than other babies, you must keep actively and consistently involved with your baby—and you must be patient. Eventually he or she will show the same signs of emotional development as all babies do.

COGNITIVE DEVELOPMENT

The cognitive is the thinking, problem-solving area of development. It is closely related to all other areas of development. Attention span, awareness of objects, interest in sights or sounds, and realization of connections between objects are phases of your baby's cognitive development. Achievement in all these phases also depends heavily on the interaction between you and your baby.

STIMULATING YOUR BABY'S DEVELOPMENT

As you can see, the kind and amount of interaction between you and your child can make a huge difference in his or her development. All babies thrive in a loving, stimulating atmosphere. They need someone who is consistently in their presence, someone who behaves in a caring way. The phrase "tender loving care" becomes even more essential to the general development of babies with Down's syndrome because their movements and reactions tend to be slower than those of other babies. And the experiences of many parents show that the learning process can be sped up through early stimulating activities. So as soon as possible, you should inquire about the availability of an infant stimulation program in your community. These programs, whether they are provided in the home or in another setting, often will enroll babies as young as two weeks old.

You may wonder what a two-week-old baby can achieve. Most parents don't realize that what other babies seem to do naturally—kick, reach, smile—babies with Down's syndrome must be taught to do. That's the purpose of infant stimulation. With the help of therapists, you will learn how to stimulate all phases of your baby's development. One set of parents who enrolled their baby in such a program told me, "Attending these classes helped us as much as it did our baby. We discovered how hard she had to work to learn very simple actions. We also received moral support from the therapists and from other parents."

If an infant stimulation program is not available where you live, there are several learning activities and exercises you can do at home to stimulate your baby's development.

For greater success and fun, be sure you do these activities consistently, and *at a time when you and your baby are both alert and responsive.* Should your baby resist any exercise or activity, discontinue it for a day or two, then try again.

LANGUAGE STIMULATION ACTIVITIES

From the first moment you hold your baby, start talking, singing, or cooing to him or her. The more verbal interaction you can have with your little one, the greater are his or her chances of developing good listening and speaking skills. Take advantage of home activities to stimulate language, especially at mealtime, bath time, and bedtime. Tell your newborn what will happen: "Now it's time to eat," or "I'm going to wash your face." It is also helpful to explain what you're doing as you're doing it.

One mother I know carried her son with her from room to room as she did her housework. "I would point to objects like furniture or pictures and name them," she remembers. She admits that at first it was difficult talking to her son because she didn't see any signs of recognition or response for some time. But suddenly, when he was about four months old, he began smiling and making noises when she talked to him.

It is also good to encourage your older children to play with their new brother or sister, and to sing or talk to the little one.

While it is true that language development depends on early verbal interaction between you and your baby, there are some things you should be aware of.

First, do not expect an immediate response. You'll need to repeat over and over the names of objects and explain again and again what you are doing. The words your baby hears should be attached to meaningful objects and activities. *Avoid using baby talk, because it will just have to be unlearned later. Speak in your normal voice.* Your time is better spent setting a good language model for your baby.

Unless there are some interfering conditions such as a hearing prob-

lem or inability to control the tongue due to weak muscles, you can
expect your little one to acquire good language skills.

MUSCULAR STIMULATION

All children learn to control their large muscles before they master
control of fine muscle movement. Your baby's first reaching action will
be a single movement involving the shoulder, arm, and hand. Later, he
or she will reach with just the arm, hand, and fingers. Then the baby
must learn to use only the hands for reaching. Finally, mastery of using
the thumbs and index fingers will come.

Many babies with Down's syndrome have *hypotonia* which means
weak muscles or poor muscle tone. If your baby is among them, there
are several exercises you can do with your child to help strengthen
those muscles.

Activities That Stimulate Large Muscle Development

Affectionate handling from day one is very important to help your
baby's muscles and to increase his or her alertness. When you have
finished bathing your little one, stimulate those muscles by rubbing
your baby's body with a towel. Other simple exercises to do at bath or
diaper-changing time are:

• Pull your baby's foot to his or her mouth and circle the mouth
with the big toe. Be sure to alternate feet.

• Circle the mouth with your baby's fingertips, or with yours.

• Rub your baby's hands and feet together, left to left, right to right;
then do two cross patterns, left to right and right to left.

These exercises bring the center of action in front of your baby's eyes,
which provides visual stimulation and aids visual and cognitive development.

To help strengthen your child's back and shoulder muscles, and to
help him or her gain head control, try the following:

• Stroke your baby's back from neck to bottom.

• Hold toys slightly above your baby's head and move them from
side to side to stimulate the turning of his or her head and trunk.

• Place your baby face down on a table or bed, with his or her head
on a well-padded edge. This encourages your baby to lift his or her
head.

• Attach bright-colored objects to the sides of your baby's crib, or across its top, to stimulate the turning of his or her head. One mother told me she used a cradle instead of a crib and strung little colored bells across it. When the baby squirmed or moved, the bells tinkled, providing both visual and auditory stimulation for the baby.

Take advantage of your baby's waking hours by keeping him or her near family activities to provide extra stimulation.

Activities That Stimulate Fine Muscle Development
Since learning to use the hands is the first step in the fine muscle developmental area, it is important that you start teaching your baby the use of his or her hands as soon as possible. You can begin by placing long, slender objects like handles of spoons in your baby's hands. Playing pat-a-cake encourages the use of both hands simultaneously, as does clapping your baby's hands to music. At first you'll have to hold your baby's hands for these activities, then gradually decrease your assistance as your baby begins to learn the movements.

To develop the pincer grasp using the index finger and thumb, place and hold your baby's fingers on toys like blocks or balls. Activities like crumpling paper, pushing buttons or piano keys, and pointing will all encourage your child to use his or her fingers. Again, begin by holding your baby's fingers, then gradually decrease your assistance.

ACTIVITIES TO STIMULATE EMOTIONAL DEVELOPMENT

Your baby's emotional development is just as important as all the other developmental areas. He or she will experience the same range of emotions as other babies have, however, your baby may not respond as quickly to activities that arouse emotions. This means you will have to play more peek-a-boo games and do more tickling, cuddling and jiggling before your baby will smile, laugh, or cry at these antics. It is important to remember that your baby's emotional development is closely tied to his or her cognitive development. It is therefore essential to keep actively involved with your baby. Although he or she may show little or no response at first, your persistence and efforts will eventually be rewarded. And when that happens, you will experience a thrill hard to describe.

ACTIVITIES TO STIMULATE COGNITIVE DEVELOPMENT

The activities you use to encourage your baby's emotional responses will also help cognitive development. Your baby's smiles, laughs, gestures, and frowns are all signs that he or she is learning to respond to the surrounding environment. Your relationship with your baby, and the quality and *persistence* of your playful interaction with him or her, are vital. So give your baby bright objects to look at, and play a variety of peek-a-boo or hide-and-seek games as often and as regularly as possible. Keep the activities fun and lively, but don't prolong them if your baby shows signs of boredom or tension.

ACTIVITIES TO STIMULATE SOCIAL DEVELOPMENT

One of the most interesting and challenging tasks of parenthood is helping our children become social human beings. We want our children to be liked, to have friends, and to be accepted by others. And we are responsible for teaching them the difference between acceptable and unacceptable behavior.

As parents of a child with Down's syndrome, you have the same challenges and the same responsibility. If you teach your child appropriate behavior, he or she won't let you down. Just remember that the teaching process may take longer.

Learning acceptable social behavior is seldom accomplished without using some discipline. You should set standards and limits for your child, and you should let him or her know what the results will be if they are exceeded. Use the same discipline techniques as you would for any other child.

You can start disciplining your newborn by not letting him or her become the hub of your family's activities, and by not letting him or her cause unnecessary changes in your family's lifestyle. Later chapters will discuss techniques for handling temper tantrums, developing good manners, and building self-esteem.

THE EFFECTS OF A DOWN'S SYNDROME
CHILD ON THE FAMILY

The arrival of a new baby is always accompanied by some automatic changes in family lifestyles. With a firstborn comes the adjustment to the new role of parents. If there are siblings, an only child becomes the eldest, or the youngest child moves to a middle position. The care and feeding of babies can disrupt established sleeping and eating patterns or social activities. As parents of a child with Down's syndrome, you may wonder what other effects your new baby will have on your family.

For many parents the greatest concern is for their relations with each other. If your commitment to each other is faltering, your baby can be the excuse for placing blame on or avoiding each other. But either of these can eventually lead to a permanent separation. Instead, talk to each other about your feelings. Try to solve problems rather than running away from them or blaming your spouse.

If your commitment to each other is steady and firm, the baby can be a source that strengthens your relationship with your spouse, helping you both to find hidden sources of courage and to develop a deeper love and appreciation for each other. Chapter 6 discusses in greater detail parental and marital stress that may be still another effect your baby will have on your family.

If you have other children, you will naturally be concerned about the effect the new baby will have on them. This is a crucial test all parents encounter because siblings' initial reactions depend on you. *They will imitate your feelings and your actions toward the baby.* If you give the baby plenty of loving care, your other children will be encouraged to do the same. If you treat the baby more as a burden than as a family member, your other children will be more likely to react negatively toward their new brother or sister.

Older children and teenagers often accept the newcomer more easily and quickly than younger children. They may also have fewer problems accepting the fact that their new brother or sister has been placed in a group home, foster home, or institution.

Parents who decided not to bring their baby home agree that their decision seriously affected other children in the family. This is particularly true if the children are eight years old or younger.

One couple explained again and again to their five-year-old son that his baby brother needed to live away from home because it was better for him and because the doctors were close to him. But for nearly a year the little boy worried whenever his parents went somewhere without him. "Are you coming back?" he'd ask.

Another family tells of their six-year-old daughter who revealed her anxiety only at bedtime. She'd ask her parents, "Will you give me away if I get sick like my baby sister?" Her concern also lasted for more than a year.

It's a difficult situation, but with patience and reassurance you can resolve this problem if it occurs with one or more of your children. Simply explain to them the truth, that you will not leave your non-handicapped children or "give them away." If the questions persist, you must continue to patiently and calmly give the same answer. Keep in mind, however, that an *overdose* of patience and reassurance can also create problems for a concerned child, particularly that of overdependence.

SIBLING RIVALRY AND JEALOUSY

Acceptance of the new baby into your family doesn't rule out sibling rivalry and jealousy. Such emotions are not unusual. Yet they can be unintentionally encouraged if you spend more time with your Down's syndrome baby than with your other children. The same can happen if your family conversations and activities revolve around the baby.

This means taking care that you and your spouse continue to express your love toward your other children, and that you continue to give each of them enough time and attention. Time spent alone with each child can especially help in expressing your love and reassurance. Talking openly about the new baby with each child, and encouraging him or her to do the same, can also help.

Large family gatherings can sometimes provoke sibling rivalry and jealousy. These gatherings are usually a time for flaunting the achievements of brothers and sisters. The obvious slowness of a child with Down's syndrome may be embarrassing to a nonhandicapped sibling.

You can help avoid sibling rivalry and feelings of jealousy by watching for certain signals in your children's behavior.

Your preschooler may suddenly engage in hostile actions like hitting, punching, or protesting. Withdrawing from family activity, ignoring the baby, or reducing his or her demands on you are also danger signals.

Children about the age of four to six may begin to display some unusual and naughty behavior as well. Self-image problems at this time are not uncommon.

Your child of elementary school age may reject any responsibility toward a Down's syndrome sibling in favor of friends at school.

Adolescents may show signs of embarrassment of their sibling, especially when friends are around. Complaining about the child or finding fault with him or her are also warning signals.

Bickering can be a problem among children of any age. Bickering is often intended to attract your attention and provoke a reaction. Therefore, when there is bickering, let the children resolve the problem among themselves if possible. Interfere only if their safety is jeopardized or if you absolutely can't tolerate any more petty squabbling.

If you notice any of these or similar changes in your nonhandicapped children's behavior, you can remedy the situation. Your first action should be one of reassurance. Express your love to each child so that he or she will feel secure. This does not mean just telling the child you love him or her, but showing that love in your actions and attitudes toward the child.

Encourage your child to talk about his or her feelings and what causes them. (Understand, however, that many children, especially small children, do not always understand why they feel the way they do, or they may not be able to adequately articulate those feelings.) Talk with your child freely about the subject, and answer honestly any questions there may be. Be sure your child understands that he or she can talk with you about the new baby, or about his or her feelings about the baby, at any time.

Explain that no one knows why some babies are born with Down's syndrome and that they will always need more help than other babies do. Explain, too, that the more help the baby gets now, the less help he or she will need later. Help your nonhandicapped children understand that you are trying to prevent their brother or sister from becoming a burden to anyone as he or she grows older.

Some families I know handled the rivalry/jealousy situation by setting aside special days for their nonhandicapped children. One set of parents for whom this has worked told me, "We let them choose activities for a day away from home, and off we'd go, leaving the baby with a sitter. All of us felt much better after an outing. We continued doing this as long as the children wanted, for close to four years." Whether or not you choose to set aside special days for your other children, remember that spending time with each of them is extremely important.

ENLISTING THE HELP OF SIBLINGS

Providing daily care for babies with Down's syndrome can be a challenge because they require more time and attention than ordinary babies.

There is one best way to handle this situation—make the care of your baby a family affair. Teach your older children to help care for the new baby. This will also help siblings learn to accept their brother or sister.

One family I know decided to take their new baby everywhere they went—to church, to parties, on shopping trips. Since she was the youngest of five children, she never lacked a baby-sitter or a chance to go some place. One of the five, a nine-year-old daughter, would often read to the baby. "I think she got more pleasure out of it than the baby did," says their mother, "because she had a captive audience."

Activities like these not only encourage bonds between the new baby and his or her siblings; they also provide excellent stimulation for the baby's development.

The important thing to remember, however, is that while you may *encourage* your other children to help care for the new baby, you should *never insist* that they help. If you insist, it can easily breed resentment, both toward you and the baby. But each time they do help out, be sure to let them know how much you appreciate their assistance, and tell them how much it helps the baby's growth and development. This gives siblings a feeling of being wanted and needed. Many parents believe there is an extra benefit for nonhandicapped siblings: they begin to realize how hard their brother or sister must work to achieve ordinary skills.

Frequent trips to the doctor with your new baby will attract the attention and curiosity of siblings so, if at all possible, encourage them to accompany you. They won't have a feeling of being left out, and they may have questions about the baby that they are hesitant to ask you.

Remember, never let your baby become a burden to your other children. And make sure they do not get the idea that they are or will be responsible for their Down's syndrome brother or sister when he or she is grown or when you are no longer able to provide the necessary care.

Explain to them that when the new baby becomes an adult he or she will leave home, just as they will.

Every now and then it is a good idea to reassess the particular activities you have asked siblings to perform in caring for their new brother or sister. Make any changes that are necessary. Peace will reign longer if you do.

HELPING YOUR OTHER CHILDREN OUTSIDE THE HOME

There is another kind of support you will need to provide for your children once they have accepted their new sister or brother into their lives: helping them explain the baby's condition to their friends. Children can often be quite cruel in their teasing. Comments like "Your brother's a retard" can hurt, but "You must be a retard yourself" can hurt even more.

Here are some ways you can help:

Let your children know that if they have been teased by their friends or classmates they can always come to you for help, support, and understanding.

Suggest to your children that they tell their friends about all the things the baby can do or is learning to do. This will help your children feel good, and it may help their friends understand that a Down's syndrome child is, above all, a human being.

You may wish to visit your children's school to talk about Down's syndrome. In most cases, teachers will be happy to have you come and speak. If you wish, bring your Down's syndrome baby with you so that your children's friends and classmates can see that the baby is really not very different from any other baby.

Urge your children to invite friends home to meet the baby. Once they have met the baby, the teasing often stops quickly. Let them watch you bathing or feeding, and let them help in some infant stimulation exercises. Encourage them to touch the baby, and (if they are old enough) to hold the baby. Some simple contact with your baby can make all the difference. Often the kids who are most relentless about teasing your children for having a "retard" brother or sister are the first ones to warm up to the baby when they actually have a chance to see and touch him or her.

It also helps if you can teach your children a simple way to explain Down's syndrome to their friends. For example, your child might say,

"My baby sister was born with Down's syndrome. That means she'll learn much slower than other kids. But nobody knows why it happens."

How your children explain the baby's disability is just as important as the explanation itself. If it is done openly and without shame, their friends will be more receptive and understanding. This is true even (perhaps especially) if their friends have been teasing them about the baby's disability.

Consider the case of Anne, the mother of an eleven-month-old baby with Down's syndrome named David. One day she and her son were sitting in their yard when an eight-year-old neighbor boy ran up to them and began chanting, "He's a retard! He's a retard!" Anne simply waited until he was through, then asked him if he would like some lemonade. He said yes. As they sipped their drinks Anne explained David's condition like this: "David has something called Down's syndrome and he will need special attention and education because he'll learn much slower than you." The explanation satisfied the youngster and he never called David a retard again.

Another aspect of helping your nonhandicapped children avoid teasing is a positive attitude. Many parents believe that siblings' attitudes toward a brother or sister with Down's syndrome determine whether or not their friends accept the baby. If your older children speak warmly of the baby, they will be less prone to being teased, and less hurt if teasing does begin. And, speaking generally, the better an attitude *you* have about your baby, the better an attitude your children will have.

Also encourage your children to simply ignore teasing, although we all know that in practice this is difficult. Still, some children, particularly preschoolers, may accept unkind remarks about a sibling with Down's syndrome with complete nonchalance.

YOUR ROLE AS PARENTS

The most important role for all parents is that of caring for their children and meeting their children's daily needs. But parents of children with Down's syndrome have other important roles.

If grandparents' attitude toward your baby is one of rejection, avoidance, or overprotection rather than acceptance, it may be because they are unsure of their role. They may hesitate to offer advice or assistance for fear that you will see this action as an intrusion. Or they may offer too much advice, or advice too often. Since everyone's emotions are on edge, you must be careful not to read things into grandparents' actions that aren't intended.

Keep the baby in the foreground of family activities. Explain that he or she needs all the extra help that's available. Encourage them to help out, and give them clues to let them know that you need their support. Then accept that support as it is offered. As for advice, acknowledge any that is given; then take whatever seems useful, and pass up whatever seems inappropriate.

You can help your own parents better understand their new grandchild, and Down's syndrome in general, by giving them this book and other materials to read. It is also important to let your parents know that they can (and should) express their feelings or concerns to you about your child at any time. They should feel free to ask you any questions they may have as well. Listen to their feelings, questions, and concerns openly, and respond to them as sincerely and as helpfully as you can. Give them support in accepting their new grandchild.

To a slightly lesser extent, this same advice also applies to your other relatives, and to friends.

COMMUNITY ACTION

You may discover, as other parents have, that you will have to get involved in community action if the needs of your child are to be met.

If infant stimulation or preschool programs are not available, you may have to persuade local school boards or social service agencies to establish these programs. During your child's school age years you will learn to work in partnership with teachers to make sure your child receives an appropriate education. If few or no opportunities exist for your child in recreation or employment, you may have to become an organizer of other parents of Down's syndrome children and together make your children's needs known. This often includes acting as a lobbyist to secure laws that will protect your child.

Being a care giver of a child with Down's syndrome means being a change maker. You must be ready and willing to change whatever needs changing and to make sure that the world in which your child lives is right for him or her.

CHAPTER 3

The First Year

Your child is unique. While there may be family resemblance, and while your child may have some of the physical characteristics of Down's syndrome, your child is still his or her own person, an individual who is different from everyone else on this planet.

No two people are born with the exact same talents, biological strengths and weaknesses, or abilities to function. Your child's growth and behavior will follow a special pattern. You can encourage, shape, and enhance your baby's individuality by providing his or her daily care with love and optimism. This loving, optimistic environment is extremely important in helping your baby get a good start in life.

Just as important is the kind of day-to-day physical care your baby receives. Usually the daily care of a Down's syndrome baby is no different from that given to other babies. But occasionally some problems arise that are unique to children with Down's syndrome. I'll go through these one at a time.

FEEDING TECHNIQUES

It's not likely that your baby will need a special diet. All you need to do is follow the feeding advice that applies to all babies. However, you should be aware of some problems your child may have learning to eat.

Your baby may have difficulty sucking or swallowing milk due to poor muscle tone. If you are bottle-feeding, the sucking motion can be stimulated by enlarging the nipple hole so the milk flows easier. Or use a longer, softer nipple, such as those used for premature babies. Rotating the bottle in a circular motion by pressing up on the palate, then down on the tongue can improve sucking. These techniques will also help ease swallowing difficulties.

If you prefer breast-feeding and the baby is having difficulty, it's because nursing requires more effort than does bottle-feeding. It may be difficult for your baby to start nursing, and once started, he or she may have problems continuing. Many babies give up after the first two or three attempts even though they are hungry. Being hungry and not able to eat is frustrating and your baby will probably start crying or screaming. However, there are ways you can encourage him or her to start nursing and to continue until he or she is satisfied.

• Lure your baby to start nursing by putting something sweet on your nipple like honey or syrup.

• Start nursing your baby as soon as his or her cries let you know it's feeding time rather than letting the cries become screams. A screaming baby may refuse to nurse.

• Supplement breast-feeding with bottle-feeding until your baby gets the hang of nursing; this may take several weeks, so don't get discouraged. Like all babies, yours will eventually wean himself or herself from nursing.

Breast- or bottle-feeding your baby may be a lengthy process, because he or she is likely to feed slowly and may require frequent rest periods during a single feeding. And don't be surprised or worried if your baby falls asleep before a feeding is completed.

There isn't much you can do about the slow eating, but there are things you can and should do to keep your baby awake during feeding time. Singing or talking to your baby, snapping the soles of his or her feet with your fingers, or wiggling the fingers and toes will help. If your baby is asleep when feeding time comes, wake him or her up gently and gradually. Be sure your baby is fully awake before feeding begins and stick to a consistent feeding schedule.

Some parents report problems with Down's syndrome babies who fail to cry when they are hungry. One mother's solution worked very well. She replaced her baby's crib with a cradle and strung tiny bells around it. Whenever her baby squirmed or moved, she would hear the chimes and check on her. If it was time to feed her, she got fed.

These solutions keep babies on a consistent schedule and provide them with regular interaction with their parents. So talk, sing, or coo to your baby during feedings. At first there will be little or no response, but don't get discouraged. Eventually you will get that first smile or funny noise, and you will shout for joy.

Parents and pediatricians alike warn against propping the bottle up and leaving your baby unattended. Not only is this an impersonal way to feed, but there is a danger that your baby could inhale milk into the lungs. This can cause problems.

You can teach your baby to hold the bottle by placing his or her hands around it. Again, you must be consistent if your child is to learn this skill. Start-and-stop tactics just don't work with Down's children.

You can begin to include mashed or strained food in your baby's diet at about age three or four months. He or she may push the food out with the tongue or have difficulty transferring food from the spoon to the back of the mouth. If this happens, press the tongue down with the spoon, then press the upper lip down and the chin up to close the mouth. Gradually the baby will learn to accept the food properly. Be sure not to use a spoon that is too big, and don't try to stuff too much food in your baby's mouth at once. It is helpful to use the same spoon at every feeding so that your baby gets used to the shape and size of the spoon.

You can begin teaching your child to self-feed when he or she is about eight months old. Here are some suggestions:

Break the activity into small steps.

Before you feed your baby a particular kind of food, point to that food and say its name. Do the same after first putting that food in his or her mouth. Do this at every feeding.

The following procedure works well:

STEP 1: Pick up the spoon, show it to your baby, and say the word "spoon"; repeat at every meal for at least a week.

STEP 2: Repeat step 1; place the spoon in your baby's hand and wrap his or her fingers around it; repeat the entire process at every meal for several days.

STEP 3: Repeat steps 1 and 2; then start raising the spoon to your baby's mouth; do this for several days at every meal.

STEP 4: Repeat the first three steps; then help your baby spoon up the food and put it in his or her mouth; repeat this action again and again, but each time give less help until the child masters the technique.

Breaking up each activity into steps helps Down's babies achieve success easier and faster. Identifying the food and the utensil will stimulate speech and language development.

Be sure to reward each accomplishment with a smile, applause, or a hug. This can work wonders.

BATHING AND SKIN CARE

It is a good idea to establish a regular routine for your baby's bath. Give the bath at the same time each day, and go through the same motions in the same sequence each day.

It is best to choose a time when your baby is wide awake so that you can practice a few stimulating exercises at the same time. Move those tiny arms up and over his or her head. Then bring the legs up toward the chest to strengthen the muscles. Sing, coo, or talk to your little one all during bath time for auditory and language stimulation.

Bathing your baby may be difficult if he or she has poor muscle tone. Instead of using the family tub, you might try bathing the baby on a soft towel or in a small sink or basin. Always use a soft washcloth or sponge. Be sure to put a towel under the basin to prevent it from slipping. You can also substitute a sponge bath for your tiny newborn until you feel comfortable using a tub or basin.

Very often these babies have dry skin problems that can become more acute during the winter months. Using a superfatted soap and lots of skin cream should ease the condition. (If it doesn't, see your pediatrician or a dermatologist.)

OTHER SPECIAL PROBLEMS

SPITTING

During the first few weeks, babies with Down's syndrome have a tendency to spit up their food. Some parents are amazed at the force behind the spitting. "Just like a bullet," one parent told me. "I was concerned about our baby not getting enough to eat and not gaining weight."

Usually no cause for this phenomenon can be found, but in almost all cases it disappears on its own with a few weeks. However, it is always a good idea to bring your baby to the pediatrician to determine if this is just spitting or truly vomiting, which can be a more serious problem.

TEETHING

Children with Down's syndrome can begin teething between the age of thirteen and eighteen months. Very often they will cut molars first. Accompanying high fever is not unusual. For most children the teething process is very slow. It can take a long time for each tooth to come through, often as much as a couple of weeks.

OTHER DENTAL PROBLEMS

Down's babies tend to have more dental problems than do other babies. The problem is sometimes caused by the underdevelopment of the upper jaw. If the lower jaw grows at a normal rate and the upper one does not, the teeth will not meet properly. This makes biting and chewing difficult. The small upper jaw can also lead to crowding of permanent teeth.

It is very important for these babies to have regular dental care and to develop good oral hygiene habits early on. This helps minimize or prevent many potential problems. The earlier you start, the better.

INFANT DENTAL DEVELOPMENT AND CARE

All newborn babies appear to be toothless, yet the twenty primary teeth that will erupt in the next two to three years are present in the jawbones at birth. In fact, the crowns of these teeth are almost completely formed at birth.

When your child's first teeth begin to erupt, it is up to you to take care of them. After each meal you should wipe the teeth and gums with a damp cloth or gauze pad. This helps remove plaque, a sticky, colorless film of bacteria that forms on everybody's teeth, which is the major cause of dental caries (tooth decay) and peridontal (gum) disease. To clean your child's teeth, you can sit on a sofa or chair with his or her head raised on your lap, or you can lay the child on a flat surface with the head raised. Since this may not be a good position for every child, be sure to consult your doctor or dentist before trying it.

Decay can happen as soon as teeth begin to appear. One cause of serious tooth decay among very young children is a condition dentists call "nursing bottle mouth." This condition occurs when a baby is given a bottle of milk, formula, sugar water, or fruit juice to drink at nap time or bedtime. If these liquids pool around the child's teeth while he or she is sleeping, the teeth are attacked by acids for long periods of time and this can cause decay. According to the American Dental Association, this risk can be reduced if you give your child just a bottle of water at nap or bedtime.

Thumb-sucking is a baby's natural reflex, and without it he or she would not seek food. It is a habit that all babies develop which makes them feel secure and happy. Usually this habit decreases after the age of two. However, if your child continues to suck his or her thumb vigorously and continuously beyond the age of four, some dental problems can occur. The pressure caused by thumb-sucking can force the teeth out of position and narrow the dental arches. Irregular teeth are not a pleasant sight, are more prone to decay, and make chewing food more difficult. Damaged teeth and narrow arches may require orthodontic treatment to improve your child's appearance and help the teeth work more effectively again.

When your baby starts teething, it is quite likely he or she will have sore and tender gums, which can cause irritability. You can relieve this tenderness by gently rubbing your baby's gums with your finger (which must be clean) or with a small, cool spoon. You can also give your baby a *clean* teething ring to chew on. If he or she continues to be cranky and uncomfortable, your doctor or dentist can prescribe a medicine that gives relief.

COMMON HEALTH PROBLEMS

While all babies seem to have their share of health problems, there are some that are more common to children with Down's syndrome.

OBESITY

As your child grows older, he or she may develop a tendency toward obesity. You can prevent this from becoming a problem by limiting the amount of high-calorie foods in your baby's diet.

INFECTIONS

Many Down's babies are susceptible to respiratory infections and pneumonia. Providing adequate humidity throughout the house with a humidifier or vaporizer can reduce the risk of such problems. Continued incidence of such infections should be brought to the attention of your doctor.

Frequent ear infections are also common among these babies, as are episodes of fluid collection in the middle ear. You should be alert to symptoms that indicate ear problems, such as crying if the ears are touched, pulling at the ears, or excessive crying when your baby has a cold. These symptoms demand immediate medical attention to avoid possible hearing problems in the future.

THYROID DEFICIENCIES

Although the physical growth of babies with Down's syndrome is naturally slower than that of other babies, it is sometimes aggravated by a thyroid hormone deficiency.

Extensive studies show that the average height for a two-year-old "normal" child is nearly thirty-five inches (89 cm), while a child with Down's syndrome at the same age averages three inches less in height, or thirty-two inches (81 cm). However, all children, including those with Down's syndrome, will show a significant variation in their growth range. This variation is influenced by the same factors. Genetic, racial, nutritional, environmental, and congenital irregularities will affect the growth of any child.

The thyroid gland is a two-lobed structure located in front of and on either side of the trachea (also called the windpipe). This gland produces and supplies thyroid hormones to the bloodstream. These hormones are needed to regulate the rate of many body functions, such as burning up food and the amount of oxygen that is used. Too much of the hormone speeds up these processes and too little slows them down.

A basic element, iodine, is necessary in the production of thyroid hormones, and most people need just a small amount of it to meet their needs for adequate hormonal production. If the thyroid gland does not produce enough hormones, a deficiency occurs known as hypothyroidism. Although this deficiency is rare among newborns, it can happen and is considered an extremely serious illness. If it is not promptly treated, growth retardation and permanent brain damage can be the result. It is very important, then, that the initial examination of all newborns includes a check for hypothyroidism. This hormone deficiency can be recognized in juveniles by delayed dentition (cutting teeth), muscle cramps, fatigue, growth retardation, sleepiness, a sensation of being cold all the time, dry coarse skin, and mental retardation. These same symptoms are observable in adolescents along with early sexual maturation.

Thyroid hormone deficiency can be treated with replacement therapy of the hormone in the form of pills that are prepared from animal origin or synthetic material. The average dose is one pill a day and it doesn't need to be taken at any specific time as is frequently the case with other medications. Very often thyroid hormone production can be restored to complete normality after a few weeks of treatment, however, this treatment almost always is necessary for the rest of one's life.

If your child shows symptoms of thyroid deficiency or if you suspect he or she was not examined for it at birth, you should ask your pediatrician or family doctor to perform the tests that tell how your child's thyroid gland is functioning. These tests measure the amount of thyroid hormone in the blood and how well the thyroid gland accumulates iodine.

HEART PROBLEMS

Congenital heart disease is common to babies with Down's syndrome. Symptoms of this illness vary from a mild murmur to a severe malfunction. These heart problems can often go unrecognized by your pediatrician at birth. However, some of the signs that indicate that something is wrong include lethargy, small size, listlessness, and a failure to cry when hungry or unhappy or in pain. Babies who seem to sleep too much, who appear drowsy even while awake, or who regularly need to be awakened at mealtime could have serious heart murmurs and should be checked by a doctor.

If your child does have a heart condition, your doctor may want to use a heart catheter process to determine what kind of problem exists. In this process a slender, flexible tube is inserted into a vein and into the heart. If the condition is severe enough, your pediatrician may recommend open-heart surgery for your child.

Deciding whether or not to authorize open-heart surgery can be a very difficult decision for parents. One Down's syndrome child of my acquaintance, a baby girl named Kerri, had a serious heart murmur. Her pediatrician used a heart catheter and told her parents that there was little chance of her survival beyond the age of two without the surgery, and only a fifty-fifty chance with it. He recommended surgery within the next six months.

After long and agonizing discussions, the parents decided against the surgery. "Those odds weren't good enough for us," they said, "and we didn't want to risk losing Kerri on the operating table. It was a tough decision."

Although their doctor recommended yearly catheter checks for Kerri, her parents also decided against them. "It's a painful procedure," they told me. "And why put her through it since she wasn't having surgery?"

Some parents have authorized the surgery, still others chose not to but did authorize regular catheter checks.

INTESTINAL PROBLEMS

A small percentage of babies with Down's syndrome are born with incomplete intestinal development. The large intestine may be in an abnormal position, or the lower part of the large bowel may not function. Such malformations can be corrected through surgery.

OTHER DISORDERS

It is not unusual for Down's babies to have constipation problems. If your child is having any problems, try increasing his or her liquid intake to include lots of water and fruit juice, especially prune juice. Serve high-fiber cereals for breakfast and again at snack time. Pieces of dried fruit make good snacks too and are a nice change from cereal. Be sure your child gets plenty of exercise. When an infant is constipated, try adding a teaspoon of syrup to an eight-ounce bottle of milk or formula. It should bring relief. If none of these home remedies solves your child's problem, you should consult your doctor before you administer any over-the-counter laxatives.

Sometimes Down's babies are prone to stomach reflex problems caused by weak stomach muscles. Because of this poor reflex, food can sometimes rise to their lungs, mix with lung fluid, and cause lung congestion. If your child has this problem, you can ease the discomfort and help to avoid further bouts by limiting his or her fluid intake. It is also helpful to keep your baby in an upright position for at least two hours after each meal so that food will be digested properly. While this treatment will help, it's best to seek your doctor's advice about the length of treatment and other effective means of dealing with this problem.

Eye problems occur more frequently among children with Down's syndrome than among normal children. The most common problems are nearsightedness (myopia) and crossed eyes (strabismus), both of which can be easily corrected with glasses. Adults with Down's syndrome seem to be more susceptible to cataracts than do their nonhandicapped peers.

It is important to remember that although children with Down's syndrome are *in general* more susceptible to these ailments than are nonhandicapped children, this does not necessarily mean that your child will have *any* of these problems. He or she may have none of them, or perhaps just one or two. But there is the chance that the child may have several of these ailments, though probably not all at the same time. It is almost impossible that your child will have *all* of the health problems described in this chapter. Most problems are more common in childhood, particularly during the first year or two of life. Some, however, can continue into the adult years.

Like all babies, your child should be brought to the pediatrician at regular intervals for well-baby checks. These checks can help prevent health problems before they occur and catch mild problems before they grow worse. You should bring your child in for well-baby checks at three weeks and again at six weeks. At about eight weeks, immunization programs should be started and routine checkups should coincide with your baby's immunization schedule. See the chart for the usual schedule for childhood immunizations. Once the immunizations are complete, your child should have a health check at least once a year.

Since routine checkup schedules can vary among pediatricians according to their policies, your doctor may have other suggestions, especially if your baby has any significant health problems. Remember, if your child has some unusual health problems, your doctor may make some changes in either the regular health-check schedule or the immunization schedule.

IMMUNIZATION SCHEDULE

Two months	First DPT (diptheria, pertussis—also known as whooping cough—and tetanus)
	First polio
Four months	Second DPT, second polio
Six months	Third DPT, last polio
One year	First tuberculosis skin test
Fifteen months	Mumps, measles, and rubella
Eighteen months	Boosters for DPT and polio
Two years	Another tuberculosis skin test (this should be done annually or as your doctor advises)
Four to six years	Continued DPT and polio, as suggested by your doctor

It is also important for your baby's well-being to have regular eye examinations, with the first one at age six months. Later on, if your little one has trouble recognizing familiar faces, repeatedly bumps into things, has a noticeable turn in one or both eyes, fails to respond to visual stimulation, or holds objects very close to the face, he or she should be given a complete eye exam.

By age three, children's visual development is sufficient enough so that an eye examination can effectively test their ability to see. Many eye care professionals recommend a complete eye examination for three year olds or for younger children if any indications of less than perfect sight appear.

TRAPS FOR PARENTS TO AVOID

Under ordinary circumstances, the responsibilities of parenthood are demanding. For parents of a baby with Down's syndrome, the situation becomes more demanding and has fewer guidelines. As a result, it is possible to create unpleasant or unrealistic situations for yourself, which is as harmful as it is unnecessary. Here are some common traps to avoid:

GIVING UP YOUR SOCIAL LIFE

After the diagnosis of Down's syndrome is confirmed and you realize that no miraculous cure will be forthcoming, you may lapse into a phase of withdrawal and isolation. Other parents have had the same experience. Some give up all social life—Saturday night bridge, volunteer activities, evenings with relatives, even church involvement. They refuse all invitations, using having to care for their Down's syndrome baby as an excuse. They wallow in pity for themselves, for their baby, and for their other children.

The urge to withdraw and to isolate yourself is natural during times of stress. And you should allow yourself *at first* to withdraw for a time —perhaps a few weeks, a couple of months at the most. But then you must return to society and a normal way of life again. Withdrawal becomes unnatural when no effort is made to rejoin the rhythm of life. You must make this effort. If the social life you led before your baby was born no longer interests you (and sometimes this can happen), then search for new activities, interests, or acquaintances.

Some parents say that something within them had to die before they could resume a social life. That "something," of course, are the dreams you had for your baby that you now know cannot and will not be fulfilled. However, once you let go of your impossible dreams and replace them with possible ones, you will experience a kind of rebirth and life will become easier.

THE SUPERPARENT SYNDROME

So much more is entailed in caring for your baby with Down's syndrome—learning about the disorder, handling unusual health problems, talking to other parents, dealing with your emotions, providing infant stimulation, and explaining to friends and relatives about this condition. And all in addition to the regular care you must provide for any baby. So it is often necessary (or at least tempting) to travel at top speed to accomplish all these tasks. And it is therefore very easy to fall into the superparent trap—and not always easy to get out.

You can avoid this trap if you follow these suggestions:

Force yourself to keep an even, steady pace, one that is not too fast. Too fast a pace can often lead to exhaustion, and in the long run you may end up getting less done than if you had kept on slowly and steadily.

Make a list of all the things you feel you should do. Then select those tasks that are an absolute *must* and do them first, or do them only. Breaking those tasks down into short blocks of time, or into smaller subtasks, really helps. Keep a journal of the completed tasks, and notice how much you have managed to accomplish.

As for those tasks that are less than absolutely essential, break them down into two categories: Very Important and Less Than Very Important. Remember that *no* task in either category is strictly urgent or even necessary, and that you can get by without doing it. (If you can't get by without doing it, move it to your list of absolute musts.)

If possible, enlist the help of others—parents, grandparents, children, other relatives, and friends—to do some of these tasks for you. Better yet, hire outside people to do some of them, if you can afford it.

Be sure to take some time off to relax, have fun, or just be by yourself or with your spouse. In fact, plan on it and put some of these pleasant activities on your "Must Do" list, if you can't seem to squeeze them in any other way. These relaxing things are important for your own mental and physical health, and they will help you overcome the Superparent syndrome.

Go through your lists occasionally—perhaps once or twice a week. Cross off items you have completed, or that you have ceased to worry about. Move items from one list to another.

Making and keeping these lists will slow you down. If you wish, you can describe in detail what you did and how you felt about doing it. The sense of accomplishment you can get from keeping this kind of a journal can be surprisingly large. And crossing completed items off your lists will make you realize just how many things you *have* accomplished.

NEGLECTING OTHER CHILDREN

Because your Down's syndrome baby is likely to demand more care and attention, you may inadvertently fall into another trap—neglecting your other children. This can cause them to develop resentment toward you and the baby.

Resentment is typically expressed in one of two ways. Either your child will reduce his or her demands on you, or he or she will exhibit annoying behavior guaranteed to attract your attention. Reduction of demands is most likely to occur when a child is of junior or senior high school age, while annoying behavior will be more common in younger children.

Be careful, therefore, to continue with pleasant family activities—picnics, vacations, dinners out, movies, even something as simple as sitting around together, talking, or watching TV. This is especially important for those activities your family has done regularly or at specified times. Don't interrupt your regular activities, but continue them precisely as before.

Do not demand that your other children be on constant call as baby-sitters. This will surely breed resentment. You can *ask* your children to sit occasionally, but do not *demand* it of any of them except in an emergency. Instead, find a sitter whenever possible. Using the excuse "we can't find a sitter" may be convenient, but don't use it too often, and even then use it only when it is absolutely the last resort.

Avoid getting so involved with your Down's syndrome baby that you ignore or pay little attention to the accomplishments of your other children. This is easy to do because they are normal and you expect them to be achievers. When they are, you are proud of them, of course, but you may fail to mention that fact because you assume that achieving comes naturally to them. Or you may assume that they know you are pleased. But don't make such assumptions; take time to give your other children the praise, rewards, encouragement, and love they need. Let them know that you appreciate every one of their achievements. Ignoring your nonhandicapped children can hurt even more when they see you giving special praise to their sibling for doing things they could accomplish easily.

Don't avoid going to school functions in which your other children participate. That's a clear message that you don't care and that you are more interested in your Down's syndrome baby. And *don't* be more interested in this baby. Spend time with all your children, and make sure each of them feels loved and cared about.

You can avoid neglecting your other children by watching for signs of resentment or withdrawal. And watch yourself. If you find that every minute of your day is spent caring for or worrying about your baby, stop and make some changes.

NEGLECTING YOUR BABY

There may be times when the care of your baby becomes frustrating and seemingly overwhelming. Day after day you have sung, talked, and cooed to this baby. You have also bounced, jiggled, and exercised the little one. Yet you can see little or no progress.

It may be tempting to ask yourself, "What's the use?" It is easy to convince yourself that your efforts are in vain. You may be tempted to stop the stimulation exercises. Or, if you have other children, you may be tempted to concentrate all your attention on them because they can give you pride, satisfaction, and other immediate rewards.

Remember that all your efforts *will* pay off. So hang in there. Your baby's progress will be slow, especially at first. But once you've gotten that first reaction—that laugh, smile, or attempt at words—you'll realize that your efforts were well spent. And from that time on, your baby will continue to respond more and more.

So make a conscious effort to compliment yourself, your spouse, and your children for all the efforts you are making with your Down's syndrome baby even if, for the moment, the baby is barely reacting to them or not at all. And when the reactions do start coming, look for each of your baby's accomplishments, and take credit for each one of them. You may want to keep a journal of your baby's progress and of all the things he or she learns to do. Remember that without your efforts, your baby could not have made as much progress.

COMPARING YOUR BABY TO SIBLINGS

Bringing up your baby is never a bed of roses. There will always be various forces tugging and pulling at you. One force at this stage of parenting is the urge to compare your baby's accomplishments to those of his or her siblings, or to those of children of friends and relatives.

But it is important to resist this temptation because it can only lead to sadness and frustration. Instead, look at each of your baby's accomplishments and compare what he or she can do now with what he or she was able to do two or three months ago. When you make *this* kind of comparison, you will be pleased with and proud of your baby's progress. You can also be pleased with yourself because you know that without your care and attention, this progress would not have been made.

Do continue to keep in mind that *every* baby, handicapped or not, develops entirely at his or her own speed. You can help your child develop as fast as possible by following the advice in Chapter 2—but your baby will still have some limits.

By the way, don't even compare your baby's progress with that of other Down's syndrome babies because the natural difference in development between any two babies can be quite large. Remember when you look at the progress checklist for Down's syndrome babies that since your baby is unique he or she may accomplish some of the tasks somewhat faster or slower than the checklist indicates.

PROGRESS CHECKLIST FOR BABY

One month	Raises head when lying on stomach
	Moves legs and arms energetically
Two months	Smiles and coos
	Rolls partway to side when lying on back
Three months	Grasps objects placed in hand
	Holds head erect
Four months	Laughs aloud
	Sits with support
Five months	Reaches for and holds objects
	Likes to play peek-a-boo

Six months	Sits with little support
	Crows and squeals
Seven months	Transfers objects from hand to hand
	Pats and smiles at image in mirror
Eight months	Crawls
	Uses pincer grasp
Nine months	Mimics sounds
	Stands holding onto support
Ten months	Drinks from cup
	Pulls self up at side of crib
Eleven months	Walks holding onto furniture
	Finds hidden objects
Twelve months	Feeds self with fingers
	Walks supported by one hand

NOTE: The ages listed above are *approximate*. Your baby will learn each of these skills at his or her own speed. However, if your child is more than a month or two late in learning any of these skills, you should check with your pediatrician.

UNREASONABLE EXPECTATIONS FOR YOUR BABY

Another force that may tug at you during this first year is expecting too much or too little of your baby. If he or she has responded to the games and stimulation exercises, you may have the urge to double your efforts with the expectation that more progress will be made. But because Down's syndrome babies, like all babies, can develop only so far so fast, past a certain point you may find that your extra efforts do not produce any significant improvement.

On the other hand, it is possible to have extremely low expectations for your baby because you have accepted the false notion that he or she can't learn to do what other children can, or because you have accepted the equally false myth that Down's syndrome children can't really be taught much of anything. This trap can be easy to fall into, especially if you have been led to believe this by a doctor or other health professionals. Remember, the "human vegetable" view of Down's syndrome people was proven to be completely and utterly false decades ago.

If your expectations for your child are too low, you may find yourself putting in less than enough energy and effort. And the less effort, care, and attention you give to your child, the slower his or her development is likely to be. So expectations that are too low can lead to a vicious cycle of lower achievement and still lower expectations.

Unreasonably high or low expectations for your child can be as dangerous as your desire to compare him or her to other children. Reasonable expectations are easier to set and reach if you remember these facts:

• Your baby is unique and has his or her own individual rate for growth and development.

• At first it will be hard to know what expectations are reasonable and which ones are not. But as the months pass, you will get a better idea of how quickly your own unique baby can develop. By comparing his or her past development with the checklist I've provided, you can get a pretty good idea of how the development will continue in the future months.

• Quite often Down's syndrome babies experience rapid growth spurts, then suddenly stop developing for a little while. Sooner or later, growth spurts will start again.

Eventually you can expect your baby to accomplish all the same skills as other babies. Just remember to be patient because it will take longer. And remember to set small goals. That makes teaching your baby much easier, more enjoyable, and much more rewarding for everyone. And it gives your baby more accomplishments for you to be pleased with and proud of.

If your expectations turn out to be unreasonable at any time, reassess the situation and modify those expectations. It is always more realistic to change your expectations than to try to force your baby to develop faster or slower than his or her own natural rate.

Occasionally illness or physical impairment may slow your child's development, or a particular activity must be temporarily abandoned or slowed down because of the undue stress it may create for the baby. In either case, or in any case where your child's development may be slowed, it is important to lower your expectations accordingly.

UNREASONABLE EXPECTATIONS FOR YOUR OTHER CHILDREN

Sometimes it is easy to forget that each of your *other* nonhandicapped children also has a unique rate of growth and development. Some parents of Down's syndrome children find themselves expecting their other children to be completely normal—that is, either to be free of problems or to develop physically, mentally, and emotionally at rates that are exactly average.

Because every child has his or her own strengths, weaknesses, and difficulties, this can be dangerous. *The expectations you have for your other children should be exactly the same as those you had for them before your Down's syndrome baby was born.* If your six year old is slow at arithmetic, very likely she is going to continue to be slow, at least for a while. Don't expect her to magically become a math whiz because she doesn't have Down's syndrome. Or, if your ten year old is tall for his age and an excellent basketball player, he is going to continue to be tall for a while, and he will probably continue to do well on the basketball court.

It is easy to begin to feel that your other children have no problems—or, worse, that they have no *right* to have problems—because they do not have Down's syndrome. This is unrealistic. Growing up isn't easy for any child, and all of your nonhandicapped children will still have their share of problems. Be sure to continue dealing with these problems just as you would have before the new baby was born. This means listening to and helping them. And it means being available to your children when they need you. Under *no* circumstances should you ignore a child's problem because he or she is normal and can handle it alone. Remember, too, that even among nonhandicapped children, rates of growth and development can vary widely.

YOUR BABY'S FIRST BIRTHDAY

As your baby approaches his or her first birthday, look back on the year and realize just how much you and your baby have both accomplished. It is a good idea to make up a written list of every task your baby has learned, every skill he or she has acquired. Very likely it will be longer and more impressive than you had thought. Rejoice in each of your baby's triumphs. If you have been keeping a journal, you may want to reread it from the beginning, noticing how much you both have learned.

After you have rejoiced in all of your baby's triumphs, rejoice in your and your spouse's. After all, every one of your baby's accomplishments is partly your doing. Make a list of all the things the two of you have learned in caring for your new baby. Give yourselves credit where credit is definitely due. Be proud of all your successes as parents of a special child.

Look over the lists at the end of this chapter. If you wish, use them to help make up your own lists. Which items apply to you? Can you add more of your own?

Now light your baby's first birthday candle and have a big celebration.

PROGRESS CHECKLIST FOR PARENTS

Have you settled down to a steady pace?
Is it easier to talk about your child?
Has that lonely, helpless feeling disappeared?
Which traps were you able to avoid?
Are you proud of your baby's accomplishments? Of your own?

PROGRESS CHECKLIST FOR SIBLINGS

Do they willingly help care for the baby?
Can they explain the baby's condition to friends?
Are they no longer embarrassed by the baby in front of friends?
Do they understand how difficult it is for the baby to achieve the skills that are so easy for others to learn?
Is their emotional behavior under control?

CHAPTER 4

The Second Year

The moment your baby was born was the moment you became his or her teacher. If you hummed, cooed, or sang to your baby, you were showing what love is about. If you tickled your child's feet and made funny noises, you were helping to develop the senses of touch and hearing. Later on, if you played pat-a-cake or peek-a-boo with your baby, you were teaching cognitive, muscular, and language skills.

Now this second year is the time to start teaching your baby self-help skills. At first your child may have some difficulty acquiring some of these skills, but with consistent and conscientious practice, and with patience on your part, he or she will master them all.

As you teach your child dressing, feeding, and toileting skills, remember that there will be times of frustration, times when your child seems to make little progress no matter what you do. When this happens, try a slower pace—but don't give up. Your child *will* learn all the skills discussed in this chapter eventually. Just keep in mind that whatever your child learns will be his or hers forever because you were consistent and patient.

TOILET TRAINING

Like all children, your child can and will learn to take care of toileting needs. The time this takes depends on how ready both you and your child are to begin this task. You must watch for some signs from your child.

If your child's diapers stay unsoiled for an hour or two at a time, or if he or she shows signs of discomfort once the diapers have become wet or soiled, these are usually indications that your child is ready for toilet training. Perhaps the most important sign of readiness is when your child understands and follows simple commands about cleanliness or tidiness—for example, "Don't put that in your mouth."

Watching for these signs of readiness is very important, because if you start the training before your child is ready, your efforts will likely be frustrating and fruitless.

HINTS FOR TOILET TRAINING

First you must establish a training schedule for your child, and you must follow it faithfully. Anything less will only increase the difficulty of the task, for both of you.

The ideal training schedule should involve three to six sessions a day, each one five to ten minutes long, and each one taking place at the same time every day. One excellent training schedule would be to put your child on the training chair at morning wake up, either before or after each meal, at midday, and at bedtime.

Through trial and error, you will learn and develop some toilet training techniques of your own. However, you may want to follow some methods that other parents have devised:

• Place your child on the training chair, say the word "potty," and point to his or her bottom.

• Allow your child to spend five to ten minutes on the potty chair. If he or she doesn't eliminate within that time, end the session anyway.

• Stay with your child at all times during these sessions.

• Explain what is happening at all times. When you place your child on the training chair, say, "On you go," and when you take him or her off, say, "Off you go."

• Keep the potty chair in the bathroom to teach the idea of privacy, and keep the bathroom door closed.

• If you decide to use the regular toilet for training, place a child-sized seat over it. Provide a footstool so that your child can climb up to the toilet. This will make the child more comfortable, and it provides muscular exercise.

- Remove your child from the toilet before flushing it to avoid frightening him or her.
- Better yet, let your child help you do the flushing and learn at the onset that this is an important part of good toilet habits.
- The sound of running water helps to "inspire" elimination.
- Don't distract your child with stimulating toys while he or she is on the toilet.
- The child's outer clothing should be easy to remove—and, ideally, easy to put back on.
- Use training pants instead of diapers, as they are easier to pull up and down. Some parents prefer to buy oversized pants for quick removal.
- As your child shows progress, show your pleasure with verbal praise, a smile, a hug, or some other reward, but don't overdo it.
- Once your child has learned to use the potty chair, teach these steps one at a time: pulling down his or her own pants and underpants, sitting down on the chair without help, wiping his or her bottom, closing the cover afterward, and pulling up his or her pants and underpants again.
- At first you will simply have potty sessions at regular intervals. But once your child has learned to use the training chair, teach him or her to use it whenever necessary.
- Try to relax and stay calm, even when accidents happen. Sooner or later your child will successfully learn to manage.
- A diet that includes fruit and roughage (fresh green vegetables, whole grain bread, and so on) will help keep your child regular. So will plenty of exercise.

Learning good toileting habits at an early age is helpful to girls when they begin to menstruate. If they are accustomed to wearing fresh, clean underwear, they will have fewer problems learning to change sanitary pads.

Toilet training is normally a slow process. Your child may progress rapidly for a time, then suddenly stop. There may even be a brief regression stage. This is normal (but not inevitable), so when this happens, try to relax. Don't push too hard, but don't give up either. Simply keep to your training schedule and continue to follow these parents' suggested methods.

Here's a piece of good news. Your child won't necessarily be slower to learn toilet training than will children who are not handicapped. In fact, he or she might even learn more quickly. I have had parents of

Down's syndrome children tell me that their Down's children were *easier* to toilet train—sometimes much easier—than their normal children.

DRESSING

The best way to teach your child to dress is to break each task into small parts, and teach one part at a time. This will seem a bit strange to you because dressing for you has become automatic. But chances are good that your parents taught you to dress yourself by teaching you one task at a time.

A good way to break down the tasks of dressing is to consciously note what you do first, second, third, and so on when you put on or take off a piece of clothing. Write down each step in order for each item. (You'll be surprised how many steps are necessary to put on or take off all the clothing you have on right now.) Remember, once you know what the steps are, be sure to teach them *one at a time*. To avoid confusion and frustration, don't introduce a new step until your child has mastered the previous one.

Dressing lessons can also be used to encourage your child's cognitive and speech development. Each day, as you help your child get dressed, name each article of clothing. Say each of its parts out loud ("sleeve, button, collar"), and point to each part as you say its name. Then explain to your child exactly what you are about to do—for example, "Now we'll put the shirt over your head."

The best way to teach your child how to put on certain clothes such as shirts and sweaters is to teach the last step first and then work backward. This technique, called *backward chaining,* has proven very successful. I will describe this in more detail.

PUTTING ON T-SHIRTS AND OTHER PULLOVER GARMENTS

Put the shirt on and leave it bunched up under your child's arms. Take your child's hands, help him or her grasp the shirt, and pull it down while you say, "Pull your shirt down."

When your child can perform this task alone, you should introduce the remaining steps.

1. Remove one arm from the sleeve and teach the child how to replace the arm as you say, "Put this arm in this sleeve." This statement is followed by "Pull your shirt down."

2. Remove both arms and repeat the instructions in step 1.

3. Hold the shirt opening over your child's head and say, "Put your head through here." Then repeat the instructions from the previous steps.

4. To avoid having your child put the shirt on backward, be sure it is clearly marked at the back. Call your child's attention to the marking and say, "This goes toward your back," as you help position the shirt correctly over the head.

This same technique can be used to teach your daughter how to put on a dress. Just remember that constant repetition is necessary for your child to refine the skill to be mastered.

PUTTING ON COATS AND JACKETS

Your child can learn how to put on a coat or jacket in one of two ways. You may want to experiment with both methods to determine which one is easier for you to teach and for your child to learn.

In one method the garment should be spread on the floor, with the openings facing up. Have your child stand above the garment at the neck end. Then help him or her bend over, slip his or her arms into the sleeves, and flip it back over the head.

To use the second method the garment is also spread on the floor, with the openings facing up. Have your child lie back on the garment and help put his or her arms in the sleeves. Then assist him or her to a standing position and rearrange or straighten the garment out as needed.

PUTTING ON SKIRTS AND DRESSES

Instead of the step-in method, it is probably easier to teach your daughter to put on a skirt by using the overhead method. This way you don't have to deal with a balancing struggle. For this method, put the skirt on over your child's head and leave it bunched around her neck. Take her hands and help her grasp the skirt hem, then pull it down as you say, "Pull your skirt down." A skirt with an elasticized waist band is easy to pull on, but be sure the elastic isn't too tight. Later on when your child is better coordinated you may want to teach her how to step in a skirt rather than pulling it overhead.

HANDLING CLOSINGS

Here are some tips to help your child learn to zip or button skirts, shirts, jackets, and coats.

• Learning to close buttons is easier if they are large, about the size of a nickel. You may want to replace small buttons on a garment with larger ones. Buttoning is made even easier if you sew the large buttons on with elastic thread.

• Teach your child to button a garment from bottom to top to improve the chances of coming out even.

• Whenever possible use Velcro tabs for closings and avoid the buttons completely.

• Make pull tabs from metal or plastic toys and fasten on zippers for easier handling.

• Pulling a zipper away from clothes or skin helps prevent it from catching.

• Fasten wooden beads or small toys to the strings of hoods to prevent them from pulling out.

PUTTING ON PANTS

Sit in a comfortable position on the floor with your child in front of you. Pull the pants over your child's feet so that they are bunched up around the ankles. Help your child stand up, leaving the pants bunched around the ankles. Say, "Pull your pants up," as you place his or her hands on the waistband and pull up together. Continue with less and less help until your child can follow these steps unaided. Then introduce the remaining steps.

1. Remove one leg from the pants, help your child to a standing position, lift the foot of that leg, and say, "Put your foot in here." Help your child maintain his or her balance while standing on one foot, and place the other foot in the leg opening. Then instruct the child to pull the pants up. Gradually offer less and less help. When your child can

manage this *entire* task by following instructions only, you both are ready for the next step.

2. Help your child put both feet in the leg openings as you say, "Put one foot in here and the other in here," and follow with, "Pull your pants up."

3. Finally, hand the pants to your child and tell him or her to put them on and pull them up. Be sure the pants are marked at the back and teach your child to look for this mark.

After much repetition, your child will eventually develop and master this skill.

PUTTING ON SOCKS

Sit on the floor in a comfortable position with your child in front of you.

1. Put one sock on your child's foot, leaving it bunched around the ankle. Place your child's hands on the sock top and, together, pull the sock up. As you do this, say, "Pull up your sock." Repeat this process for both feet. Gradually reduce the amount of help until your child can do this alone.

2. Place the sock only over your child's toes. Put his or her thumb inside the sock, and say, "Pull up your sock." Repeat this for both feet. Continue this until your child automatically puts his or her thumbs into the sock and can pull it up without your help.

3. Leave the sock off your child's foot but bunched up. Put your child's hands on the sock, with the thumbs on the inside. Say, "Pull up your sock." Help your child get the sock over the toes at first if he or she needs help. Repeat for both feet. Gradually withdraw your physical assistance until your child can do this all alone.

4. Finally, teach your child how to bunch up the sock, first by doing it together, and then by gradually giving less and less help. Continue to say, "Pull up your sock."

Your child is likely to learn more easily and quickly if you begin the teaching with an older child's cotton socks. The larger socks are easier to put on and take off, and cotton socks are easier to handle than the stretch ones.

PUTTING ON SHOES AND BOOTS

At age two your child may not have the dexterity to learn the difficult and frustrating task of putting on shoes or boots and lacing them. However, you can begin by pointing out the difference between the right and left shoes by marking the inside edges with tape or waterproof colored marker. Show your child these marks as you slip the shoes on and explain how the marks must match up to get the shoes on the right feet.

You can also give your little one a headstart on learning how to lace the shoes by explaining exactly what you do each time you perform this task.

If your child has problems keeping the shoes laced and tied, you can substitute quarter-inch elastic for laces and sew the ends together. The elastic stretches and the shoes can be slipped on and off without lacing and tying.

Once your child has learned all the steps in putting on a particular item of clothing, gradually reduce the verbal cues from a step-by-step description to simply "Put on your shirt." Eventually you can simplify this further to "Get dressed."

Allowing your child some freedom each morning in selecting the outfit for the day will help him or her learn color coordination. The decision-making opportunity will also engender good feelings, and it will help your child develop a positive self-image.

Too much freedom of choice, however, can be frustrating and anxiety producing for both you and your child. One ideal solution is to offer your child the choice of either of two shirts, two pair of pants, and so on. This allows you to select color combinations that will look good, while allowing your child to choose a favorite item of each pair. As you present the choices, describe the items to your child: "Would you rather wear this green shirt today, or this blue-and-white striped one?"

If, after offering your child two choices for several weeks or months, you believe he or she can handle three choices, try that. Naturally, as your child grows older, you will want to offer more and more freedom in choosing outfits. By the time your child is five or six years old, he or she should be selecting daily outfits and dressing without help. You should, of course, make suggestions or critique those outfits if necessary.

An excellent and extremely thorough guide to kids' clothing and grooming, *Kids' Chic*, written by Gloria Gilbert Mayer and Mary Ellen McGlone and published by Evan, discusses in detail the arts of choosing and buying your child's clothes wisely, getting the best value for your money, teaching your child color coordination and grooming skills, and helping your child to look his or her best.

GROOMING AND HYGIENE

Helping your child learn the various phases of good grooming and hygiene will be easier if you establish a routine. This means teaching the same tasks at the same time every day. If you can avoid it, don't change or interrupt the routine as this will slow your child's learning.

The sooner your child learns to wash his or her hands after using the toilet and to brush his or her teeth after eating, the more likely he or she is to retain such habits. So start teaching your child basic hygiene soon after the second birthday. If you do, he or she will eventually take pleasure in staying clean and looking attractive. This pleasure also helps your child develop a good self-image which is so very important as he or she grows older.

Be sure to keep equipment within easy reach. Keep a sturdy step stool near the sink so your child can reach the faucets and see in the mirror.

Many parents tell stories to their toddlers while teaching them grooming and hygiene. However, do not distract your child with toys from the task at hand.

FACE WASHING

To start teaching your child to wash his or her face, use the following show-and-tell technique. Begin with step 1; repeat it each day, gradually giving less and less help until your child can perform the task with verbal instructions only. Then add step 2, again repeating the step with less and less help until your child has mastered it. Continue with this process until your child has mastered all the steps together. At each stage, explain what you and your child are doing as you do it.

1. Point to the washcloth, say, "Washcloth," put it in your child's hand, and together rub it gently over his or her face.

2. Next, wet the washcloth, squeeze it dry, and repeat step 1.

3. Point to the dry soap, say, "Soap," put the bar in your child's hand, and together smell the fragrance.

4. Tell your child to wet the washcloth and squeeze the water out. Give whatever help is needed, and be sure *you* control the water flow.

5. When he or she can follow step 4, show your child how to rub soap on the wet cloth.

6. Help rub the soapy cloth gently across your child's face.

7. Teach your child to rinse both the cloth and his or her face.

8. Teach your child how to use the faucets, but don't expect mastery of this for a long time, probably not until age four or five.

Once your child can follow all these steps with nothing more than your verbal instructions, gradually reduce those instructions until you can simply say, "Wash your face."

As your toddler accomplishes the practice of face washing, you may have to accept a result that is less than perfect, especially at first. So, much patience and persistence are needed and it is a good idea to reward your child for his or her efforts with smiles, hugs, and words of praise.

HAND WASHING

Again, use the show-and-tell method for hand washing. Repeat each step time after time, each time withdrawing a little more of your physical assistance, until your child can complete the step at your request. Then add the next step and repeat the entire process. With each step, explain what is happening and why it is important or useful.

1. Teach your child to turn on and adjust the faucets if you have not done so already. You can expect to give a great deal of assistance over a long period of time before this skill is mastered.

2. Have your child hold his or her hands under the running water to wet them. If necessary, begin by holding them in yours.

3. Rub soap over your child's palms; gradually teach your child to do this alone.

4. Holding your toddler's hands in yours, rub his or her palms together, then rub the backs of the hands and the wrists. Gradually reduce your amount of physical help.

5. Show your child how to rinse his or her hands, and then how to dry them.

At first, you will need to control the water pressure to avoid unnecessary messes, but after a while your child will learn to adjust the faucets without your help.

Remember to teach your child the names of his or her body parts that are being washed, and the names of the objects that are being used for washing. And don't forget to reward your child for tasks accomplished.

To get dirty hands really clean, help your child wash a toy or a plastic dish in a sink full of soapy water.

When your child can wash his or her hands with only verbal instructions, gradually reduce those instructions to "Wash your hands." Some parents prefer to teach their children how to wash their hands before they teach face washing. You should teach these two skills in whatever order seems best for your child.

Here are a few more tips on hand and face washing:

• Keep a step stool next to the sink to encourage self-help. Climbing on and off the stool also helps stimulate large muscle development.

• Use colorful towels printed with pictures. Name the things in the pictures as your child uses the towel.

• Once your child can follow the request to wash his or her face or hands, be sure to see that this is done in the morning, before meals, before bedtime, and whenever they get dirty. Also teach your child to check in the mirror after washing to make sure that his or her face is clean—and to wash again if it is still dirty.

BATHING AND SHOWERING

To teach your child bathing techniques, you can use the show-and-tell method as well. But do not begin to teach your child about showering and bathing until he or she has fully mastered hand and face washing. With bathing there are some additional things to keep in mind:

• Before you teach actual washing, teach your child to use the faucets and to control water flow and temperature. This can be very important, as a child who is not skilled in controlling water temperature can get scalded. Until your child learns to turn the faucets on and adjust the water flow and temperature, it's a good idea for you to do that.

• Also, before you teach your child bathing, start teaching him or her about using a stopper or drain-closing device, operating the shower on-off switch, and knowing when the tub is full enough for the water to be turned off. He or she will need your assistance for a long time before these skills are mastered.

• Place a bathmat or another high-friction mat on the bottom of the tub so that your toddler will not slip and fall.

• You can ease your child's fear of bath water or showers by bathing or showering with him or her at first.

• Encourage your child to have fun during bath time. Use bubble bath if you like. Encourage the use of bath toys, but avoid water guns. Allow your child to splash and play and, at least at first, to stay in the bath or shower as long as he or she wants.

• Make sure your child learns not to urinate in the bath or shower.

• Don't forget to teach your child what to do with his or her dirty clothes.

HAIR CARE

Haircutting tips

• Cut your child's hair while it is wet, but remember that hair is shorter when it's wet.

• To prepare for that first professional haircut, take your child with you when you or your spouse visit the beauty salon or the barbershop.

• Be sure to give your child a haircut that is flattering. It is *not* true that the style of a haircut is not important until your child grows older.

Combing and Brushing

Stand behind your child as you both face the mirror and show how hair is combed. Be sure to explain what you are doing and why you are doing it. The next step is to let your child learn to handle the comb. Place a medium-sized comb in his or her hand, and with your hand covering your child's, guide the comb up and through the hair. Continue helping and explaining until your youngster can complete the task with just a single verbal cue of "Comb your hair."

Parting the hair is difficult to learn at age two, so you may want to avoid styles that need parting. If styles without parts are not flattering to your son or daughter, then you should do the parting. Don't be surprised if your child doesn't master this skill until he or she is seven or eight years old.

Once your child has learned the combing process, simply substitute a brush for the comb, making sure that the brush is the right size to be manipulated. Your child's dexterity with either a brush or comb will depend a great deal on his or her motor coordination. The better coordinated he or she is, the easier it will be to use a brush or comb.

Shampooing

Your child may not have the dexterity to master shampooing until age seven or eight or even older. However, now is old enough to start learning the steps involved with shampooing. So each time you give your child a shampoo, explain exactly what you are doing, step by step. Here are some tips that will make shampoo time a little less difficult for both of you.

• Shampooing in the bathtub is easier if you resurrect an old infant seat for your child to sit in. Tilt it back so your child's head is in a comfortable position.

• Wrap your child in a big towel and lay him or her on the kitchen counter with the head protruding over the sink. You may want to use another towel under your child's neck to cushion the contact between the neck and the edge of the sink.

• Put only a small amount of water in the tub at first and let your child lie flat on the bottom for a shampoo.

• Water is easier to control if you use a sponge for rinsing.

Many parents entertain their children with stories during the shampoo. Others create soap sculptures with their children's hair and let them see the results in a mirror. Don't hesitate to use other techniques you think of to help make shampooing fun for your child. Remember, the more fun you can make it, the more your child will want to learn to shampoo without your doing it. And, as always, be sure to reward good behavior.

Don't be surprised if your child doesn't master the skills of hair care for a long time. Keep repeating the show-and-tell process and don't give up. The verbal, auditory, and muscular stimulation your child receives during the shampooing are what count most now. But your child *will* learn to brush, comb, and shampoo eventually.

FEEDING

You have discovered by now that the messiness of self-feeding goes hand in hand with your child's attempts to become a do-it-yourselfer at mealtimes.

If you experience an irresistible urge to feed your child, rather than let the youngster do it alone, *don't give in.* Instead, concentrate on helping your child refine the skills he or she has already accomplished: holding a cup or spoon, getting food onto a spoon and into the mouth, and so on. As your child becomes more skilled in the art of self-feeding, the messiness will decrease.

Expect some setbacks or temporary regressions in self-feeding. These will pass, however. Continue to help your child refine his or her skills, and in time your child will get better and better at self-feeding.

A sudden spurt of accomplishment is also possible. I know of one Down's syndrome child who suddenly picked up a spoon and began feeding herself, even though her parents never taught her how to use the spoon—she was simply copying what she'd seen her parents do.

After your baby's first birthday you can begin teaching him or her to drink from a cup without your assistance. There is no doubt that at first this will involve plenty of mess and spillage. But be patient, and once again use the show-and-tell method.

1. Show your child how to hold a cup or glass. To begin, you should wrap your hands around your child's. After a time, give less and less physical help.

2. Next, teach your child how to lift an *empty* cup to his or her mouth.

3. When your child has mastered the use of an empty cup, put a *small* amount of liquid in the cup and help raise the cup to the mouth. Gradually reduce your assistance. Be sure to use something your child will be eager to drink—juice, milk, or something else appetizing. Plain water is less messy but is less appealing as well.

4. Gradually increase the amount of liquid in the cup or glass as your child's drinking skills get sharper.

You will probably want to use small paper cups at first. They are lightweight, nonbreakable, and easy to handle.

While your toddler eats or drinks, you may want to keep a newspaper or a plastic sheet around the chair. This makes cleaning much easier. Serving food in a deep dish can help, too; it keeps spillage down.

It is also helpful to drape a towel or a large handkerchief around your baby's shoulders to help catch spills. Be sure to keep a second towel handy to wipe up spills that go elsewhere.

GROWTH AND DEVELOPMENT

During your child's second year, he or she should continue to expand verbal and motor skills while also learning to develop appropriate behavior patterns.

The key to how well your child acquires these behaviors and skills is your own efforts as parents. There is little doubt that you will have to spend as much time helping your child during these second twelve months as you did during the first twelve. That's because you will be expecting your youngster to accomplish more complex skills such as crawling, standing, walking, and talking.

To acquire these skills, your child may need a great deal of encouragement, motivation, and stimulation. This is particularly true if his or her muscle strength is weak. Remember that Down's syndrome children usually acquire speech and motor coordination at an older age and slower pace than other children do.

However, if you are firm, patient, and confident, and if you keep your sense of humor during this developmental stage, both you and your child will succeed.

PROMOTING YOUR BABY'S SPEECH DEVELOPMENT

Your child will acquire speech and language through interaction with other family members. From the moment your baby was born, you should have been talking to him or her and encouraged others to do the same. This verbal interaction should be ongoing. Make it a part of your daily activities and you will provide the stimulation your child needs to acquire speech.

Talk to the baby about the things he or she is seeing, doing, or touching. Explain what you are doing. Be sure to attach words or labels to objects and actions. Use phrases or complete sentences so he or she learns how to put words together.

Listening is as important as talking to your child. Encourage any attempts he or she makes to communicate. When it happens, be lavish with your rewards—a smile, a big hug, lots of verbal praise, or some combination of the three. These provide stimulation as well as encouragement.

If your child makes mistakes in speech, as all children do, *don't* correct them. Providing a good speech model is more effective than criticism at this age. Eventually your child will learn to correct his or her own speech mistakes.

Speech therapists advise reading to your child as a method for stimulating speech development. One set of parents followed that advice by giving their son Davey several picture books shortly after his first birthday.

"We chose books that had just one large, colorful object on each page," said Davey's mother, "to help him learn different shapes and the names of different objects and animals. The speech therapists advised us to point to an object or animal and to say only that word. If we wanted him to learn animal noises, we imitated just that sound."

This advice proved effective for Davey. By the time he was two years old, he could say, "Mama" and "Daddy," and could imitate seven animal noises.

Encourage your other children to get involved in reading to their little brother or sister. This provides extra stimulation for your baby, and it helps your other children feel helpful, wanted, and close to the baby.

Verbal interaction between your child and other siblings has great possibilities for stimulating speech. So encourage your other children to talk, to tell stories, and to sing to your Down's syndrome child.

As you help your child with speech development, try not to speak for him or her. Instead, provide the opportunity for response and development of speech skills.

All parents are tempted to use baby talk with a young child. But you should resist that temptation, because your child will pick it up. And the longer you use baby talk, the longer it will take your child to unlearn that baby talk and speak like an adult. Insisting on appropriate speech for your baby builds a good habit that will help his or her social acceptance in the future.

PROMOTING YOUR BABY'S MOTOR DEVELOPMENT

Children with Down's syndrome usually are slower than other children to develop gross motor development skills such as crawling, standing, walking, and running. However, this varies significantly from one child to another, and it depends a good deal on your child's muscle tone. The weaker the muscle tone, the more necessary are longer and more intensive stimulation exercises.

By their second birthday, many Down's syndrome children can pull themselves to a standing position and stand alone for a brief time. Here are some exercises you and your child can do that help acquire standing skills and beginning walking skills:

First you must make sure that your child learns the sensation of standing on his or her feet. To do this, prop your child against a wall, hold the feet on the floor, and push down gently on the hips to help straighten the knees and trunk. During this activity, give your child something to do, such as holding a bright toy, to help overcome the fear of losing balance. Once your child learns to stand alone, he or she probably won't waste much time before starting to walk. Some parents say they bounced and jiggled their babies before helping them learn to stand. This helps to strengthen their legs.

Although walking and standing seem to be related, another skill, unique to walking, must also be learned: the ability to move the body forward. Letting your child push a chair around the house is an effective way of teaching forward body movement. It also teaches your child how to shift weight from leg to leg.

Although most children acquire basic gross motor skills (standing, walking, and so on) before they are ready to learn fine motor skills (grasping, finger feeding, and so on), children with Down's syndrome may not follow such a progression because of physical defects, heart problems, or weak muscle tone.

If your child isn't ready for gross motor activities, you should begin engaging the youngster in exercises that will develop his or her fine motor skills. Finger feeding, playing nursery rhyme games like Itsy Bitsy Spider, crumpling paper, and helping your child pick up small objects are just a few methods of building fine motor skills. But try not to overdo these activities, because you and your child may get bored. If progress is slow, don't give up, but don't push too hard either. Each small gain your child makes is a stepping-stone to future accomplishment.

USING DISCIPLINE WISELY

Growing up is complicated for all children, and it can be more difficult for a child with Down's syndrome. But it is especially hard on a child when his or her parents avoid taking appropriate disciplinary measures. Undisciplined children, retarded or not, can look forward only to an undisciplined adulthood that inhibits their social acceptance.

Many parents of children with Down's syndrome wonder when they should begin to discipline their children. The answer is from the first moment the child behaves in an objectionable manner. If you as parents wonder if special disciplinary methods are necessary for your Down's syndrome child, the answer is no. Your child can be disciplined in the same manner as any other child.

It is important for your child to learn that discipline is part of life. You can be a strict or a lax disciplinarian, *but you cannot be inconsistent.* It is through consistency that you teach your child the difference between acceptable and nonacceptable behavior. If you are having a good day, don't overlook or excuse behavior that you would correct if you were having a bad day. Likewise, don't be more demanding or harsher in your discipline when you are in a bad mood. Either of these reactions on your part will only confuse your child.

Be sure your child knows why you are administering discipline and always explain what it is he or she has done, and why it is objectionable.

If you have other children, you must help them understand that their brother or sister must be disciplined for misbehaving, just like any other child.

Here are some other useful guidelines for discipline:

• Set limits for the entire family and adhere to them.

• The same discipline should be administered to your Down's syndrome child as to your other children. Everyone should be treated equally, and there should be no favoritism.

• Help your child understand that he or she has rights, but that infringement on the rights of others is not acceptable.

Discipline is a crucial factor in helping your child develop appropriate behavior. The earlier you initiate such measures, the sooner your child will acquire behavior that will help him or her become socially accepted.

Discipline is only one way to help your child acquire acceptable behavior. Setting good examples is another. The well-known warning "Do as I say, not as I do" may have little effect on your Down's syndrome child simply because he or she, like any other child, is a great mimic. Your child will tend to do what you do, no matter what you say.

Here are some hints that other parents have found helpful to develop appropriate behavior patterns in their children:

• Give your child a toy telephone to play with while you are on the phone.

• Insist that your child verbalize requests. Don't give in to finger pointing.

• If your child throws food on the floor, quietly get a cloth and clean up the mess. Have your child help clean up as soon as he or she is old enough. Then remove the child from the table.

• If your child is rebellious and gets into everything, try to avoid situations that are tempting. Keep breakable and spillable objects out of reach if possible.

• Temper tantrums need an audience to exist—so try ignoring them. I observed this incident at a convention for parents of Down's syndrome children. A mother and her young son were walking down a hall. The boy complained that his legs hurt. "We'll sit down soon," said his mother. At that, the boy jerked his hand from his mother's clasp, sat down on the floor, and started screaming and rolling about. His mother continued walking, never once looking back. She hadn't gone more than a few feet before her son calmed down and ran to her. She took his hand, and they continued to walk to a nearby bench and sat down.

• If you can't ignore a temper tantrum, try disappearing into another room for a few minutes.

• If your child is angry, but not throwing a tantrum, try holding him or her closely, and try rocking. Hum or sing a song until the youngster calms down.

In general, children misbehave when they want attention. If you *constantly* reprimand your child for inappropriate behavior, you are in fact rewarding that child for misbehaving with your attention. Often a better method is to ignore the misbehavior and reward appropriate behavior. This is ideal in those cases where your child is misbehaving but not causing anyone harm. However, when the misbehavior does cause harm to others, it should be punished.

To keep a sense of perspective and a sense of humor about all this, it might help for you to keep in mind how frustrating it must be to *almost* be able to walk, talk, or do anything else.

NURSERY SCHOOL

Since most infant stimulation programs do not serve children beyond the age of two, you should begin searching for another program in which to enroll your child before he or she reaches the age of two. This early search is important for two reasons. One, you'll want to make sure that a nursery school is not only available, but can also provide the program your child needs. Two, if you know in advance which nursery school your child will attend, you can prepare your youngster and yourself for the transition from infant stimulation to nursery school. Many states offer nursery school programs specifically designed for children with handicaps that are essentially a continuation of infant stimulation activities. These programs are extremely important to your child's continued physical, mental, and emotional development.

Unless the right kind of nursery school is not available where you live, it is almost always better for your child to be enrolled in a nursery school program. He or she will learn and grow more there than is likely by staying at home twenty-four hours a day.

If you do not have access to a nursery school in your community, you may have other options. Perhaps you can make arrangements to keep your child enrolled in an infant stimulation program. Find out if there are other parents in your area whose handicapped children need but are not receiving a nursery school program. You could all join forces and petition your local officials, like those in government and education, to start a nursery school. That's how most programs now available for handicapped children got started. Or, perhaps, surrounding communities offer nursery school programs that your child could attend.

If you are like most parents, you will worry about sending your child away from home to nursery school at the tender age of two. But if you take the time to visit different programs that are available and select the one that will be most beneficial to your child, you should feel more comfortable with the idea. Remember, these programs will help your child continue to learn, grow, and develop.

LOCATING AND CHOOSING A NURSERY SCHOOL PROGRAM

To locate a nursery school, you can start by asking the staff from your child's infant stimulation program for help. They should be able to give you a listing of what is available in your area. If they cannot give you the help you need, then you should contact your local school district. Start with the superintendent of schools or the director of special education. If these people cannot help you then you should try these resources: a local social service agency, a county chapter of the Association for Retarded Citizens, the National Down Syndrome Congress, or the United Way. You could also check the yellow pages in your telephone directory. Look under the headings "Schools—Academic—Preschool" or "Schools—Special Education."

Before you choose a nursery school program for your child, it is wise to visit every one that is available. Observe how the teachers interact with the children and how the children interact with one another. Talk to staff people and ask them any questions you wish. Notice the condition of the room and the equipment—the shape it is in and what is available.

Here are some things to keep in mind when selecting a nursery school program for your child:

• The teachers must have academic backgrounds in early childhood development, especially as it relates to children with special needs.

• Class size should be small enough to allow for individual needs and development. There should be enough teachers and aides to provide the individual attention that children with special needs should have.

• The classroom should be cheery, light, and uncrowded. It should offer a warm, caring, and happy atmosphere.

• Furniture and equipment should be plentiful, in good condition, and appropriate for your child's age group.

• You should have frequent opportunities to talk with teachers and aides about your child's program and progress.

• Teachers and aides should demonstrate a warm and caring attitude toward students.

• The program you choose should be one that is most fitting and beneficial for your child's level of functioning.

• The distance of the program from your house can be important.

Make sure your child can tolerate the bus or car trip to and from the school each day.

• Find out who has the responsibility of providing the transportation —you or the school.

• Be sure to inquire about any fees the school charges. The most expensive program doesn't necessarily mean your child will benefit more.

When choosing a nursery school for your child, you should keep these two most important goals in mind: (1) the program should meet your child's special needs in speech, language, and motor development, and (2) the program should provide your child with the opportunity to learn and develop appropriate social skills.

There are two major types of nursery school programs to choose from: regular or special. A special nursery school admits only children with mental and/or physical disabilities. In a regular nursery school, children with disabilities are, to the extent that is possible and appropriate, educated along with children who are not handicapped.

A common disadvantage to regular programs is that less attention is given to the special needs of Down's syndrome children. However, these programs will offer your child a greater opportunity for language development and the chance to interact with nonhandicapped children. This is a significant advantage; in special schools, there is usually little or no opportunity for Down's syndrome children to talk and play with their nonhandicapped peers. (It's also good for normal kids to have the chance to interact with other children who are handicapped.) This interaction therefore helps handicapped and nonhandicapped children understand one another and learn to get along.

But the advantages to a special school are that normally there are only six to eight students in a class, and that students are taught by a special education teacher who also has a full-time aide. Since these schools and programs are designed specifically to serve the needs of handicapped children, the low child-teacher ratio enables each child to receive the individual attention he or she needs.

Before your child enters a nursery school, whether it is a special or regular program, he or she should be given an evaluation test to determine his or her level of functioning. Quite often parents are asked to contribute additional information to the evaluation. This is the time to explain the skills your child has and has not achieved, likes and dislikes, and what seems to trigger unusual or negative behavior. You should explain to all the people who will be working with your child anything that you believe will help your child adjust to the class, or that will help the teachers have a better understanding of your child and his or her needs.

If you are not given the opportunity to share information about your child with teachers and staff, you should demand that chance. After all, who knows your child better than you do? Far too often professionals tend to disregard the information that parents have to offer, claiming that they are being overprotective. You should not let that kind of attitude prevent you from sharing information about your child that will help smooth his or her transition into the program. A smooth transition and a good adjustment help to promote a positive learning experience for your child—which is, after all, why you are sending him or her to school.

MAKING THE CHANGE

Before your child actually begins attending nursery school, it is necessary to prepare for this change. Take your child for at least one visit to the school and spend an hour or two there. Two or three such preliminary visits are ideal.

Drive your child to the school a few times before school begins. If he or she will be taking a bus to school, ride along on the bus for the first two or three days, if possible. These efforts will help your child become familiar and comfortable with the route to and from school.

It is also helpful to make your child generally more comfortable with being out of the house. If you have not already been taking your youngster to the zoo, to church or synagogue, to stores, and to friends' houses, do so now, before school begins, so that he or she can feel comfortable with taking trips and being in different environments. Making a few special trips to fun places like the park and the zoo will especially help, since your child will learn to associate being away from home with having a good time. Even extra walks around the block can be positive experiences for your child. As always, as you take these trips, point to objects, kinds of people, and animals, say their names, and explain what they are and what they do.

In short, do anything you can for your child to make him or her comfortable being away from home and in a new situation. This will ease the trauma of suddenly changing his or her daily routine.

CELEBRATING YOUR BABY'S SECOND BIRTHDAY

Like many parents, you may be amazed at how quickly the months have gone by. You found the inner strength to continue helping your baby develop and grow—and now the child can probably put on his or her clothes, speak quite clearly, and eat with little or no help. Your youngster may even do things you thought were never possible. All these accomplishments probably will need some refining, but that, too, will happen.

Now that your baby is about to begin the third year, what did you as parents accomplish? What did your baby accomplish? And what did your baby's siblings accomplish?

How many items on the following list can you check as measures of your family's accomplishments?

PROGRESS CHECKLIST FOR PARENTS

Do you give your child credit for things he or she has learned?

Do you reward each accomplishment with a smile, a hug, or words of praise?

Is the temptation to give up or despair decreasing?

Do you no longer worry if your child doesn't always meet your expectations?

Do you and your partner both spend as much time as possible with your child?

Are you breaking learning tasks into small steps and teaching one step at a time?

Do you recognize signs of your child's accomplishments, no matter how small they are?

PROGRESS CHECKLIST FOR BABY

Twelve to eighteen months

Holds cup or glass
Uses spoon
Crawls and slides

	Reaches for objects
	Stands alone momentarily
Fifteen to twenty-one months	Likes to climb
	Walks with support
	Can drink from a cup with help
	Feeds self with spoon
	Says, "Mama" and "Dada"
	Imitates sounds
	Tries to dress self
	Shows signs of toileting readiness
Twenty-one to twenty-six months	Dresses self but can't do buttons
	Puts on shoes but can't tie laces
	Attempts to run
	Walks unaided
	Climbs up stairs
	Obeys simple commands
	Is making progress in toilet training
	Can say twenty to thirty words
	Combines two or three words

PROGRESS CHECKLIST FOR SIBLINGS

Do they help entertain the baby?

Do they assist with teaching the baby various skills?

Is there little or no sibling rivalry?

Have they outgrown feelings of overprotection or resentment toward their Down's syndrome brother or sister?

Now, throw a big party for your baby, for your other children, and for yourselves.

CHAPTER 5

From Toddler to Five Year Old

Nearly every parent I talk to says that the two- to five-year-old stage of their children's development is filled with surprises that are pleasant, comical, frightening, exciting, infuriating, and sorrowful.

This is a time when your child, like every child, wants to explore his or her world and become a part of it. It is also a time for you as parents to gradually relinquish your child to that world. This exploring and relinquishing can sometimes put you on a merry-go-round of emotions. You know your child must have the opportunity to satisfy his or her inquisitive nature, but at the same time you may be reluctant to provide that opportunity.

If you are overcautious or too restraining, you will merely delay the inevitable. Your child will explore, experiment, and imitate as easily without your encouragement as he or she will with it.

This stage of child development is also a time of transition for you both. If your youngster is enrolled in a program for two or three year olds, you should begin inquiring about the available education programs for older children.

YOUR CHILD'S GROWTH AND DEVELOPMENT

It is possible that your child will begin the third year somewhat small and underweight, very likely caused in part by feeding problems. Allowing your child to snack between meals to compensate for the lack of food at meals has its plusses and minuses. It will certainly help weight gain. But snacking can easily become a habit that can result in later years in your child becoming overweight. Children with Down's syndrome do have a tendency to become overweight and even obese as adolescents and adults, and this is caused in most cases by simple overeating, not by anything glandular, so you should monitor your child's weight and eating habits. And, since these children tend to have some difficulty with gross motor coordination anyway, the more weight they gain, the more difficult it is for them to move.

In general, you should allow snacking if your child is underweight. But you should limit it once your child reaches a normal weight, and you should limit it strictly or eliminate it altogether if your child shows signs of growing overweight.

As is the case with any child, it is always best to serve snacks that are nutritious, such as fresh fruits and vegetables, cheeses, lean meat, whole grain bread, and so on. Cookies, candy, and other sweets add calories, but they add very little nutrition and they will help your child develop a sweet tooth which may carry over into adulthood.

Since Down's children tend to have problems with their growth and development, the importance of consistent and thorough health examinations for your child cannot be overemphasized. Generally, your child should have a health exam at least every two months between the ages of two and three, and at least once a year thereafter. However, your pediatrician may insist on examining your child more frequently depending on the state of his or her health. Unusual or unexpected changes in your child's behavior or disruptions in growth may be signals of serious health problems. If your child tires easily, seems to be very lethargic, shows excessive irritability, or shows little gain in weight or height, make an appointment with your child's doctor immediately. Such symptoms are easier to diagnose and treat at the onset. Likewise, if your child has respiratory problems, be on the alert for sneezing, sniffling, and coughing. When these occur, get your child to a doctor quickly—within a day or two, if possible.

HOW TO EASE YOUR CHILD'S FEARS ABOUT HOSPITALIZATION

Going to a hospital for medical attention is an apprehensive situation for most adults. For children it can be very frightening. They are separated from their parents, the environment is unfamiliar and not at all like home, and there are strangers everywhere. But it is the medical equipment that probably terrifies a child the most. If your child needs to be hospitalized at any time, here are some tips that will help you to prepare him or her for the new routine.

It is not a good idea to have lengthy discussions about hospitalization several days before it happens. You will only add to your child's apprehension. Instead, on the day before the confinement starts, explain in a calm, quiet manner why it is necessary to go to the hospital.

The day before (or perhaps an hour or two) hospitalization is to begin, take your child on a tour of the hospital. Meet some of the staff and visit the areas in which your child will be cared for or treated. If medical tests will be required, explain what those tests are, why they are necessary, and what procedures will be used. If you can't explain because you aren't sure of an answer, find out that answer—don't guess or make an answer up. Tell your child that you will not be allowed to go with him or her into surgery, but that you will be nearby. Point out where you will be. If the treatment is going to hurt, let your child know. Explain that there may be a bandage, for example, on his or her tummy.

Visit with the medical staff and explain your child's likes, dislikes, habits, and fears. This will help the staff understand your child, which in turn can help ease the apprehension he or she may have.

During the hospital tour, and any time thereafter, encourage your child to ask any questions, and answer those questions openly, honestly, and as best as you can.

Once hospitalization actually begins, accompany your child everywhere your presence is permitted. While your child is being examined or a test is being done, explain what is happening and why it is necessary. When the time comes for you and your child to be separated, be sure to give him or her a big hug.

If at all possible, try to arrange things so that both you and your spouse can accompany the child to the hospital. And remember to consistently reward your child for good behavior throughout the hospital stay. When your youngster is calm and quiet, or sits still and doesn't cry, or is generally cooperative, be sure to give smiles and words of praise.

It should go without saying that if your child needs to stay in the hospital overnight or longer, you and your spouse should both visit frequently.

If you believe it is necessary to explain to your child's teacher about the hospitalization, insist that there be *no* class discussion about it. These discussions will only increase your child's fears, and it may cause fear in his or her classmates as well.

Keep in mind your child's age and ability to comprehend as you explain about the stay at the hospital. An explanation should be simple enough for your child to understand—but at the same time no simpler than is necessary. And remember a happy child is a better patient than one who is distraught with fear.

Although all the information in this section is especially important for children ages two to five, it also applies to older children and adolescents.

ALLOWING YOUR CHILD TO TAKE RISKS

From toddler to five year old is a time when your child will get involved in some escapades or daring activities. All parents realize that this world we live in is not as kind or predictable as we would like it to be. Yet our children must learn to live in it, whether or not they are handicapped.

To help your child cope with this world means you will have to let him or her take some risks. It also means some risks will be taken without your approval. This is pretty much inevitable for all children, whether or not they have Down's syndrome.

One child I know, a three year old named Jeremy, decided to climb up an extension ladder onto the roof of his parents' house. Although neither parent understood how he managed that feat, they now make certain the extension ladder is stored safely away when it is not being used.

Another, five-year-old Jason, loves to climb swing poles. Although this caper may not be as dangerous as Jeremy's, it does test his parents' patience.

In both these situations the boys seemed so pleased with their accomplishments that their parents decided not to discipline them. They did, however, give their children a clear explanation of the dangers of their ventures.

Allowing a child to take some risks is part of his or her growth and development. There is probably no way of preventing your child from taking some unauthorized risks. What you *can* do is structure some risky situations to help your youngster learn how to handle them. Here are a few suggestions:

Leave your child alone in a room for brief periods of time. Then gradually lengthen the amount of time.

Let your child practice climbing a tree, a ladder, or a pole while you watch. After a few successful tries, allow this without supervision.

Letting your child take risks will no doubt expose him or her to some danger—but at the same time your youngster will experience the dignity and satisfaction of accomplishment.

It is not always easy to determine how much risk to permit your child to take. In general, though, you should allow any risks where the chance of serious harm is very slight, for example, risks that could result in a scrape or a bruise, but that pose no real danger—running down a hill, or climbing a low wall, or jumping rope. A scrape or a bruise will hurt, of course, but children get such cuts and bruises all the time, and your child will recover from such a minor injury very quickly. In fact, getting a bruise here and there and then getting over it can be an important step in your child's emotional growth.

However, if your child takes a risk that could do real harm, take him or her aside and explain exactly what could happen and why. Then explain exactly what the punishment will be if that risk is taken again. Be sure your child understands. In some cases, your child will take the risk anyway, in which case you should use discipline exactly the way you said you would.

You should act this way in cases where genuine and serious danger is involved—for instance, if your child wants to hang upside down from a tree branch, or play with an electric outlet, or play with matches. It is your responsibility to keep things like matches out of reach of your child. Just as Jeremy's parents removed the extension ladder once they realized their son could climb it, so must you help your child avoid harm by keeping dangerous objects out of reach.

HOME ACTIVITIES TO STIMULATE GROWTH AND DEVELOPMENT

If your child is enrolled in a nursery school program, you should continue home activities that will stimulate physical growth and development. If the school program provides gross and fine motor exercises, ask the teacher for suggestions about duplicating them at home, and/or for other exercises that will benefit your child. These extra at-home activities do provide reinforcement which most children with Down's syndrome need.

If your child is not enrolled in a nursery school program, then stimulation exercises at home become even more important. Here are some activities that will help stimulate your child's growth and development:

- Teach your child to ride a tricycle.
- Have your child imitate the movements of animals.
- Invent games in which your child must step over hurdles such as boxes or tires, or in which he or she must climb stairs, hop, jump, or climb up and down a step stool. These all help develop balance, coordination, and strength.
- Enroll your child in a swimming class for toddlers.
- Buy action records, toys, and games—things that require your child to walk, run, dance, or otherwise develop muscles and coordination. Have your child practice these activities alone sometimes, and sometimes you should join in. (But before you spend a great deal of money, go to your local library and ask the children's librarian for suggestions; then check a few sample items out. What your child actually likes may be different from what you think he or she will like. Some communities may have a lending library of records, books, games, and toys for handicapped children. Check with your local chapter of the Association for Retarded Citizens, United Way, the National Down Syndrome Congress, or with your local social service agency to see if there is such a library in your area.)

None of these activities is fun to do alone all the time, so join your little one, and for a few minutes each day experience the excitement and delight of child play.

SOCIAL GROWTH AND DEVELOPMENT

All children, including those with Down's syndrome, go through specific social growth stages, and all children need love, understanding, patience, and judgment from their parents at each stage. There is little doubt that the art of parenting would be much easier if children would only behave. Nevertheless, all children seem to play in the mud just after they have been cleaned up, spill milk on a freshly scrubbed floor, and start a squabble when parents are on the telephone.

All such behaviors are part of the complicated process of growing and learning. In fact, these behaviors are signals of the various stages of development that all children experience. If you are aware of these stages, you will have a better understanding of your child and his or her behavior. These stages, and the behaviors involved, are common to all children, but Down's syndrome children may go through them at a somewhat later age.

THE OBSTINATE STAGE

If one of the first words your two year old learned to say was no, don't be surprised or alarmed. The child has reached the obstinate stage, which probably will last for another year or so. Saying no is one way a child begins to express independence. Starting to walk, talk, and self-feed are other signs of becoming independent. You can expect the obstinate stage to recur during the teenage years.

THE AGE OF IMITATION

You will recognize this stage when your child is between five and six. He or she will begin to mimic the behavior and speech patterns of friends or classmates. It is a time of wanting to do what everyone else is doing. For example, if your child is not asked to accompany his or her siblings to the swimming pool, you can expect the youngster to try going alone, no matter if he or she knows the way or not.

THE AGE OF PALS

When your child is between seven and nine, you may notice close friendships developing with other children, usually with classmates who are of the same sex. Your daughter may have several girlfriends or your son will have many boyfriends. Sometimes these friendships will narrow down to one or two children. They enjoy each other's company, try to imitate one another, and may even share a few secrets.

DISCIPLINING YOUR CHILD

The years from toddlerhood to age five are the ones in which proper discipline can be most important and most useful in helping your child develop appropriate behavior. Here are some things to keep in mind when dealing with misbehavior and discipline.

When your child responds to disciplinary measures by saying no, you should not let this habit deter you, especially if your child is in the obstinate stage. Ignore the no, and discipline your child exactly as you otherwise would have—no more and no less.

The difficulty with disciplining your child is the fear that he or she may not understand why you must use discipline or why you won't allow misbehavior. But each time your child does something wrong, explain exactly what it was that was wrong, why it is wrong, and what disciplinary actions are the result then and will be the result in the future. With repeated explanations, your youngster will soon begin to realize that certain actions will result in some privileges being denied or taken away. In fact, you may discover that he or she understands more about the process of discipline than you suspected.

If your immediate reaction to your child's misbehavior is one of yelling "No, no," you are in fact teaching the child how to use that word. This is a common trap that many parents get caught in. But each time you feel like yelling or screaming at your misbehaving child, try standing face to face with him or her. You will find it very difficult to give in to that urge to scream.

A statement like "Don't do that" is not usually a satisfactory method of explaining your disapproval of your child's misbehavior; nor is it a satisfactory method of disciplinary action. So do not be surprised if your youngster responds to your "Don't do that" by ignoring it, or with a question like "Why not?" When this happens, you should explain as best you can and in whatever terms your child can understand. ("Because" and "Because I said so" are not satisfactory explanations; avoid using them.) However, if your child continues to respond with a "Why not" no matter how well you explain, he or she is probably trying to delay the inevitable—the discipline. When this happens, you must be firm with your child and not let yourself be manipulated by the questions.

Remember, when you disapprove of the behavior that is occurring and it is not harmful to your child or anyone else, simply try to ignore it. Misbehavior is one way your child can get your attention and your attention will merely reinforce the misbehavior. Instead, reward your child's *good* behavior with a smile, a hug, or verbal praise. I really cannot overstress the importance of giving these rewards for good behavior often and consistently. Every time you praise your child's good behavior, or reward it with a smile or a hug, you are helping to reinforce that good behavior.

For discipline to be effective, you and your spouse must agree on when and how it should be administered. Then you should firmly stick to your agreement under all circumstances. Without this agreement, you will merely confuse your child, or you may teach him or her to take advantage of any inconsistency.

TEMPER TANTRUMS

The best method for dealing with temper tantrums is trying to head them off. Boredom, frustration, loneliness, or being overtired can all lead to tantrums. Look for symptoms of these feelings, and when they first appear, try to change the feelings by reading your child a story, playing a game (preferably a new or favorite one), or going for a walk together. If your child is overtired, put him or her into bed, then tell a story or sing a song.

If your child actually does throw a temper tantrum, you may want to try these methods that other parents have found effective:

• Since it's good to let off steam now and then, sometimes just let your child scream (preferably away from the rest of the family).

• Ignore the tantrum but not the child. Try to find out why the tantrum is occurring or what is causing it. If possible, deal with the cause.

• If you can't discover what's causing the tantrum, put your child alone in a room until the tantrum is over.

• If your child is throwing a breath-holding tantrum put a cold cloth on his or her face.

An unsuspected health problem can sometimes cause a tantrum, as in Sandy's case. Her parents thought she was a stubborn child because she refused to obey them. When they disciplined her, she always resorted to temper tantrums. But during a routine health check, the doctors discovered that the little girl had a problem that affected both her ears. Fluid tended to collect in the middle ear, which caused a hearing loss. It turned out that Sandy just wasn't hearing her parents' requests and commands. Surgery corrected this problem and restored her hearing, which significantly reduced her tantrums.

PERSONAL POSSESSIONS

To become a responsible adult, your child must learn to care for and share his or her possessions. These are the years when it is best to teach caring and sharing to your child. When you begin to teach your child how to hang up clothes or put away toys, keep in mind his or her limitations. At first the efforts probably won't meet your standards, but it is the effort that is important, and it should be recognized and rewarded with praise, a smile, or a hug. In time your child will measure up, because recognition and gentle encouragement are always excellent ways to motivate a youngster toward improvement.

Some parents told me they did not spend much time teaching their children how to care for their clothes and toys or keep their rooms clean. Yet the children seemed to know what was expected of them and behaved accordingly. The parents were not sure if their children had a built-in sense of neatness, or if they acquired these habits by watching others in the family.

Remember, though, that this imitation works both ways. If you and your partner have a messy house or do not pick up after yourselves, it is going to be very difficult, if not impossible, to teach your child neatness. He or she is likely to imitate your actions, no matter what you say is right, or wrong.

The reward system is an effective way to teach your child the importance of caring for and sharing possessions. But try not to let your child become dependent on rewards. You should gradually increase the significance of the task to be performed, and at the same time decrease the size and importance of the reward. At first you might offer your child a special privilege or treat, such as a movie or a delayed bedtime, for sharing or putting away toys. But eventually the only reward should be praise and a smile or hug.

Here are some suggestions to assist you help your child develop caring and sharing habits.

Never redo a task your child has completed. If you do, you will only encourage a sense of incompetence and failure.

Give your child an alternative—for example, "As soon as you pick up your toys, you can go out to play." This encourages your child to make choices.

At first you may want to name the items that your child picks up or count them as they are put away. This is fun, and at the same time it encourages neatness, teaches your child the name of objects, and reinforces the skill of counting. After you have done this a few times, have your child name the objects or count along with you. Eventually you can remain silent and your child can do the naming or counting alone.

HELPING YOUR CHILD DEVELOP A GOOD SELF-IMAGE

With your help your child can develop a good self-image by being treated with respect, by being made to feel special, and by being given a sense of security. Your child will recognize your respect when

- you use words like "Please" and "Thank you."
- you correct his or her misbehavior in private rather than in front of others, whenever possible.
- you knock on the door before entering your child's bedroom.
- you ask permission to borrow any of his or her possessions.
- you say, "That's not a nice way to behave" rather than, "You are a naughty child."
- you let your child know that it's the behavior you disapprove of, not him or her as a person.

To help your child feel special, try these suggestions:

• Introduce him or her to your friends whenever the occasion allows it. Have your spouse do the same.

• Include your child in conversations.

• If a conversation is directed toward your child, let him or her respond without prompting from you. *Never* respond on your child's behalf.

• Give praise for a job well done, even if it does not meet your standards. Give your child credit for meeting your expectations for *effort;* the standards will be reached with consistent repetition.

Your child will develop a sense of security from being held closely, from the love and attention you give, from the nearness of your physical presence during playful interaction, and from the sound of your voice.

As you help your child to develop a good self-image, keep in mind that this development does not happen overnight. It takes time—but it is time well spent.

ACCEPTING A NEW BABY

All children need preparation for the arrival of another baby in the family. How that arrival is explained depends on the child's age. You should be open with your child and answer any questions in a way that helps him or her understand what will happen to the family.

An older child will probably ask detailed questions about the baby, wanting to know how the baby got inside the mother, how it eats, how it will get out, and so on. Your answers to such questions should depend on your child's ability to understand them. You should not be surprised if your child asks these kinds of questions over and over, even if you have explained the answers before. If you are asked a question repeatedly, continue to patiently explain the answer to your child as best you can—unless you feel that the repeated questions are merely an attempt to get your attention, or are a form of manipulation.

If your child does ask the same question repeatedly, you may want to ask gently, "What is it you don't understand or are worried about?" or "What else would you like to know about the subject?" or even "Is there something about the answer that worries or scares you?" Your child might not be able to articulate an answer to any of these questions, but fairly often children may be able to express what they have in mind.

In all cases, you should of course tell your child the truth about pregnancy and birth, and about the rudiments of sex if that seems appropriate. However, you may need to simplify your answer considerably.

It is very important that you do give your child an explanation, and that you discuss what will happen well in advance. The *unexpected* appearance of a new brother or sister can be a traumatic experience for any child. Letting your child share in the excitement and anticipation that accompany the birth of a baby will help with the acceptance of the newcomer.

Once the new baby arrives, your Down's child will likely be curious at first. He or she may try to treat the baby like a doll or toy. But soon your youngster will realize that the baby is another person, just like he or she is.

Because the new baby will need and receive special attention, some rivalry problems can occur. If this happens in your family, you can help solve it by allowing your child to help care for the new baby. This will also aid your child to learn to accept responsibility, which in turn helps build his or her self-image and self-worth. But you should not expect acceptance of the new baby to occur immediately. It will take time—several weeks, perhaps.

ENCOURAGING SOCIAL GROWTH

Your child's social growth can be stimulated with educational toys, games, records, and books. But be sure you select only those that he or she can cope with. Remember, a toy recommended for ages three to four may be more appropriate for a five year old with Down's syndrome than one recommended for four to six year olds.

There is a wide variety of educational supplies available, including some specifically designed for handicapped children—but they can be quite expensive. So, before you buy any, you may want to follow some or all of these steps:

• Ask your child's teachers for advice and recommendations.

• Check with associations for retarded citizens.

• Go to your local library which may have some educational books, toys, and games to check out. Take some of these home and see which ones your child reacts best to. Ask the librarian for help and suggestions.

• Go to a special library for handicapped children if there's one in your area, check out some of its materials, and ask the librarian for recommendations.

There are many activities you can share with your child at home that do not involve outside products or materials but that help stimulate his or her social growth. Here are some suggestions:

• Sing activity songs with your child.

• Have your child show you some of his or her drawings (or in the case of a younger child, scribblings). Make up stories based on the drawings and tell them to your child.

• Start a scrapbook of your child's drawings. Let your youngster help you put the book together, and let him or her decide what drawings go where.

• Point to or hold up objects and name them. Ask your child to repeat the names or to say them with you. After a time, you may want to have your child speak in complete sentences, "I see a book."

• Show your child pictures of animals. Name the animals and make the sounds they do. Encourage your child to do the same, first with you, then alone.

• Encourage your child to share experiences with you, to tell you what he or she saw, heard, thought about, and learned that day. *Listen* to what your child tells you. If you ignore your child, only half listen, or merely pretend to listen, your child will know it, and feel bad about it. Respond positively to what your child tells you, and ask questions about his or her activities.

• Ask your child to draw pictures to show how he or she feels. This is especially helpful if your child is angry or upset.

• If your child *is* angry or upset, find the cause and discuss it.

Don't underestimate your child's ability to observe and imitate. If you are often angry or quarrelsome, your child will learn to be the same. So be careful of the examples you set.

Social growth also means learning to behave in public. If you want your child to learn appropriate public behavior, you must take him or her into public places. Take your child with you to church, to friends' houses, to the park, to restaurants, and to stores. Bring your youngster to your workplace, if possible, for a few minutes either during work or after hours. Encourage your spouse to do the same.

You will likely encounter some occasional embarrassing situations, but these, too, are learning experiences for your child. Just be sure that if your child does exhibit inappropriate behavior, you explain exactly what it is that *is* inappropriate, why you consider it inappropriate, and what you will do if it happens again. Then, if your youngster does repeat the behavior, be sure to use the discipline that you said you would.

But remember also to *consistently* reward your child for appropriate behavior with smiles, hugs, and verbal praise.

DRESSING AND GROOMING SKILLS

During this stage of your child's development, you should continue with the learning and refining of good grooming and hygiene skills. Your youngster should be able to acquire the skills of combing and brushing his or her own hair, using a toothbrush, and dressing and undressing without your help.

Now is the time to start teaching your child how to work shoelaces, buttons, snaps, and zippers. Here are a few tips that can help:

• To teach your child how to work buttons, snaps, and zippers, start by placing the garment flat on a table face up. Let your youngster practice on a variety of different items—shirts, pants, coats, and so on.

• Until your child has fully mastered the art of getting a zipper started, safety pin the garment shut at the bottom so that the zipper cannot quite travel all the way downward. This enables your child to practice zipping the zipper up and down without having to get the zipper slide on track. Your child can put on and remove the garment as if it were a pullover.

• Until your child can tie and untie shoelaces alone, buy shoes without laces. Once your child has mastered putting on and taking off socks, he or she should be able to do the same with loafers and slippers. When your child can put on shoes without assistance, it is time to start teaching how to lace shoes. You should delay teaching your youngster how to tie bows until he or she has mastered lacing.

LACING SHOES

To begin teaching how to lace shoes, have your child practice on a large lacing frame or toy shoe. These aids can be purchased at toy shops that specialize in educational toys and other equipment for children. Or

you could have your child practice lacing on a shoe belonging to someone in your family. Remember, the bigger the shoe, the easier it will be
for your child to manipulate the laces.

Here are some hints to help you help your child learn to lace shoes.

Sit in a comfortable position with your child in front of you. Put the
lace tip in his or her hand and help thread the tip into the bottom two
eyelets, pulling the lace a short way through. Measure the lace ends for
even length, then thread one end into the second opposite eyelet. Do the
same with the other lace end. Repeat this until the shoe is laced. Be sure
to explain what you are doing and give verbal instructions like, "Put the
shoe lace in here." Remember to keep these lacing sessions short at first
to avoid frustration for both of you.

Tying a bow seems to be the most difficult to learn and take the
longest to successfully accomplish. Here is a short easy way to tie a
bow. To start, tie a simple hitch with the laces, then form a loop with
both strings instead of one. Place one loop over the other, thread it
through and pull both loops tight. Be prepared to repeat this again and
again, keep the sessions short, and most important of all keep calm.

FROM NURSERY SCHOOL TO PUBLIC SCHOOL

The first day of school for any child can be a traumatic event, both
for the child and for the parents. It can be difficult that first time your
toddler waits on the corner for a bus, or trudges down the walk with
other children to a brand-new adventure.

If your Down's syndrome child has been enrolled in a nursery school
program, you have already passed that milestone of the first day off to
school. Next you and your child must face another milestone, the transition to public school. This will probably be more difficult for you than
for your child. The difficulty lies in the fact that you have probably
become comfortable with the care and instruction your child has received at nursery school, you know and trust the teachers, your child
has made progress, and you and your child have settled into a comfortable routine.

Now you are confronted with a change in that routine, and you must
learn to deal with a new and perhaps formidable system of service. Yet
this transition from nursery school to public school can be exciting,
challenging, rewarding, and educational for both you and your child.

For your youngster it will be a new adventure. For you it will mean getting acquainted with a new service system and a new jargon that is peculiar only to educators. You must also become familiar with the special education laws that guarantee not only your child's rights to receive an appropriate education, but your rights as parents to have a say in your child's educational program.

UNDERSTANDING SPECIAL EDUCATION LAWS

In 1975 the Education for All Handicapped Children Act was enacted into law. This act, better known as PL (Public Law) 94–142, states simply and clearly that "all handicapped children ages three to twenty-one have the right to a free and appropriate public education which must be provided in the least restrictive alternative and to the degree possible in a regular school setting with nonhandicapped children." This means that your child cannot be excluded from a public school education, and that some form of appropriate education, public or private, is mandatory. The two key phrases in that law, "free and appropriate education" and "least restrictive alternative," are extremely important to parents like yourselves.

In the first phrase, *free* means that whatever your child's educational needs are, your local public school system *must* provide his or her education at no cost to you. The word *appropriate* is interpreted to include both educational and other related services that will benefit the whole child. Examples of related services are special transportation, therapeutic service such as physical, occupational, or speech therapy, and psychological services.

"Least restrictive alternative" refers to the setting in which your child is educated. It is often mistakenly equated with the concept of "mainstreaming," which implies that your child must be educated in a regular classroom with his or her nonhandicapped peers. This is not true. What "least restrictive alternative" actually means is that your child *must* be educated in an environment that offers the fewest constraints to his or her learning processes. In other words, your child's educational program must be provided in a setting that offers the greatest opportunity for the acquirement of the skills that he or she needs to become a contributing member to the community. That setting may or may not be in a mainstream classroom. "Least restrictive alternative" does, in fact, protect your child from being haphazardly dumped into mainstream classes.

PL 94–142 requires that free and appropriate public education be available for your child through his or her twenty-first birthday. The vast majority of Down's syndrome children will continue in school until this time and will graduate from high school at age twenty-one.

However, some states have extended the upper age limit of twenty-one by one or two years. Other states have lowered the minimum age of three to birth. This means, for example, that some states provide free and appropriate education for handicapped children from the time of birth to age twenty-five.

Be sure to check with your local director of special education for information about this age limit in your state.

Although PL 94–142 is primarily intended to benefit children, it also contains provisions that make it a "Bill of Rights" for parents. These provisions guarantee you, the parents, the following rights:

To participate in the development of your child's educational program

To review and inspect all of your child's educational records, and obtain copies of these records

To determine your child's primary language, which *must* be used by your child's teacher(s) as the major means of communicating with your child

To be notified in writing when changes in your child's education plan are being considered

To appeal through legal process any decisions made by the schools in regard to your child's education with which you disagree

To request that information be removed from your child's records which you believe to be inaccurate, misleading, or discriminatory

In addition to the rights of a free and appropriate education, and the least restrictive alternative part, PL 94–142 also guarantees your child the following rights:

He or she cannot be excluded from public school programs and services.

Your child must be given an individualized education plan, which is a written statement of the services he or she will receive. This statement must contain learning objectives, progressive steps to meet those objectives, and a time frame for achieving them. You have the right to review this plan at any time.

Your child has the right to a fair evaluation, which means that no single test or evaluation procedure can be used as the sole criterion for determining your child's educational program. This means that he or she must be given two standardized evaluation tests, neither of which can discriminate against your child on the basis of handicap, or racial or cultural background. All tests must be given in your child's primary language, the one he or she understands and uses regularly.

Your child has the right to due process, which means that you can, when necessary, use legal procedures to obtain or determine his or her educational programs.

When your child is considered for educational services, he or she must be evaluated or assessed in these areas: physical growth and development, cognitive and academic functioning, social and emotional development, fine and gross motor skills, perception in sensory motor skills, vocational interests and skills.

Your child must be reevaluated every three years to determine if a change is needed in his or her educational plan.

There are other special education laws which vary from state to state, so be sure you get copies of these laws from your state department of special education and study them thoroughly. Your child's education depends on how well you know these laws and your rights under them.

UNDERSTANDING EDUCATIONAL JARGON

An important part of understanding the special education law is learning and understanding the jargon that educators use. Some of the most commonly used jargon includes:

- IEP—individualized education plan
- LRA—least restrictive alternative
- Litigation—filing court action suits by an individual or individuals
- Child find—a process in which school systems try to identify handicapped children and youths through age twenty-one
- Mainstreaming—the integration of handicapped children in classes with nonhandicapped children
- Core team—a group of three professionals who are initially responsible for reviewing referrals to special education classes

• Short-term objectives—the methods used to achieve the annual goals of your child's educational plan

• Review conference—a meeting between parents and educators to review or to revise the individualized education plan for your child

WORKING WITH EDUCATORS

PL 94–142 gives you the right to help plan your child's educational program. This is an important right granted *only* to parents of children who are handicapped. It should be taken seriously because your child's education rests on your shoulders as much as it does on those of his or her teachers. So in addition to understanding the special education law and the jargon that special educators use, you must learn to work in partnership with your child's teachers, and together plan the best program for him or her.

This partnership may not be easily established because educators and parents often create barriers between themselves that prevent them from working together. You may find that your child's educators are trying to impress you with their academic knowledge. They may use terminology that is difficult for you to understand. They may try to exclude you from participating in the decisions that affect your child's educational program. They may even assume that only educators are capable of making decisions about the educational destinies of children. Like other parents, you may resent such assumptions. After all, you have had the responsibility of making all kinds of decisions for your child from the time he or she was born. You may ask what other parents have asked, "Why should educators think we are no longer capable of making decisions for our children now that they are in school?" The best way to overcome this attitude of educators is for you to become very assertive and exercise your rights, politely but firmly.

Parents can also be guilty of creating barriers that can prevent them from working effectively with educators.

It is not uncommon for parents to view educators as godlike, or as having all the answers, and therefore being capable of making all decisions concerning a child's education. Such a viewpoint is unfair to educators and children alike. Educators can't possibly know all there is to know about a child in order to make a decision. The child, in turn, may be shortchanged if educational decisions are made on less-than-accurate information.

Some parents I know tend to make unreasonable demands on educators' time and attention by requesting unavailable information, or by insisting on an unrealistic or unworkable educational program for their child.

Other parents have been unwilling to accept any advice from educators, believing that to do so would threaten their integrity and authority. These parents adopted an attitude of "No one is going to tell me what is best for my kid."

When the barriers created by educators are combined with those created by parents, the result can only be a no-win situation, and the only person who is really going to be hurt is the child.

Here are some suggestions that should help establish a cooperative working relationship between you and your child's educators:

• Insist that any relevant information that educators have be shared with you so you can make appropriate decisions.

• If you don't understand the terminology, say so and ask for an explanation.

• Exercise your right to be involved in decisions affecting your child by attending all meetings related to his or her education.

• Insist that you be allowed to help select educational goals and objectives for your child.

• Try to avoid getting into a competitive relationship with your child's educators. It is an easy situation to get into, but much more difficult to get out of. When differences of opinion occur, look for ways to compromise. As much as possible, try to work *with* your child's teachers rather than against them.

DEVELOPING REALISTIC EDUCATIONAL GOALS

You and your spouse have the right to participate in your child's educational program. One phase of this participation is the development of realistic educational goals. For children with disabilities, their major educational goal should be to live as independently as possible in their community. What your child learns in school must be the necessary skills to live as a responsible adult member of the community.

It is your responsibility to make sure that your child's educational goals are met. This responsibility is less awesome and easier to assume if you become familiar with the process of how educational goals are developed.

These goals for your child must be based on both formal and informal evaluations. For the formal evaluation, your child must be given several tests to determine his or her physical, mental, and social abilities. None of these tests can be given without your consent, which should be in writing. This will protect you and your child in case there is a misunderstanding later on. Informal evaluations are based on observations made by teachers, you and your spouse, and support personnel such as the school principal, occupational, physical, or speech therapists, and psychologists.

When the evaluations are completed, a multidisciplinary team consisting of teachers, you and your spouse, and support personnel study the information from the evaluation tests (both formal and informal) to develop educational goals for your child. The team should take into consideration: your child's past performance; your opinion on what is important for your child to learn; and your child's specific strengths and weaknesses.

Once the multidisciplinary team has thoroughly studied the information concerning your child, it begins to write learning objectives in each of the learning domains. While there are various ways of describing these learning domains, they are commonly broken down as follows:

- Expressive and receptive language development (talking, listening)
- Gross and fine motor skills (body development and senses)
- Self-help skills (dressing, eating, toileting)
- Social and affective skills (getting along with others, manners)
- Cognitive skills (counting, telling time, music)

Your child's learning objectives must be written in behavioral terms that are easily understood and easy to measure for progress. An example of a well-written learning objective is: "The student will be able to put on his or her jacket correctly 85 percent of the time when asked to do so. The student will accomplish this objective within three weeks after instruction starts."

This statement clearly outlines what skill will be learned, how well the student will learn it, and how long it will take to learn the skill. In addition to this information, each learning objective must also state in writing who is going to teach the skill, what time of day it will be taught, and how much time will be spent teaching it.

These learning objectives should correspond to your child's lifelong goals of living as independently as possible as an adult. As each learning objective is written, you and other members of the multidisciplinary team must ask yourselves this question, "How will this learning objective help the child in the future?" For example, if one of your child's learning objectives is to draw a straight line, how will that skill benefit him or her as an adult?

PRIVATE SCHOOLS

Thus far this chapter has discussed only public schooling, though much of the material in this chapter applies as much to private schools as it does to public ones. Although the vast majority of Down's syndrome children do attend local public schools, there exist a good number of private schools that serve primarily or entirely handicapped children. Most of these are day schools, though there are a few boarding schools as well. These private schools are normally quite expensive.

For a listing of names and addresses of private schools, contact your local branch or the national headquarters of the Association for Retarded Citizens. And you also have the option of sending your child to a regular private school where he or she can be mainstreamed.

OPTIONS FOR PARENTS

Your local school district has the responsibility of providing special education and related services to any child who needs these services, even if he or she doesn't attend public school. In other words, "the least restrictive alternative" means that your child should acquire knowledge and skills in the most "normal" environment. If you expect your child to function in the normal world, it makes sense for your child to be largely educated in that world, in the classrooms along with nonhandicapped peers.

Special education classes provided before PL 94–142 were for the most part segregated from the normal or mainstream classes. This meant one of two things happened. Special education students attended classes in separate buildings that housed only special classes, or these students attended classes in a public school building but were isolated from the other students because the special classrooms were located in remote areas of the building. Having been a special education teacher in the early to mid-sixties, I still have vivid memories of trying to accommodate my students in a dark murky basement and renovated broom closets. Such isolation is now extinct.

Instead, under PL 94–142 special education classes are provided in a variety of mainstream settings within regular public school buildings. Under this arrangement your child could attend any one of the following:

• A regular class with no special services, but in which his or her progress is monitored by classroom and special education teachers.

• A regular classroom with necessary support service provided by therapists or counselors.

• A regular classroom with part-time placement in a special class for handicapped children.

• A special classroom with integration into other activities with non-handicapped children at least twice a day.

You should keep in mind that these settings or arrangements may vary among the different states and are known as the "ladder" approach to special education. The distinct advantage of this approach is that it allows your child to move up or down the ladder of classroom arrangements as his or her educational needs change. The other advantage is the interaction that occurs with nonhandicapped students.

In some areas, public schools still provide special education classes in buildings that accommodate only special education students. Parents who choose this segregated environment for their children believe it has two advantages over regular class placement: there is more individual attention and the entire faculty has special education training.

If your child is mainstreamed, there is the risk of teasing or bullying by nonhandicapped children. On the other hand, since ridiculing, teasing, and bullying seem to be a part of social behavior, it may be helpful for your child to be confronted with it and to learn to deal with it at an early age. (It is quite likely he or she will continue to encounter such behavior throughout the period of public school education.) You can help your child cope with this negative behavior in the same manner as you would help him or her cope with peer harassment. This is discussed in Chapter 7.

In a segregated class your child, having little or no chance to interact with nonhandicapped peers, is ill prepared to deal with society's quirky behavior. Unfortunately, this behavior is one of the hard realities of life, and sooner or later your child will be exposed to it and will have to learn how to deal with it.

Clearly, there are advantages and disadvantages to both mainstream-

ing and segregated special education. Not every school system will be able to offer you a choice between the two. But if a choice is available, you will need to weigh the factors carefully to determine which option is best for your child.

Once you have made a choice, it is not irrevocable. It is possible for your child to be mainstreamed for part of his or her education and enrolled in special education classes during other years.

SUMMER SCHOOL

There is little doubt that summer school is important for children with Down's syndrome because it helps them maintain the skills and knowledge they acquired during the regular school year. If the summer school curriculum is based on the five general areas of learning mentioned on page 102, then you should expect your child to learn additional skills. Even if the summer curriculum focuses on just one or two areas of learning, your child can still benefit from attending these classes. A limited program for these children during summer is better than none at all simply because it reinforces the skills they have acquired.

Generally summer school sessions are six weeks long and last either half a day (about three hours) or a full day (six hours). Since summer school is not mandatory according to PL 94–142, it may or may not be available in your community. If it is and you want your child to participate, you must be sure to include a summer school program in the individual education plan.

LEGAL OPTIONS

If your child needs special education and related services but attends a nonpublic school, your local public school must provide the special services your child needs at the nonpublic school. However, you have the option of refusing any special services offered by the public school for your child at the nonpublic school site. If you consent to have special services provided for your child at a site other than a public school, you and your child have the same rights under PL 94–142 as if he or she were attending a public school.

When you differ with your child's school about the services your child is receiving, you should try to resolve those differences on an informal basis. These are examples of situations that may create a difference of opinion between you and the school. You do not think that the transportation services are adequate. You think your child needs more services than he or she is receiving, such as speech therapy daily rather than twice a week. You question the validity of the school's assessment of your child and you want another one performed at no cost to you.

To resolve these or similar situations on an informal basis, you simply discuss them with your child's teacher and school principal. This is almost always the simplest, most direct, and best method for resolving difficulties or disagreements. However, if your efforts toward an informal resolution are unsuccessful, you have the following options:

Due process hearing An impartial hearing officer makes a decision after hearing comments from you and school representatives.

Appeal to state commissioner If you are not satisfied with the due process hearing, you may appeal to the state commissioner of education who will review the case and issue a written decision.

Lawsuit If the decision rendered by your state commission of education does not satisfy you, you may want to initiate a lawsuit in district or federal court.

Section 504 This section of the Rehabilitation Act of 1973 offers a procedure for cases in which a person is discriminated against solely on the basis of a handicap. An example of such a discrimination would be if the school does not make an appropriate modification such as a ramp for wheelchairs. If you believe that your child is being discriminated against simply because he or she is handicapped, you can file a Section 504 complaint. To do so, address your complaint in writing to the local Office for Civil Rights in your area. (See Chapter 12 for information on writing this letter.)

DENTAL CARE FOR THE TODDLER

Most children (including most Down's syndrome children) have all of their primary teeth by the age of three. These teeth are just as important for chewing, speaking, and appearance as are the permanent teeth.

Primary teeth also keep space available in the jaws for permanent teeth. If your child loses a primary tooth too early, nearby teeth are likely to spread into that space. When this happens, there will not be enough space for the permanent teeth, which will then erupt out of their proper position.

When all of your child's primary teeth have come in, it is time for you to begin brushing and flossing them. Be sure you use a toothbrush with *soft* bristles, a straight handle, a flat brushing surface, and a head that is small enough to reach every tooth. Your child should use this same kind of brush when beginning to brush without your help.

The American Dental Association recommends this method as the best way to brush teeth.

• Place the head of the toothbrush alongside the teeth, with the bristles angled against the gums.

• Gently scrub back and forth with short strokes.

• Brush the inner, outer, and biting surfaces of each tooth.

• Use the front "toe" of the brush to get at the inside area of the front teeth.

Flossing your child's teeth helps remove the plaque that hides between the teeth and under the gum line, areas not easily reached by a toothbrush. Here are some hints for successful flossing:

• Break off about eighteen inches of floss and wind most of it around the middle finger of one hand.

• Wind the remainder around the same finger of the other hand.

• Hold the floss tightly and gently insert it between the teeth. Be careful not to snap the floss down into the gums.

• When the floss reaches the gum line, curve it into a C shape and slide it into the space between the tooth and the gum until you feel resistance.

• Scrape the floss up and down against the side of the tooth. Repeat this process for each tooth.

As you start brushing and flossing your child's teeth, remember to use the show-and-tell technique, just as you did when teaching the self-care skills of feeding and dressing. Brushing and flossing are not easy self-care skills to master, so don't be surprised if your child is five or six years old before being able to brush without help. Even then, he or she must still be watched to make sure that the brushing is done thoroughly. If your child can brush independently, you should still continue to do the flossing since most Down's syndrome children don't master this until about the age of eight.

Preschool children tend to wear out a toothbrush rather quickly because they brush with imperfect strokes or chew on the bristles. It is therefore a good idea to replace your child's toothbrush frequently. Bent or chewed bristles will not remove plaque, and they could hurt the gums.

The preschool years are a good time to help your child establish good eating habits because it is easier for you to control the diet at this age than it is later on. In addition to balanced meals, be sure your child eats sensible snack foods. At this age all children need in-between-meal snacks because they can seldom get all the nutrients they need at mealtime. However, if your child snacks too often, especially on foods that are high in sugar content, his or her teeth will be more susceptible to decay.

Fluoride is very effective for preventing tooth decay. It strengthens the tooth enamel and makes the teeth more resistant to acid attacks. Your child can get the protection of fluoride in several ways, the most effective being to drink fluoridated water. According to the American Dental Association, children who from birth drink fluoridated water will have 65 percent fewer cavities, and when these children are teenagers, 20 percent of them will still be cavity-free.

If there is no fluoridated water in your area, then your dentist may prescribe fluoride tablets, rinses, or gels for home use. You can call your local water department or state health agency to find out if the water in your community is fluoridated or not.

Brushing the teeth with fluoride toothpaste is also helpful, but some of the available brands do not prevent tooth decay. Those that carry the seal of the American Dental Association have proven to be effective in reducing decay, so be sure to look for that seal on the carton or tube of toothpaste before you purchase it.

VISITS TO THE DENTIST

The ideal time to schedule your child's first visit to a dentist is before all of the primary teeth have erupted. You may have reasons to delay this first visit, but don't wait too long. Most dentists recommend that all children see a dentist for the first time no later than six months after the primary teeth have all come through. The earlier you begin these visits, the better chance your dentist will have to prevent problems. Of course, any time a child injures a tooth or has a cavity, a dentist should be seen immediately.

The dentist you choose should be a pedodontist, one who specializes in treating children, especially children who are handicapped. If your own dentist or your child's pediatrician cannot recommend a children's dentist, you can try these resources:

- Ask your neighbors and friends.
- Telephone your local dental society.
- Call your local health department.
- Telephone the nearest hospital or check with a local dental school.
- Look in the yellow pages of your phone book.

After choosing a dentist, it is a good idea to explain about your child's disability before making that first visit. It will help the dentist understand the child and ease any of your youngster's fears.

You should help your child understand that this first visit to the dentist is an important adventure. Explain to your child that the dentist is a friendly person who helps other people take good care of their teeth. You should try to make this explanation in a positive, matter-of-fact way, using words that your child understands. Whatever you tell your child, don't use statements like, "It won't hurt," which suggest that the visit will be unpleasant.

You may want to ask the dentist for hints on how to prepare your child for the first dental visit. Remember, if your child's first visit to the dentist is a positive experience, it will help shape his or her attitudes for future visits.

CHAPTER 6

The Parental Role

There will always be moments of fear and joy, sorrow and happiness, discouragement and delight, and anger and humor as your child goes through the difficult process of growing up. Whatever emotions you find yourself experiencing, try not to let them overwhelm you to the point where you adopt either a saint or a martyr role. Neither of these roles is realistic, and they will not be beneficial either to you or to your child.

These roles can be avoided if you remember not to set a goal of absolute perfection for yourself as a parent. For example, don't set a goal of never scolding your child or of always controlling your temper. Such goals probably won't make you a better or more loving parent, and they are close to impossible to attain anyway. More important, you also run the risk of teaching your child to expect everyone to treat him or her the same way.

There is little doubt that the problems you must face with your child are real and that the emotions you will experience will be strong. But remember, many of those same feelings would arise whether or not your child had been born with Down's syndrome.

If you are angry and feel like blowing your stack, it's all right to do so *occasionally.* That will take care of your emotion for the moment, at least, and blowing your stack is better than taking an action you may regret later. It also lets your child know that you are not all-wise, all-patient, or generally perfect. If you express your anger *once in a while,* your child will learn that you are just as human as he or she is.

You probably can't escape the surges of emotion that accompany being the parent of a child who is handicapped. What you *can* do, though, is remember that time is your friend, and that the emotional chaos you find yourself in every now and then will eventually pass.

DEALING WITH COMMON PROBLEMS, WORRIES, AND CONCERNS

As your child grows older, you may harbor some resentment toward him or her because the care involved demands so much of your time. By demanding so much, your youngster may seem to be depriving you of much personal pleasure. It is also easy to wonder if you are doing too much or not enough for your child.

These emotions are common among parents like yourselves. Yet having them does not mean you are an unloving or uncaring parent. What it does mean is that you are struggling to bring your life to a balance again. This is fundamentally a positive act, and a good sign.

To recapture your balance, you and your spouse must be open with each other and talk about your feelings. The longer you postpone such discussions, the harder it will be to start them. Ultimately, this can create a rift in your relationship. So speak your mind freely, and encourage your partner to do the same. And when he or she talks, *listen* attentively and compassionately.

Try joining a group for parents of children with Down's syndrome if you have not already done so. Sharing experiences and talking about your concerns with other parents is good therapy.

Some parents find relief and support by keeping a daily or weekly journal in which they record actions they took or incidents that occurred, and how they felt about them all.

Raising children puts stress on any family. Your family will be no different, except perhaps in the frequency and kinds of situations that cause stress. The best ways to relieve family stress are the tried-and-true ones all parents use. First of all, you and your spouse should give yourselves time to relax, take it easy, and have fun. If you don't have this time now, make it for yourselves. If you "can't" spare the time, spare it anyway somehow. Ignore a social obligation or let your house stay a little cluttered for a few days. This time to relax and enjoy life—and each other—is important to your own happiness and well-being, and even to your sanity. It is not a luxury but a necessity. One good way to make time for yourself and your spouse is to enroll your Down's syndrome child in an after-school program.

DIVIDING ATTENTION AMONG YOUR CHILDREN

Because a child with Down's syndrome often demands a great deal of attention and care, most parents fear they may neglect other children in the family. By making the care of your Down's syndrome child a family affair, you can avoid neglecting your other children. If they are old enough, encourage them (but don't insist) to help with diapering, feeding, and dressing their sibling. Set aside a time when everyone can be together to read, to play a game, or to go for a walk. Encourage (but never force) your other children to read, talk, sing, and tell stories to their Down's syndrome sibling.

When one of you—Mom, for instance—prepares your child for bed, then the other parent should spend that time with your other children. And don't forget to reverse the roles every now and then.

Several parents told me about an interesting way in which they solved this problem. They regularly set aside some time—say, a full or a half day a week, or an hour or two every few days—to spend just with their other children, doing something of interest *chosen by the children.* During this time their Down's syndrome child is cared for by a relative, friends, or a sitter.

As your Down's syndrome child grows older, remember that it is unfair to make any comparison with any of your other children. In fact it is unfair to compare *any* of your children against one another, as each child will have his or her unique abilities and limitations.

Don't give in to the temptation of expecting your normal children to be superkids, simply because they don't have Down's syndrome like their brother or sister. And don't expect your other kids to compensate for the lack of ability you see in your handicapped child. These sorts of expectations are heavy and unrealistic burdens for any child to bear. And don't expect your spouse or yourself to be superparents, either, to make up for your Down's syndrome child's slowness. The superparent role will be too much for you both to bear.

Your expectations for your nonhandicapped child must be realistic and achievable. It is fine to expect many achievements from your child, but there is a point beyond which expectations stop motivating your child and instead begin to be debilitating. The expectations that you and your spouse have for your child should be as reasonable for him or her to meet as your expectations for your nonhandicapped children are for them to meet. You should expect your Down's syndrome child to do what other small children do—learn to speak, learn to crawl and walk, learn to obey requests and commands, and learn all the basic self-care skills—but you should allow this child more time to learn. You should give your child every opportunity to become as self-sufficient and independent as possible, but you should not ask anything that is genuinely beyond his or her abilities.

Be careful, too, not to dote on any of your nonhandicapped children. It is easy to begin to lavish your attention on a normal child simply because that child is not handicapped. It's also easy to dote on a child who is especially bright, good-looking, or athletically adept. But resist this temptation. Instead, reward each of your children for their own particular achievements while avoiding favoritism toward any particular child.

If all this sounds like a difficult balance to attain, the fact is that it sometimes can be. However, you will learn from your experience what expectations are too high and which ones are too low. You'll definitely make some mistakes, but that's fine. Don't condemn yourself (or your spouse); instead, learn from those mistakes and adjust your expectations accordingly.

UNDERSTANDING THE DEVELOPMENTAL STAGES OF YOUR CHILD

All children develop physically in an organized, progressive manner. The differences from child to child will occur in the length of the developmental stages and in what levels of achievement are reached.

During the first year or two, your child's progress could be very close to what is considered normal for all children. This is especially true if the baby has had the advantage of infant stimulation classes.

The emotional and social development of all children also follow an organized, progressive pattern. Chapter 5 discussed three early stages of development; the obstinate two year old, the imitative three and four year old, and the "best pal" seven to nine year old.

The eight- to ten-year-old child will experience the stage of parental preference, that is, the child clearly will prefer to spend more time with the parent of his or her own sex. This preference indicates an awareness of sex differences and of sex roles and a desire to learn more about them.

When your child reaches the teenage years, you can expect a repetition of the obstinate stage. This obstinacy is your child's way of asserting and achieving independence. Remember, though, it may take your child a little longer to advance from one stage to another.

Here are three important items to keep in mind as your child grows older:

• Children outgrow rules and guidelines just as they do clothes, so be sure you revise them every now and then.

• Growing up isn't a race, so don't try to rush it.

• No stage lasts forever.

Just as the development of your child follows the same progressive pattern as other children, so do his or her needs and wants. Your child needs what every child needs—love, understanding, discipline, and guidance. Encourage the development of interests and hobbies, and provide opportunities that will help your youngster acquire physical skills —swimming, for example. Your child needs the chance to make decisions and accept responsibilities that will give him or her a sense of self-worth. Your child wants and needs social acceptance. And, like all children, your child needs a good, appropriate education that will develop his or her abilities. The ultimate need all children (and adults) have is to live a life that is rewarding and fulfilling.

TRAPS FOR PARENTS TO AVOID

SIBLING RIVALRY AND JEALOUSY

When a second child is born, all parents take on another role: that of peacemaker and peacekeeper between their children. The age space between the first and second child will determine when you take on this role. Usually it is about the time the second child begins to invade the first child's turf. Once this invasion happens, you can expect sibling rivalry and jealousy to continue for a long time, simply because it is a part of growing up for all children.

When rivalry flares up between your children, let them try to settle their differences without your intervention. If that does not work and you must interrupt, then you may want to try these techniques:

• Send all the children involved to their rooms with instructions not to come out until they are ready to apologize to one another.

• If there is a toy or other object causing the disagreement, take the object away yourself and have the children go to separate areas for a cooling-off period.

• When you see a clash coming and it seems as if it may be inevitable, try distraction, like asking for help. (Don't try to distract your children with a treat of some sort, or they will soon learn that starting to quarrel will earn them a reward.)

• Like tantrums, rivalry thrives before an audience, so when an argument begins you may want to leave the room—or better yet, tell your children that they can argue if they like, but only if they do it privately in another room.

• Kids often squabble when they are bored. When this happens get them interested in a new activity.

QUARRELS WITH YOUR SPOUSE

The occasional quarrel is unavoidable, and it can even be beneficial, at least in letting off steam. But keep in mind that when you do quarrel with your spouse, you may frighten your child. This could lead to crying, screaming, pleading, or even a tantrum on your child's part. While all children can be disturbed by parental squabbles, Down's syndrome children tend to react more emotionally.

The solution here is not to avoid quarrels when they are "necessary," but to have them away from your child so as not to upset him or her. This is especially important if the quarrel has something to do with your child because if you are heard arguing, your child may feel guilty about "causing" the argument. This can do real harm to your child's development and self-esteem, especially if the quarrels are frequent.

Arguing away from your child doesn't mean simply going into the next room. When your child hears you screaming at your spouse downstairs, or through the door, he or she is going to be at least as frightened as if you were standing right there—maybe even more so. So if a disagreement with your spouse threatens to turn into a real fight, see if you can take a walk or a car trip, where your child can't see or hear you scream at each other.

By the time your child is nine or ten, it is no longer so important to argue elsewhere. In fact, by that age, it is probably best to let your youngster know that grownups do have disagreements and yell at each other once in a while.

Having a *great many* arguments, however, not only will disturb your child and make him or her feel guilty or insecure; it is also not very good for you or your spouse. If you find yourselves arguing frequently, regardless of the cause, you may want to speak with a marriage counselor or psychologist.

FEAR OF TAKING YOUR CHILD INTO PUBLIC PLACES

Years ago, society's attitude toward people who were different was one of "keep them out of sight" because they were seen as misfits. No one wanted to be reminded that ours is not a perfect society. Because of this attitude, parents of Down's syndrome children quite naturally felt guilty and embarrassed for having produced misfits. Rather than have their secret known, they kept their children out of sight as much as possible.

Fortunately, society's attitude has been gradually changing simply because parents began to assert their rights and the rights of their children. With this changing attitude, it is easier for you and your child to be seen in public.

The best way to overcome any apprehensions you may have is to take your child out. Many parents told me they felt uncomfortable forcing themselves to go out in public, but they also felt good because it was another step forward in their growth as parents. "It's another in the series of changes you must make if your child is to become all that he or she can," they told me.

Society has still not accepted Down's syndrome people 100 percent. While society tolerates and offers limited acceptance to these children, they are not often seen as valued contributors to community life or to society in general. Because of this attitude, parents of Down's syndrome children must win a place in society for their children. Winning this place may be one of the most difficult tasks you will have to take on— but it is not an impossible one.

Taking your child to public places is not only a major step in his or her intellectual, emotional, and social development, it is also a major step in helping the child win a place in society. But taking your youngster to public places does entail exposure for both of you to the occasional negative reactions of other people. You will be hurt and mystified by these reactions at first, but you must learn to deal with them.

One way of dealing with friends and neighbors is to take the time to explain your child's disability to them. Tell them that, given a chance, your child can learn many things and that, handicapped or not, he or she has the same desires and feelings as other children—in short, that your child is human. Tell them what you are doing to help your child overcome specific deficiencies in speech or motor development.

One family I know invited some friends and neighbors to their house for a coffee party. They also invited a representative from the local Down's syndrome parent group to explain the syndrome and answer questions. This not only taught the neighbors a great deal and eased many of their fears, but it showed them that the parents were friendly, intelligent, and forthright people. The coffee party wound up encouraging good-neighbor relations as well as understanding.

Unkind remarks, stares, or whispers from strangers in public places are more troubling. These can be dealt with in one of two ways. You can ignore such actions, or you can take a minute to briefly explain your child's condition. Some parents advocate giving an explanation because it helps people understand and become more accepting toward a person with handicaps. Other parents prefer to let such unkind actions pass rather than reward the rudeness with their attention.

You can help your child with Down's syndrome to live and cope with negative reactions from others by teaching him or her to ignore them. However, your child could, like many other Down's syndrome children I know, be acutely aware of the negative reactions from other people and react to the situation by simply walking away. I have observed this sensitivity in children as young as eight years old, and the older the person is the more sensitive they seem to be.

Whenever you, your partner, or your other children are confronted with the thoughtless actions or remarks of other people, talking it over among yourselves helps ease the discomfort you may feel.

THE DESIRE TO RUN

At times you may have felt that the problems of raising your Down's syndrome child were more than you could bear. You may have secretly wished you could run away from it all. When the urge to escape overtakes you, try these alternatives instead:

• Look for accomplishments you and your child have achieved. (Hopefully you have been recording these accomplishments in your child's baby book. If you haven't, get a baby book and get started now.)

• If you are moving at top speed and still can't get everything done, slow down a little. Complete only the most necessary tasks. One mother I know limited the amount of time she would spend on a particular task. For example, she allowed herself an hour for cleaning the kitchen. If she completed the cleaning in less time, she spent the rest of the hour on herself, reading or just relaxing. If she couldn't finish in an hour, she stopped anyway.

• See if you can arrange for an after-school program for your child, or for a "special friend" to spend time with your child.

• Don't forget to make sure you are meeting your own needs as an individual and as part of a couple. Be sure to provide for your own happiness.

• Arrange for respite care for your child. (This is discussed in detail later in this chapter.)

• Complete an unfinished project, or start a new one.

• Take up a new interest or hobby—perhaps something you've always wanted to do but never got around to.

• When you feel like you absolutely *have* to get away, do it—take a short vacation. But plan it in advance and let your child know exactly what will happen.

• Remember that being a parent is difficult, no matter what the circumstances are.

• Remember, too, that time does heal. As the days and weeks pass, you will no longer feel as panicky as you might today.

FEELING TRAPPED

Sometimes the biggest trap of all is simply the feeling that you *are* trapped. For some partners, a particular problem can occur so frequently, or the different problems (whether or not they involve their Down's syndrome child) may seem so numerous that they will feel trapped or helpless in the face of them.

The most important thing to remember in such cases is that you are *not* trapped. You are not serving out a life sentence of misery, nor has a Superior Being inflicted any kind of vengeance on you. The bad feelings you may have now will pass sooner or later, and there will come a time in the future (and very likely in the near future) when you will feel happier and more secure once again.

Parents who feel trapped are often putting too much pressure on themselves—by doting on their children, or by trying to be superparents, or by seeing themselves as martyrs or saints. If you are putting too much pressure on yourself, you will normally feel much better, and much less trapped, if you simply reduce that pressure and relax. Take it easy for a few days or, better yet, take it easier in general.

Many communities offer weekend retreats especially for parents of children with handicaps. There the time is spent doing a variety of physical fitness, recreation, or relaxation activities that promote self-discovery. Check to see if there is one in or near your community.

DEALING WITH MARITAL STRESS

The effect that your child has on the relationship between you and your spouse can be positive or negative. If your relationship is strong, the chances of your child having a negative effect are less. If a tenuous relationship exists between the two of you, the challenges of raising your Down's syndrome child can put a great deal of stress on both of you. But there are ways of dealing with the problems that arise between you and your mate.

WHO IS TO BLAME?

You must understand that nothing you or your spouse did or did not do caused your child's handicap. Nor could you have prevented it from happening. It is purely and simply a faulty separation of chromosomes. Still, at times it is tempting to lay blame either on yourself or your spouse. This is understandable because whenever something goes wrong, as human beings we want to know why. All the parents I have talked with said that at one point or another they too tried to lay blame on someone.

But you should neither blame your spouse nor accept any such blame yourself. Placing or accepting blame serves no useful purpose whatever and it can cause or increase bad feelings between you and your spouse.

FINANCIAL BURDENS

Quite often the health care needs of a Down's syndrome child place a heavy financial burden on the family which in turn can strain marital relations. Constant worry over financial resources can be a major cause of marital stress.

You and your spouse must come to terms with the actual cost of your child's health care and your own actual earning power. Simply worrying about finances will not help to solve any problems. If the costs of your child's health care exceed your earning ability, you should not hesitate to seek help elsewhere—from relatives, from your community, or from your child's doctor or hospital.

Often a hospital or doctor will charge based on your income, or on your ability to actually pay the bill. Thus an operation that might normally cost four thousand dollars might cost you and your partner only one thousand, or even less. Sometimes payment can be delayed, or made on the installment plan. Speak with your child's doctor, or with the hospital's accounting office, to see what can be worked out.

Bank loans are also an option, of course. Loans are frequently given for medical expenses—not just for houses, cars, and so on.

And don't be afraid or ashamed of looking to your community agencies for financial assistance. That is what they are there for. Contact your local or state health department, your local social service agency, the local children's aid societies, and the children's section of the welfare department; any of these may be able to provide financial assistance. You could try calling the United Way, the Association for Retarded Citizens, or the Down Syndrome Congress chapters in your area for additional financial resources. Remember, in approaching these agencies you are not a beggar asking for a handout, but a concerned parent seeking help with the medical expenses for your child. See Chapter 11 for information on obtaining assistance from the state and federal governments.

Some parents who are told that their child will need surgery or some other expensive medical procedure seek a second medical opinion to see if a different and less expensive procedure will suffice. There is nothing wrong with doing this, and in fact sometimes it is a very good idea. At best, it will give you another, less expensive option; at worst, it will confirm the first medical opinion and give you peace of mind.

Whenever your doctor recommends a medical procedure you should ask, "What will this cost?" and "Is there something just as good but less expensive available?"

One way or another, though, your energy is always best spent seeking solutions and assistance for your financial problems. It is *not* well spent arguing with your spouse about finances or worrying about them privately.

SUPERPARENT SYNDROME

Many parents tend to assume that they can and should provide all the care their children need at all times—and that they should provide this care with love, devotion and, if necessary, sacrifice. In real life, however, few parents actually measure up to this role. You probably won't either—not so much because your child is handicapped, but because the saintly, sacrificial role is not a realistic one. It is, in fact, only an image (and a false one, at that) of what many parents think they *should* be.

Expecting to be perfect parents—to be always cheerful, available, and loving to your child—is known as Superparent syndrome. It is *not* a positive state of mind, but a set of unreasonable expectations that will likely cause trouble for both you and your child.

Parents who believe that their every waking moment should be devoted to the care of their Down's syndrome child, or to their children in general, will be doing little good for their children and will be putting excessive and unnecessary strain on their marriage. Because no one can actually fulfill the role of the superparent, accepting such a role can lead to frustration, exhaustion, and depression. It can also lead to your child depending on you too much and too often. Since you strive to constantly give your child the absolute best care, he or she soon learns to expect the best at all times, not only from you but from others. When the youngster *doesn't* get the best from other people who certainly aren't going to meet the superparent standards, he or she is likely to be confused, unhappy, or frustrated.

Some parents believe, consciously or unconsciously, that they are the only ones who can properly care for their child. The child in turn accepts that idea, and eventually the parents and child begin to become completely dependent on one another. This is not a healthy relationship, especially since your child needs to become more and more independent and outward-directed if his or her emotional growth is to keep up with physical growth.

The cure for the Superparent syndrome is the same as its preventative measure—learning to let go. Deliberately give up some of the responsibilities of caring for your child with Down's syndrome. Have friends, relatives, neighbors, a paid sitter, or a reliable day care program be in charge of your child. Begin gradually, entrusting your child to others for only an hour or two at a time at first. Then lengthen the time you spend away from your child.

Be sure to spend this time doing things that you enjoy or that are important to you. Do *not* spend this time thinking or worrying about your child, or buying gifts or treats to ease any guilt feelings you may have. This will only help further your child's dependence on you. While your child is in the care of others, occupy your self with other people and other things. This may be difficult at first because you may feel guilty about leaving your child in the care of someone else. But eventually you will discover that another care giver can meet your child's needs, and you can relax. This will give you peace of mind and will ease any strain that may have resulted from your superparent role.

Caring for your child and meeting his or her needs on a daily basis are the major responsibilities of all parents. But it is easy to forget that you and your spouse also have needs that must be met. You cannot brush your own needs aside because your child's needs are "more important." If you do, you will only wind up feeling emotionally drained, frustrated, and depressed. You must be just as careful to meet your own needs and the needs of your spouse as you are to care for your Down's syndrome child and your other children.

It is easy to forget about your own needs, or to feel that there is simply no time to meet them, especially if you have adopted a sacrificial attitude toward your child. But it is extremely difficult, if not impossible, to keep a healthy relationship with your spouse, and to stay happy and healthy as an individual, if you are ignoring your own needs. Remember, you and your spouse need to give and receive support, respect, understanding, and love to and from each other. And you need time to talk with each other—about your feelings for each other, and about how you feel as parents of your Down's syndrome child. So do talk and express your feelings. Allow and encourage your spouse to do the same —and really listen. Keep in mind that there are no right or wrong feelings, only sincere ones.

Remember, too, that you also need time—time to think, time to relax, and time just to be together—*away* from your children. Allow yourself this time on a regular basis. In fact, plan and insist on it. Adjust your schedule so that you always have this time to look forward to, preferably every day. If you still find yourself feeling irritable, frustrated, or exhausted, see if perhaps more time with your spouse will make you feel better. Be sure you spend this time on *yourselves,* doing things that are enjoyable or important to *both* of you.

Everything I have said here about time with your spouse also applies to time spent alone. Most people need at least a few minutes each day when they can be completely alone with their own thoughts, away from the pressures of everyday living. This time spent alone is as important as time spent with your spouse. So be sure to make this time for yourself as well.

What can you do with this time? Lots of things. Continue with a hobby or an interest, or start a new one. Take a class in a subject that has always interested you. Do volunteer work, or take up some form of exercise. Take long walks. Or just be alone with yourself and relax. Chances are you will think of a number of other rewarding and relaxing things to do while you're away from your children.

One alternative that is particularly useful for parents who are temporarily overwhelmed by the responsibilities of raising a Down's syndrome child is *respite care,* which is discussed on pages 128–29. This can be of special benefit when your child is a source of high personal or marital stress.

Another option is enrolling your child in an after-school or "special friend" program.

Always keep in mind that although your child's care will always be your most immediate concern it should not be the focus of all your attention.

Parenthood means teamwork. If one of you is ready to look for ways of helping your child and the other is still trying to deal with the grief over the lost dream child, decisions will be difficult to make as a team. Now, as never before, each of you must take on your fair share of parenting responsibilities. Sharing an equal division of labor, listening, and understanding can go a long way to fulfilling your needs as parents, and to increasing your love for each other. But if stress or problems between you and your spouse arise or continue, don't simply give up or think "This relationship is hopeless." Instead, seek the help of a marriage counselor, a family therapist, or some other psychologist, and see if working together you can improve the situation.

HAVING ANOTHER CHILD

If you are thinking about having another child, you cannot help wondering if he or she will be born with Down's syndrome. Though it is possible to estimate your chances of giving birth to another baby with Down's syndrome, there is no way to absolutely prevent the syndrome from occurring.

You will recall from Chapter 1, where they are described, that there are three types of Down's syndrome: trisomy 21, translocation, and mosaicism. Roughly one person in six hundred is born with Down's syndrome, and 95 percent of these births are caused by trisomy 21. Four percent are caused by translocation and about 1 percent is caused by mosaicism. Genetic testing will determine what form of Down's syndrome your child has, a topic I will discuss in detail later in this chapter. Only one of these conditions, translocation, is hereditary and can be transmitted by either parent.

Many people who are normal in every other way have translocation and are thus "carriers" of the condition. If you have translocation you can pass it on to your children, but this is only a possibility and not a certainty. And if you *do* pass it on to a child, he or she either may have

Down's syndrome or be perfectly normal and simply carry the translocation condition just as you do.

Because translocation is hereditary, if your child has this form of Down's syndrome, you and your spouse run a much higher risk of having another Down's syndrome child than does a couple in which neither partner is a carrier. Unfortunately, there are no statistics available to tell you exactly how much greater your risk is.

If your child does have the translocation form of Down's syndrome, you and your partner should both have genetic tests to see which of you is a carrier. You should keep in mind, however, that the risk of having another Down's syndrome child is related only to the parent who is the carrier. For example, suppose you and your first male partner had a child with the translocation form of Down's syndrome, and after genetic tests it was determined that your male partner was the carrier. If, later, you have another man's child, that child cannot inherit translocation (unless, of course, your new partner also has translocation).

If your child's Down's syndrome is caused by trisomy 21, the chances that your next child, or any future child, will also have Down's syndrome are roughly 1 in 150. At present, no one knows why the risk goes up so much once you already have one child with trisomy 21.

Very little data is available on mosaicism since it is so very rare. If your child's Down's syndrome is the mosaic type, it is simply not known what the chances are of your having a second baby with Down's syndrome.

The main factors you should consider when deciding whether or not to have another child are your and your partner's ages. Research clearly demonstrates that older parents are more likely to give birth to Down's syndrome babies. For example, if a prospective mother is thirty-five or older and the prospective father is forty-nine or older, this couple is at very high risk to have a child with Down's syndrome.

Yet, additional research shows that a significant number of couples in their early to late twenties are also having Down's syndrome babies.

Too, when deciding whether or not to have another child, you should check to see if there is a history of Down's syndrome in your or your spouse's family.

SEEKING GENETIC COUNSELING

Most parents of Down's syndrome children would do well to seek genetic counseling before deciding to have another child. A genetic counselor can be found by asking your pediatrician or family doctor or, if you prefer, calling your county or state health department. Also, most medical schools and university hospitals offer genetic counseling to the general public.

You should be aware of what happens when you seek genetic counseling. A team of people gathers factual information that is used as the basis for the counseling sessions. This team consists of the parents and any or all of the following professionals: family physician, medical specialists (obstetrician, pediatrician, and so on), special laboratory personnel to study chromosomes, a human geneticist, a social worker, a psychologist, and a nurse.

You and your partner will be expected to supply the team with all the information possible about your immediate families as well as your aunts, uncles, cousins, nieces, nephews, grandparents, and perhaps even great-grandparents. You should be prepared to give as much information as possible about family members' birthdays, ages at the time of death, causes of deaths, and which members may have had Down's syndrome. You will also be asked to supply full medical records of your family members, or let the team members know where these medical records can be found and examined. It is possible that all this information may not be available; however, you should make every effort to find and supply as much as you can.

At some point you and your partner will be given physical examinations. Laboratory tests, including a chromosome analysis will also be done. The chromosome analysis usually takes three to six weeks to complete.

When the laboratory results are available and all the other essential facts have been gathered, all the members of the team, which is usually directed by a physician, will evaluate this information. Once the evaluation is completed, genetic counseling begins.

The actual counseling is done by the team member who is best able to talk to you and your partner about the results of the evaluation. Counseling sessions are usually one to two hours long and in most cases one session is adequate.

Both of you should participate in these counseling sessions together. If you have older children, encourage them to participate as well. This will help answer any questions they may have about their risk of being future parents of children with Down's syndrome, and it will help them understand more about Down's syndrome in general.

The counselor will provide you with a reliable estimate of your chances of having another child with Down's syndrome, giving you the necessary factual information so that you can make an informed decision about having another child. But, remember, only you and your spouse can actually make the decision whether or not to have that child.

At any time during your genetic counseling, don't hesitate to ask your counselor any questions you may have. Since the cost of genetic counseling varies among communities, it's a good idea to find out, at the onset, what financial commitments will be expected of you.

AMNIOCENTESIS: IS IT FOR US?

If you and your spouse decide to have another child, your genetic counselor may suggest amniocentesis as a precautionary measure. The counselor can arrange the procedure, which is a simple one. Some of the amniotic fluid that surrounds the baby in the mother's womb is withdrawn with a syringe during the fourteenth to sixteenth week of pregnancy and then examined. If the results of the examination indicate that the baby has Down's syndrome, you have the option of deciding whether or not to terminate the pregnancy. This, of course, is not a small or a simple decision to make, and it will have to be guided by your religious, moral, and ethical convictions.

Although amniocentesis is a simple procedure, complications can occur. Sometimes the amount of fluid taken is insufficient, and the test must be repeated. Occasionally cramps or bleeding may occur after the process is completed. On rare occasions (about 0.1 percent) there is a risk of intrauterine infection or spontaneous abortion occurring as a result of the procedure.

Researchers from Stanford University discovered in 1984 that cells from a fetus appear in the mother's bloodstream as early as the twelfth week of pregnancy. This discovery may make possible an alternative to amniocentesis: a simple blood test which will detect the presence of Down's syndrome in the unborn child.

Additional research, conducted in 1984 at Cleveland State University, shows that the presence of a particular protein in the bloodstream of either parent may be the newest indicator of who is at risk of having a child with Down's syndrome. Further research will attempt to answer questions about the chemical nature of this protein and its reliability as a predictor of the syndrome.

RESPITE CARE

A variety of services have been developed for parents of Down's syndrome children since the early seventies. One of the newest services is *respite care.* This service provides relief from parental care-giving responsibilities on a short- or long-term basis.

All parents benefit from an occasional break from the constant demands of parenting. This can help to maintain your perspective and enhance your relationships with your spouse and with your other children. Respite care is helpful, too, during a family emergency or crisis. And respite care is a great way to help you simply catch your breath and take a break.

If opportunities for respite, such as relatives, sitters, and neighbors, are not available for your child, you should investigate other respite sources in your community. These may include:

At-home aides. Trained aides will come to your house to help you care for your child or provide care while you and your spouse are out. In this case, respite is normally provided for a few hours at a time. Occasionally live-in aides are available, but this can be expensive.

Respite provider home. Your child will live in the home of another family. Care may be provided overnight, for a weekend, or longer, depending on your situation. Usually several children will be cared for at once by the family.

Foster care. Foster care is similar to the care provided by a respite provider home. Some families with a foster child will accept other children on a short- or long-term basis.

Respite care agency. Some group homes keep respite beds available.

Day care respite. This type of short-term care is available during day and/or evening hours. It is normally provided by a group of parents on a cooperative and often rotating basis. A traditional day care program may also be used to provide respite care.

Other respite sites. Respite care may be provided in your area by nonprofit agencies like the Association for Retarded Citizens, in some public or private institutions for people with disabilities, or in community residences for children and adults who are disabled. Check with the particular organizations for details.

Before you decide on any respite care program, be sure to visit the site you are considering to see if it will meet your child's needs and provide the kind of environment you want and approve of. Use the guidelines listed in Chapter 2 to help you make your decisions. If you are hiring an in-home aide, be sure that the person has experience and proper training. Ask for references *and check them.*

If your child will be spending more than a day or two in a respite care home or facility, it is a good idea for you both to go there the day before respite care begins. This way your child can meet with staff people and other resident children and generally get a feel for the place and the people.

For more information on respite care, and on the options available in your area, contact your local social service agency, Association for Retarded Citizens chapter, National Down Syndrome chapter, or your state health and welfare agency. Be sure to inquire about the costs of each program, which can vary significantly from one option to another.

SPECIAL PROBLEMS OF WORKING PARENTS

If you and your spouse both work outside of the home, do not let this interfere with your child's growth and development.

If you have a new baby, do not ignore the infant stimulation classes. Instead, find someone (a friend, a relative, or a paid sitter) who will attend those classes with your baby. If you cannot afford to pay a sitter, perhaps you can trade some service (cooking dinner twice a week, cleaning house, fixing the car, working in the yard, and so forth) for the sitter's care. And be sure to practice the infant stimulation exercises when you are home with your baby in the evening and on weekends.

If you have an older child, you may be able to arrange day care for the entire time both you and your spouse are away at work. Don't forget to check out after-school and "special friends" programs. If no such program is available at your child's school, perhaps one is available at another facility in your area. If none of these options is possible, see if one of you can work part-time, or if one of you can change your work hours to better suit your child's needs.

If a change or reduction in work hours simply can't be arranged, you may need to hire a sitter for those hours when neither you, your spouse, nor day care can provide care for your child. You should search diligently and conscientiously for a good and caring sitter. Interview potential sitters carefully, and be sure to ask for and check references. Keep in mind that the more handicapped your child is, the more difficult it may be to find a good sitter. So be willing to look hard, and be willing to pay a reasonable salary.

Be sure the sitter knows of your child's particular needs, problems, and handicaps. Be sure, too, that he or she knows what to do in case of emergency—fire, illness, or anything else. I recommend giving the sitter a written, signed statement granting permission to seek medical attention for your child in an emergency. Also make sure the sitter has the telephone numbers where you, your spouse, and other family members can be reached in an emergency.

If possible, administer any medication your child needs before you go to work. If this isn't possible, make sure the sitter is well versed in giving your child the medicine. And if your child is older, make sure he or she understands in advance that the sitter will be doing this.

Remember, it is unfair to make an older child be the sitter all the time. But it's all right to ask for this help occasionally, especially in emergencies. Or, if you like, *offer* your older children the chance to care for their younger brother or sister for pay. Be sure to pay them what you would normally pay a sitter. But don't *insist* that they take the job. If they turn it down, simply hire someone else.

Remember, too, that your child's sitter is entitled to an occasional vacation. This is true whether the sitter is a friend, a relative, someone you have hired, or one of your children. If a friend or a relative is sitting for your child as a favor, be sure to show your appreciation. Give that person a small gift or a dinner out once in a while. This is just as true and just as important if the sitter is one of your children.

Child care is sometimes difficult to arrange during the summer months. Many communities offer summer day camp or recreation programs especially designed for children with disabilities. These are sometimes offered by local parks and recreation departments. And many public schools offer extended special education programs during the summer months.

TIPS FOR DIVORCED PARENTS

Divorce can be hard on any couple and on any child. For Down's syndrome children, the separation of parents can be especially difficult. If you and your spouse do separate, either temporarily or permanently, the following tips will be useful:

• It is imperative that you both explain to your child why one parent will be leaving home. When doing this you should include an explanation of visiting rights. Your child may not appear to understand, especially at first—yet he or she probably understands much more than you think. Whatever you say, be open with your child and be prepared to repeat the explanation again and again. Encourage your child to ask the two of you questions about the situation, and answer those questions as openly and honestly as possible.

• Whether you are the custodial or the absentee parent, you have the responsibility of maintaining a relationship with your child and of helping your child maintain a relationship with your ex-husband or ex-wife. Try to be flexible so that *everyone's* needs are met. Remember, your child's handicap does not prevent him or her from forming a deep attachment to both of you.

• As you adjust to single life, do not neglect your own needs and interests as an adult. Go ahead and fulfill those needs without a feeling of guilt or selfishness.

If you are the custodial parent, you may find these suggestions helpful:

• Trying to be all things to your child is unrealistic, and in fact impossible. Single parents are especially prone to Superparent syndrome. But don't fall into this trap. Do what you can for your child and let that be enough.

• Don't dote on, spoil, or become too worried about your child because now he or she is "all you've got." Too much attention or protection can only harm the development of your child's personality and independence, and it can lead to an unhealthy dependence on you—or to your own unhealthy dependence on your child. Try to avoid the roles of martyr and saint for the same reasons. And keep in mind that your child is not all you've got left. You've still got the rest of your life ahead of you, and your divorce or separation is not the end of the world. (If you feel otherwise, it wouldn't hurt to speak with a psychologist or counselor about your feelings.)

• Find and join a support group for single parents. This support can be enormously helpful. You will realize you are not alone, and you will be able to learn from other single parents. You may even make some friends. In larger cities, the Association for Retarded Citizens or the National Down Syndrome Congress may sponsor its own support groups for single parents of handicapped children.

• Try to be flexible in arranging visiting rights for the other parent. Remember, this is for your child's benefit.

• As the custodial parent, you have the major responsibility of disciplining your child. Don't let discipline slide because it is more important now than ever for your child.

• Summer vacations, when your child is out of school, can be very difficult. You might want to arrange with your ex-partner for extended visiting rights during these times. These should be on terms that are favorable to all three of you.

• Your child needs role models of the other parent's sex. See if you can find a relative of that sex to spend time with your child, or contact the local branch of Big Brothers/Big Sisters. *Don't* rush into remarriage or another relationship simply because it will be "good" for your child to have someone of the opposite sex around. This could lead to emotional stress for everyone.

For parents who do not have custodial rights, here are a few tips:

• Your child needs you as a father or mother, even a part-time one, more than he or she needs an entertainer. If your visiting rights are limited to short periods of time, make the most of them by strengthening your relationship with your child. While entertaining activities such as movies are pleasant, you should also look for opportunities to talk with your child, to teach new skills and information, and in general to keep your parent and child relationship strong. This can include both organized programs and time spent together at home, on walks, and so on.

• Make a special effort to be available at times other than visiting periods—on your child's birthday and other holidays, for meetings with your child's teachers, for religious events and celebrations, and in emergencies of all kinds.

• If at all possible, it is a good idea for you and your former husband or wife to agree on ways for you to keep in touch with your child between visits. This helps ease tensions, avoids possible arguments, and keeps your child from being used as a bargaining chip or from being caught in the middle.

CHAPTER 7

Years Six Through Nine

Children with Down's syndrome will always, to some degree, be different from average children. This difference will most often be noticed in
the facial features, and the poor verbal skills that plague many of these
children also sets them apart from the general population. To the extent
that your child's differences can be minimized or decreased, so will his
or her social acceptance be increased. There is also a direct relationship
between social development (appropriate behavior) and social acceptance. The more appropriately your child behaves, the better he or she
will be accepted by society. For these reasons, social development and
social acceptance become critical issues for your son or daughter.

DEVELOPING SOCIAL SKILLS

The two most important factors that determine how well children
accept one another are personal appearance and age-appropriate behavior. Since appearance and behavior are social skills, the sooner your
child acquires them, the better are his or her chances of making friends.
Like all children, your child wants and needs to be accepted, and to
have friends. And some practical efforts on the part of you and your
spouse can help your child gain that acceptance and those friends.

CLOTHES

If your child has not yet shown any interest in clothes, now is the time for you to help develop that interest. You should teach your son or daughter how to choose clothes in colors, styles, and fabrics that are flattering, age-appropriate, and also in style. You will be amazed how something as simple as a pair of fashionable sneakers will escalate your child's acceptance among his or her peers.

Looking good means feeling good about one's self. Probably the best way for your child to acquire a clothes sense is to take him or her shopping rather than making the purchases yourself and then bringing them home. As you are shopping, explain about what colors, designs, or fabrics look well together. You may want to call your child's attention to the prices of various items, and instead of paying the bill yourself, let your child give the money to the cashier. (It is a good idea, though, for you to stay close by and monitor the transaction.) These experiences can help your son or daughter learn the skills needed to make good decisions.

POSTURE

The most expensive or flattering clothes won't do much for your child if his or her posture attracts negative attention. Watch how your child sits, stands, and walks. Can any of these attitudes be improved? If so, now is the time to make that improvement. The longer you wait, the more ingrained the inappropriate posture becomes and the harder it will be to correct. Bad habits in sitting, standing, or walking *can* be corrected, unless of course they are due to a physical cause. A good starting place to teach your child correct posture is for you the parents to set an example. Remember, Down's children are great mimics, and they can and do acquire many skills (and many bad habits) simply by observing their environment and the people in it.

BEHAVIOR

Inappropriate behavior can also prevent your child from gaining the acceptance of his or her peers, and of the public in general. An unnaturally loud laugh, a temper tantrum, or poor table manners may be overlooked every now and then at home. But if your child exhibits such behavior in public, he or she is quite likely to attract stares or even unkind remarks.

When you two are out in public, let your child know the kind of behavior you will and will not tolerate. The best way to learn just what kind of behavior is expected is through experience. Take your child with you to church, shopping, and on trips, and use the situation to teach him or her how to behave. You may have some embarrassing moments at first, but eventually your son or daughter will start exhibiting the kind of behavior you approve of.

Children with Down's syndrome must indeed go to greater lengths to acquire acceptance and gain friends. This may not seem fair, but it is a reality. On the other hand, knowing that you have gone that extra mile to help your child gain the social skills he or she needs to move through society with grace and dignity should be very comforting to you.

IN THE NEIGHBORHOOD

Besides good behavior and attractive appearance improving your child's chances of being socially accepted, he or she must learn the fine art of successful social integration. And your own neighborhood is a good place to continue the lessons learned at home. These suggestions can help you help your child acquire the necessary skills to socially interact with neighborhood children:

• Be sure your child understands the ideas of sharing toys, taking turns at games, and of winning and losing them. Teach your child to do all of these.

• At first you may want to encourage neighborhood children to play with your child by inviting them for planned activities like going for a walk or playing in a nearby park. Also successful is organizing parties, lunches, and trips to the zoo, the movies, and so on.

• When the children become acquainted and begin playing together on their own, encourage them to include activities at which your child is proficient.

• If your child uses sign language to communicate, teach the other kids how to sign.

• When your child goes to the neighbors' to play, you should limit the visiting time at first, then gradually increase it as his or her social skills improve and the neighbors become more accustomed to your child.

• Be sure you are available in case an emergency arises when your child is visiting at neighbors' houses. If he or she has a medical condition that excludes certain kinds of play activity, explain this to neighboring parents.

When your child learns to successfully interact with the kids on the block, remember that he or she is gaining skills that will help for a lifetime.

COPING WITH PEER HARASSMENT

Since the early seventies, our society has enacted legislation that protects the civil and legal rights of people who are mentally retarded. And yet we have difficulty accepting them as social human beings. One reason for this nonaccepting attitude of able-bodied people toward disabled people is doubt. We see these disabled people as a burden and question their worth to us. Another reason for this nonacceptance is discomfort. Many people not comfortable around others who are different or disabled tend to deal with their discomfort either through avoidance or harassment. Until this attitude is changed, it is quite likely that your child will at one time or another encounter harassment from his or her nonhandicapped peers.

As parents, you can be effective in changing this attitude in your community. You can go that extra step to make sure your child has all the social skills he or she needs for social acceptance. You can encourage the development of friendships between your child and his or her nonhandicapped peers. And you can do as other parents have done and continue to do: you can speak out, voice your opinion on anything that affects your child, from the way tax dollars are spent to the methods for teaching your child in school. You can join forces with other parents and develop a public awareness campaign that helps the community see and understand your children for what they *can* accomplish, not for what they cannot do.

There is no easy way for you to help your child cope with peer harassment. Some parents encourage their children to avoid the harassers. Others attempt to explain to the harrying children what Down's syndrome is and the problems that it causes. Still other parents try to resolve the issue by talking to the parents of the children who are doing the tormenting, explaining what Down's syndrome is and how the harassment affects their children. You will likely find that different circumstances call for different approaches. Keep in mind, though, that *all* children, whether they are handicapped or not, find themselves confronted with teasing and harassment by their peers. These situations can never be avoided entirely and, to some degree, if your child did not have Down's syndrome, other kids would find something else to tease him or her about.

COPING WITH THE WANDERLUST SYNDROME

The wanderlust syndrome is identified by one characteristic—your child will simply disappear or wander off the minute your attention is drawn away from him or her. You will become aware of this syndrome when your child is about six years old. It seems to gain momentum and reach its peak at about age eight, then starts tapering off. Many parents believe this wandering is precipitated by boredom, by natural curiosity, by loneliness, or by a desire to do what other kids in the neighborhood are doing.

Take the case of seven-year-old Jason, who lives in a northern suburb of Minneapolis. One summer afternoon his ten-year-old sister and her friends went to a local swimming pool. Jason was not allowed to accompany them because his mother feared for his safety even though he could swim. She was concerned, too, about the supervision, or the lack of it, that his sister could provide. Barely five minutes after the group left, Jason disappeared. His mother, suspecting he was following his sister, walked in the direction of the pool and found him. He had managed to change into his swimming trunks, find a towel, and get halfway to the pool in less than five minutes.

Other parents have told me about their children taking off for school playgrounds or for the houses of school friends several blocks away.

Sometimes their children just wandered from house to house in the neighborhood.

Ask your neighbors to call you or bring your child home if they notice him or her wandering around. Some parents living in small towns alert the local police department to be on the lookout for their children, and they ask to be notified if the children are found wandering. One family established boundary lines within their neighborhood, using houses or other buildings as markers beyond which their child was not supposed to go. "We pointed out these markers to our son and explained again and again why he shouldn't go beyond them. It helped —sometimes," they commented.

If your child shows signs of the wanderlust syndrome, you will have to ask yourself what the cause is. Is it curiosity, or a prank? Is the child bored, lonely, or merely miming the actions of other kids? Chances are that the answer is some combination of these. Try to discover what the reasons are by discussing it with your child. Explain why such behavior is not acceptable, especially if you suspect it is his or her way of playing a joke on you.

If the wandering is caused in part by boredom or loneliness, you can help solve these problems by enrolling your child in recreational programs designed especially for children with disabilities. Special Olympics, swimming, and dance classes are some common examples. Check around to find out where these programs are given.

If you live in an area where such activities are not available, you may want to consider joining forces with other parents and petitioning your local school or parks and recreation department to provide some programs for your children. This is how a great many of these programs get started.

You may want to have your child wear an identification bracelet to help ensure a safe return if his or her wanderlust goes beyond the neighborhood. And although you should limit your child's wandering as much as possible, remember that this is simply another stage of development and, like all the other stages, the child will outgrow it sooner or later.

HELPING YOUR CHILD AVOID
THE SCAPEGOAT ROLE

Some parents have discovered that not only are their children confronted with peer harassment, they are also blamed for things that go wrong in the neighborhood. If a window is broken, a toy missing, or a yard damaged, the blame is sometimes automatically laid on their child.

Both adults and other children are guilty of this. Adults may do it by leaping to the conclusion that your child cannot recognize the difference between right and wrong. This is untrue, and you may want to explain to your neighbors that your Down's syndrome child *is* quite capable of learning and following appropriate behavior patterns.

Children have a different reason for blaming your child for some damage or disruptive deed: if they can convince adults that your child is the perpetrator, they will get off the hook. This may sound terribly meanspirited, but almost all children who do something wrong will try to put the blame on anyone else they can, especially if they think they have a good chance of getting away with it. Occasionally children will do something wrong specifically to blame someone else and try to get that person into trouble. This could happen to your child.

Some parents try to prevent incidents from happening by confining their children to the home yard. Other parents help their children avoid the scapegoat role by taking the trouble to find the real offenders, and making them known to the victims.

Of course, no child is perfect, and there are probably going to be times when your child *is* at fault. (But, just as you shouldn't jump to the conclusion that your child is always innocent, don't jump to the conclusion that he or she is always guilty. Learn the specific circumstances and talk to your child about what happened before you start blaming anyone.) When this happens, you should make restitution to whomever was harmed. Replace, repair, or pay for any damage done, and apologize for your child's behavior. Be sure your child apologizes directly (preferably in person) to the victim. Explain to your child in no uncertain terms why those actions were wrong and what will happen if he or she ever repeats them again. Teaching the difference between right and wrong, and between appropriate and inappropriate behavior, will help reduce your child's chances of becoming a scapegoat.

Sometimes other kids will try to talk your child into doing something wrong. You must make sure your child understands that he or she should not give into such goading. You should also help your youngster understand that being teased and being a scapegoat are, unfortunately, part of growing up.

Eventually your child will learn to recognize situations that could lead to potential trouble. He or she can learn to avoid such situations by simply walking away from them.

HELPING YOUR CHILD DEVELOP
SELF-CONFIDENCE

There are two main reasons that parents have difficulty helping their children develop self-confidence. The first is a desire to do everything for their children just because it is faster and the task is completed to meet parental standards. A common example of this expressed by parents was teaching their children how to dress themselves. "It was easier and less frustrating for us to put the child's shirt on rather than let him or her learn how," these parents said.

If you are a victim of this attitude, you must understand that you are denying your child the experiences necessary to survive, both in childhood and adulthood. Doing things for your child won't necessarily make his or her life easier—and it may make it harder. The more you do for your child, the less chance there is of learning those skills independently. And the fewer skills a child has, the less self-confidence he or she will have, and the smaller his or her chances will be for a productive, happy, self-reliant adult life.

A second attitude many parents find themselves guilty of is not helping their children learn to accept themselves as worthy human beings even though they are handicapped. You can take some positive actions to help your child acquire self-confidence. Let your child take a few risks; it is all a part of growing up. *(You* may age during this process, too.) Assist your child to learn to help him or herself. While the youngster is struggling to complete a task, keep nearby, but keep busy with your own chores. That way if help is needed by your child, you are available. But don't give help too easily. Let your child struggle and work at a task for a while. If you think he or she can succeed without your help, say so. Say, "I think you can do it alone. Keep trying." Be positive and supportive in your comments. And if your child really *does* look like he or she needs help, give it. The trick is to give help when it is genuinely needed, and to provide encouragement, but *not* assistance when your child can complete a task alone.

If you are busy with your work, and your child asks for assistance, do not give it immediately. Instead, respond with, "I'm busy now, but you keep trying." Then give help when you can—*if* it is necessary.

Brothers and sisters can also help your child develop self-confidence and skills. One family told me of the prowess their nine-year-old son developed on the trampoline with the help of his athletically proficient older brother.

Being sure of one's self and one's ability are difficult attitudes for all children to learn. But they must learn them for their own well-being. And when your child says, "I can do it myself," you will grin with pride, knowing your child has overcome one more of life's difficulties.

HELPING YOUR CHILD DEVELOP COMPETENCE AND RESPONSIBILITY

As you help your child develop self-confidence, you will also be helping him or her to acquire competence. The old adage that practice makes perfect is most applicable here as your youngster learns a myriad of new skills associated with school, with recreation, or with tasks around the house.

Your child will need a great deal of encouragement to try a new skill such as riding a bicycle or learning to swim, and you can expect to spend a good portion of your time teaching that skill until it is mastered. Remember, too, the importance of breaking the skill into small phases and teaching one phase at a time. (This technique is discussed at some length in Chapter 4.) Be sure to let your child know that you have confidence in his or her ability to learn new skills. And be lavish with your praise as your child completes each of the individual phases in learning new skills.

One of the most awesome tasks all parents face is teaching their children to become responsible human beings. Teaching your child to accept responsibility means more than the expectation of completing an assigned task like hanging up clothes or keeping a room clean.

Accepting responsibility means your child must learn to care not only for him or herself, but for other people and for the environment. This may seem to be an extraordinarily large assignment for you and your child. Perhaps it is, but it is also necessary if you want your child to become a socially accepted and responsible person, both as a child and as an adult.

How do you teach your child responsibility? Chances are you have been doing it since the day he or she was born. Remember all those times you cuddled your little one, all the songs you sang, all those stimulating exercises you did together? With each cuddle, each song, and each exercise you were communicating how much you loved and how much your child meant to you. This is the first step in teaching your child about responsibility.

To become a responsible person, your child must learn the importance of caring about other people. This can happen only when your child knows that he or she is cared about. The care and concern you show toward your child helps increase this sense of responsibility toward others because he or she learns from your actions that everyone is a worthwhile human being.

When you teach your child to complete certain chores around the house, you take another step down the path of his or her becoming responsible. Chores like hanging up clothes, picking up toys, or taking out garbage help your child learn two very important facts: one, that he or she has a responsibility toward the care of the surrounding environment; and two, that he or she is capable of doing many things. At the same time the youngster will gain a sense of accomplishment, which further encourages a feeling of responsibility. Your child must learn to contribute to the family, and that his or her contribution *does* make a difference to the family's well-being. As your youngster learns the importance of this, he or she will begin to realize how much people need one another, and the child's sense of responsibility will continue to grow.

When your child does make a contribution to family life by completing assigned chores or tasks, be sure to express your appreciation for these efforts. Whether or not the chore is completed according to your standards, let your youngster know you respect the effort he or she has put forth. (But also encourage improvement.) Your expression of appreciation and respect gives your child still another opportunity to develop a sense of responsibility. It is when your son or daughter feels respected and appreciated that he or she can begin to express these same feelings toward other people. And by expressing these feelings, your child's sense of responsibility for other people begins to grow.

Teaching your child to become responsible goes beyond teaching neatness, orderliness, or the fulfillment of your expectations. One family's experience demonstrates the sense of responsibility Down's children are capable of acquiring:

Sandy is a twelve-year-old girl. She and her parents were attending a wedding reception, and as the guests mingled about their attention was drawn to one fellow who was having difficulty walking. No one offered to help him as he reeled toward a chair and sat down. Sandy darted to the man, patted his hand, and said, "Hi." She continued talking to him and patting his hand for a moment, then rejoined her parents. No one else ventured near the fellow. Sandy's parents found out later that he had cerebral palsy, which explained his ungainly walk.

LEISURE ACTIVITIES

The quality of life for anyone depends as much on how well one learns to use leisure time as it does upon one's academic, vocational, or career accomplishments. It is just as important to participate in a large variety of leisure activities as it is to go to school or work each day. In fact, it is essential that all of us relieve our daily routine of school or work with leisure activities. Games, sports, hobbies, community affairs, even watching television gives us a necessary respite from our workaday world, a chance to recharge our batteries.

Play is often called the work of childhood because children do learn from their play experiences. These experiences become even more important for children with Down's syndrome because of the learning difficulties they encounter. The more your child participates in play or leisure activities, the greater are the opportunities to acquire new knowledge.

There are other benefits your child will gain from recreation and leisure activities: he or she can develop social relationships, engage in self-expression, discover creative talents, and reveal unique strengths or abilities that are seldom exhibited outside of leisure or recreational experiences.

You should help your child become involved with leisure activities that are enjoyable, that are age-appropriate, and that allow individual progress. Any activity that meets these criteria will improve self-image and self-confidence.

Encourage your child to participate in a wide range of activities, from those he or she can enjoy alone to those requiring two or more participants. Whenever possible, your child should be allowed to get involved in activities that include nonhandicapped peers. Such interaction not only helps your child gain competence and self-confidence, it should also improve verbal and social skills.

Many parents encourage their children to get involved in competitive activities. Competing in games with nonhandicapped children can be beneficial to your child because it can stimulate his or her social growth. Your youngster will also discover that nonhandicapped kids do accept kids with handicaps. You may, however, have to set some limits on the nature or degree of your child's participation. These limits will depend primarily on motor coordination, ability to interact socially, and general health.

If your child is not capable of competing on a par with able-bodied kids, you really should not expect him or her to do so. Such expectations are unrealistic and will not help your child to develop a good self-image, simply because it is a losing situation right at the start. Although every child must learn that winning and losing are parts of growing up, it is not fair to place your child in situations where the only alternative is losing.

However, if you really believe your child should be integrated into competitive activities with nonhandicapped peers, and if he or she really wants to be a part of those activities, there may be other opportunities available that are noncompetitive.

For example, perhaps your child can learn to distribute equipment like bats, balls, and towels to other players as they begin a practice session or a game, perhaps help keep score. A friend of mine told me about a Down's syndrome teenager who learned to help with weigh-ins for his high school wrestling team.

To find out how your son or daughter can participate on a noncompetitive basis with nonhandicapped peers, ask your child's classroom teacher or physical education coach.

If you prefer not to have your child compete with able-bodied kids, there may be other opportunities in your community that offer competitive activities just for children with disabilities. Special Olympics is a well-known example. Public schools often sponsor Special Olympics programs as part of their special education curriculum. Other organizations like city parks and recreation departments of The Association for Retarded Citizens also provide Special Olympics activities. One of the largest manufacturing companies in Minnesota, Honeywell Corporation, sponsors an annual one-day Special Olympics event. It is a gala festival attended by thousands of disabled kids from all parts of the state.

Many communities provide a variety of activities designed especially for children and adults who are handicapped. Scouting, day camp, visual and performing arts, sport teams, and dancing clubs are among the more popular activities offered. At a recent national convention I attended, the opening ceremonies featured a mixed choir of young adults, all of whom were mentally retarded. They sang flawlessly and unfalteringly to an audience of four thousand people. At this same convention I watched a square dance group from Florida perform. About half of the twenty-four dancers (all adults) had Down's syndrome. Their precision, timing, and intricate dance steps held a crowd of two hundred absolutely spellbound during their hour-long performance.

Check with your local board of education, United Way office, or branch of The Association for Retarded Citizens to see what is available in your area.

These specially designed recreation activities can help your child gain benefits other than fun and entertainment. High on the list is the emphasis that is placed on the strengths and talents he or she already possesses. Your child's participation begins at whatever level he or she can perform, and then expands or improves on that performance. For example, if your son can play softball only if he uses an oversized bat, he would continue to use that bat and then gradually start learning to use a regulation one. This allows him to progress at an individual pace, and his success or failure can be judged from a set of personal performance standards rather than from a set of group standards.

Special activities will also help your child learn the fine art of competition and of fair play. Still another benefit your child will derive from these special activities is the chance to develop more social relationships.

Helping your child develop an interest in hobbies is another valuable resource for using leisure time. A family living in rural Minnesota told me about their son's interest in stock car racing. He was allowed to accompany his father into the racing pits, visit with the drivers, and watch their performances from that vantage point rather than from the bleachers.

Sailing is the hobby of another family I know from New Jersey. The parents began taking their son on short junkets when he was two years old. Now at age thirteen, he is a dependable, enthusiastic sailor who not only knows how to cast off, rig the sails, and drop anchor, but can do it all very effectively.

Participation in leisure activities, whether or not they are specially designed, brings your child closer to society's expectations of people. We are all expected to use our leisure time appropriately and effectively. But the degree to which we meet this expectation depends on our individual abilities. In that sense, then, everyone has special needs, not just people who have Down's syndrome or other disabilities.

RELIGIOUS EDUCATION

Whether or not religious education is necessary for your child depends on whether you as parents believe it is. Most parents I talked to were firmly convinced that religious education is important to the education of the whole child. If you and the rest of your family regularly practice the religious beliefs of your choice but do not include your Down's syndrome child, it is very likely he or she will wonder why. You can be sure that your child will ask you for an explanation. Down's children don't appear to be very observant at times, but don't let that deceive you.

Ask your priest, minister, or rabbi for advice about religious education for your son or daughter. It is quite likely that a class may be available, simply because religious leaders are recognizing their responsibilities toward people with disabilities. If there are no classes, perhaps your child can be enrolled in ones provided for nonhandicapped children. Many parents prefer this arrangement because of the opportunity it provides for social interaction.

Whether or not your child can participate in the various rituals associated with your religious beliefs, or in the rites of passage such as confirmation or bar or bas mitzvahs, must be decided by you, your religious adviser, and if possible your child.

In case there is nothing in the way of religious education available in your community, you may have to resort to home tutoring.

I recently read an article that illustrates just how much a Down's syndrome child can achieve when the appropriate resources are available. A fifteen-year-old boy successfully completed his bar mitzvah, a ceremony that usually occurs at age thirteen. He not only wrote his ceremonial speech, he delivered it without a single mistake.

HEALTH CARE

While adequate health care is important for any child, it becomes mandatory for children with Down's syndrome because they seem to be more susceptible to health irregularities. Descriptions of these irregularities and suggestions for dealing with them are discussed in Chapter 3.

Even if your child is not bothered by unusual health problems, you really shouldn't adopt a relaxed attitude toward his or her health care. Regularly scheduled visits to your pediatrician are very important, and they are probably the best preventative actions you can take to ensure your child's well-being.

DENTAL DEVELOPMENT

The care of your child's teeth is also very important to his or her total well-being and good health. Chapter 3 discusses dental development and ways for you to help your child develop good oral hygiene habits before the sixth birthday. After that age, significant changes in dental development occur that affect all children for a lifetime.

Beginning at about age six, your child's dental development will undergo several important changes. The jaws will start to grow to provide room for the permanent teeth. As the jaws grow, the roots of the primary (baby) teeth begin to dissolve and the permanent teeth prepare to erupt.

Usually the first permanent molars, sometimes called the six-year molars, erupt at about age six. However, these teeth can appear as early as age five and sometimes later than age six. These teeth are especially important because they help define the shape of your child's lower face, and they can affect the position and health of all other permanent teeth. Since six-year molars do not replace any primary teeth, this means they are permanent and must last your child a lifetime. Therefore, proper care and treatment of six-year molars is critical.

If a primary tooth is lost before its permanent replacement has erupted, it is a good idea to take your child to the dentist. He or she may recommend that a space maintainer be inserted; this helps reserve the space intended for the permanent tooth. You should also consult your dentist when your child has a primary tooth that does not fall out. It may have to be removed by the dentist to prevent irregular eruption of the permanent teeth.

ORAL HYGIENE

At age six your child should be able to brush his or her teeth without any assistance from you. However, the youngster may still need to be reminded to perform this task. It is probably a good idea to occasionally supervise the brushing just to make sure that it is done properly and thoroughly. Flossing the teeth is a much more difficult skill to learn, so don't be surprised if your child doesn't master this until age eight or even older. But with practice, persistence, and patience, he or she will be successful. Of course, your supervision is still necessary to make certain that flossing is not only done, but done correctly. You will probably have to continue this supervision until your child brushes and flosses after each meal and before bedtime with only a reminder from you. The reminder may need to be continued through your child's adolescence.

It is extremely important for your child to establish a brushing and flossing routine because clean teeth are less likely to decay and more likely to last longer. Remember, too, that your child's diet plays an important part in the prevention of tooth decay. It is a well-known fact that too much sugar, either natural or refined, can harm the teeth. Eliminating sugar from your child's diet is hardly possible because it is contained in many different kinds of food. Look at the labels on various foods you purchase. Ingredients like sucrose, dextrose, fructose, and maltose are all forms of sugar. What you can do is encourage your child to eat fresh fruit and vegetables that have low sugar content. You should also help your child avoid sticky sweets that tend to cling to the teeth and prolong the acid attack caused by sugar, which in turn promotes decay.

Now is the time for your child to begin daily use of a fluoride mouth rinse in addition to brushing with fluoride toothpaste. You will probably have to teach your child how to use a mouth rinse and also supervise him or her closely until this is learned. If your child has mastered rinsing after brushing, there should not be a great deal of difficulty learning to use a mouth rinse. The difficulty will probably lie in the taste of the rinse and the tingling feeling it leaves in the mouth.

DENTAL VISITS

At age six, your child's teeth should be cleaned professionally by a dentist to remove plaque and stains. Just how often your child will need professional cleaning will be determined by the condition of the teeth. The professional cleaning removes plaque that can build up on teeth whether or not they are brushed every day. Of course, the less your child brushes, the greater is the amount of plaque buildup, which in turn can cause more tooth decay. Professional cleaning of your child's teeth should become a regular part of his or her oral health care beginning at age six and continuing into and through adulthood.

SPECIAL DENTAL PROBLEMS

Although your child may start out with healthy teeth and gums, any or all of the following special problems can be encountered as he or she grows up.

Malocclusions

This is a condition in which the teeth are crowded, crooked, or out of alignment. It can occur at any age but is more likely to develop between the ages of six and twelve when the permanent teeth are erupting. Malocclusion can occur if the jaw is too small, if the primary teeth are lost too early, or if your child continues thumb-sucking beyond the age of four. Chapter 3 discusses the dental problems that can result from extensive thumb-sucking.

Irregular teeth can be corrected by having them straightened. The age your child should have this done depends on the nature of the malocclusion and its cause. Most children are treated for malocclusion at about age twelve.

There are several reasons why crooked or irregular teeth should be corrected. First, they are difficult to keep clean because certain surfaces of the tooth cannot be reached with ease. Chewing becomes more difficult, and if your child selects only those foods that are easy to chew, his or her diet may not measure up to nutritional standards. Crooked teeth may be a sign that your child's jaws are not growing properly. Irregular teeth will affect your child's appearance and could cause emotional problems. When your child's teeth are properly positioned, they not only enhance his or her entire appearance, they also function as they were intended to. If your child has a malocclusion problem, this can be treated by your dentist, or ask for a referral to an orthodontist, a dentist who specializes in treating malocclusions.

Oral Injuries

Injuries to the teeth can occur easily, especially during childhood. Rough-and-tumble games, a fall, or a blow to the mouth during contact sports all can result in serious tooth injuries. Not only can a tooth be cracked, broken off, or knocked completely out of the mouth, it can also die from hard blows.

If a tooth is knocked out, rinse it in cool water, but *do not* scrub it. Put it in a cup of water or wrap it in a wet towel, and rush your child and the tooth to the dentist. If he or she can tend to your child within thirty to ninety minutes of the accident, there is a good chance of saving the tooth by replanting it in the jaw.

Toothache

When your child gets a toothache, call your dentist at once. Don't try to alleviate the pain with home remedies. However, the American Dental Association does recommend the following emergency treatment that you can give until your child sees the dentist:

If you can see a cavity in the aching tooth, flush it with warm water to remove any food or other debris. Then apply oil of clove directly to the aching tooth. You can also give your child aspirin to relieve the pain, but never place aspirin directly on the tooth.

Remember, these are only temporary emergency measures. You should call your dentist and take your child in for treatment as soon as possible.

Gumboils

A gumboil is the signal of an abscess caused by infection within the tooth. As pus collects, it works its way through the root of the tooth and into the jawbone. If your child has this problem, call the dentist immediately because abscesses must not be neglected.

GENERAL HINTS FOR PARENTS

You now know that the road to parenting your special child has many bends and curves, and that it takes some very special effort to move along that road. But haven't your special efforts been accompanied by very special rewards for both you and your child? Remember the exquisite joy you felt when your youngster said that first word, took that first step, began dressing without help, or completed a myriad of other "first" accomplishments during the past several years?

Your special efforts not only helped your child achieve each of these accomplishments, they helped you to cope with the uncertainties you encountered along the way. One significant uncertainty that most parents face is learning how to understand their children, particularly if they have poor verbal skills. This uncertainty can be overcome if you learn to watch your child and his or her actions. The old adage that actions speak louder than words is surely descriptive of the following incidents:

• A two-year-old girl I know surprised her parents with her imitations of popular rock singers.

• A father told me about his ten-year-old son who after watching an older sister build a cabin of toy logs duplicated her act without any assistance.

• A twelve-year-old boy I am acquainted with competed against his nonhandicapped peers in a school science fair and won the second place ribbon.

All of these children have Down's syndrome. Not only did they surprise their parents by these things, but the parents then had a much better understanding of the interests and capabilities of their children.

It will take some special effort on your part to understand your child, and watching his or her actions does help. Keeping a sense of humor also helps. If you can look for the bright side of the different situations you encounter, they will be much easier to deal with. You will also discover that the bends and curves in this road you are traveling down will continue to become less threatening, less confusing, and less uncertain.

CHAPTER 8

Years Ten Through Twelve

During this stage of your child's development, you and your spouse will continue to help your son or daughter develop good habits, increase his or her responsibilities, and investigate the opportunities for prevocational training.

One of the most important facts for you to remember about your child during these preteen years is that regardless of the disability, he or she is, and will continue to be, a human sexual being. Your child will experience the same sexual desires as his or her normal peers.

Another especially strong need for your child at this age is the desire to belong, to have close friends. Your child will want to expand his or her social circle beyond the family unit, beyond the immediate neighborhood, and beyond teachers and classmates at school. By now he or she has probably made friends with people like the mailman, the gas station attendant, and the storekeeper down the street.

Your child is now entering the prepuberty stage of development. These years can be exciting and pleasant for both of you *if* you learn to adopt a relaxed attitude toward your child and toward the changes he or she is going through. Make an effort to take each situation as calmly as possible, and remember to look for the humorous side of things, no matter how frustrating or unpleasant they seem to be. Most important of all, take time to enjoy your child, because he or she is growing up fast.

SIGNS OF GROWING UP

During these preteen years you will begin to notice changes in your child's physical, mental, and emotional development. The physical changes are the most noticeable at first simply because they are most obvious. The mental and emotional changes are usually more subtle and not quite as easy to spot. However, all of these changes usually occur simultaneously.

The early signs of physical changes for girls are breast development and the onset of menstruation. For boys it's voice change and facial hair growth. Other signs for boys and girls are pubic hair growth and a greater tendency toward masturbation.

Among the mental changes your child will exhibit are greater curiosity about body parts, increased awareness of the opposite sex, teasing the opposite sex, overpossessiveness of personal belongings, wanting more privacy, and adopting mannerisms of people outside the family circle, such as classmates or television personalities.

Your child may display any or all of these emotional changes: bouts with moodiness, wanting to be alone, refusing to play with younger children, selecting a best friend of the same sex, and developing a more-than-casual interest in the opposite sex.

As your child enters this growing-up stage of development, he or she will also become aware of the changes that are occurring, especially the physical ones, but probably won't understand what is happening or why it is happening.

SEX EDUCATION

The topic of sex education evokes many mixed emotions for parents of Down's syndrome children. Along with these emotions comes a variety of questions: Who is responsible for your child's sex education? How much should he or she be told? What information is appropriate?

Even though your child is handicapped, he or she must learn to face the sexual realities of life. You the parents have to realize that your child is likely to be interested in sex and *does* need to know about sexual matters. If you try to convince yourselves that your child isn't interested in "that" or doesn't need to know about "those things," you are creating a dangerous trap both for yourselves and your child, and you are denying reality.

The question of who is responsible for your child's sex education must be decided by you and your spouse. If you believe it is your role, then you must resolve any personal fears or inhibitions you may have toward the subject before you can effectively teach your child. His or her attitude toward sex, and how comfortably the facts of sexuality are accepted, depend on your own level of comfort with those facts. Therefore it is important to overcome any uneasiness you may have about discussing the subject with your child.

You may decide that your child's sex education is the responsibility of the school. These days the health curriculum during the sixth grade in most mainstream elementary schools includes a unit on sexual development. Yet these same classes are not always available for the students who are mentally retarded. If the school your child attends follows such a policy, you can challenge it on the basis that sex education is self-help information that your child needs to know in order to learn appropriate behavior and not be exploited.

If you are reluctant to assume the total responsibility of your child's sex education and yet are not comfortable leaving that responsibility entirely up to your child's teacher, you could try a cooperative approach. With this your child's teacher introduces the subject at school, then you the parents reinforce that information by discussing at home.

When to start your son or daughter's sex education is just as important as who will teach it. Experts in the field do not believe one particular time is better than another. Instead they suggest that parents should, from the very beginning, help their children develop healthy, wholesome attitudes toward body parts and body functions. You should realize, though, that you can't avoid discussing the topic of sex with your child forever. Sooner or later you must deal with it.

A good time to start dealing with your child's sex education—or at least preparing yourself to deal with it—is when your child reaches the age of nine. This is the time to decide who will be responsible for teaching your child and what it is that should be taught.

To determine what your child needs to know now, you should give careful thought to what he or she must know in order to survive in the community after reaching adulthood. You can then select those facts you believe are essential for your nine year old and begin discussing them. These facts should include menstruation, masturbation, sex differences, and body changes and appropriate behavior.

You should begin preparing your child at this age for puberty and the body changes that will occur. You should explain the hair growth that will appear in the armpits and in the pubic area. Your daughter should understand what to expect when she begins to menstruate. Your son should be told about the hair that will also start growing on his face and chest. He should be told that his voice will change. Explain to him what wet dreams are, and that they happen to all boys. Assure him that he need not feel guilty about having them. (It is possible that he may have guilt feelings because the ejaculations are sometimes accompanied by pleasant sexual feeling or dreams that he may not understand.) Remember that your child's sex education should deal not only with sex per se, but with social relationships and emotional fulfillment.

Whether you introduce the facts about reproduction depends on how much your son or daughter at age nine can really comprehend. You cannot expect your child to learn all in one easy explanation. It will take several times, and facts about reproduction can be introduced in one of these later explanations.

There are several books listed at the end of this chapter that should be helpful to you as you begin to prepare your child's sex education program.

MENSTRUATION

Teaching your daughter about menstruation may or may not be an easy task. It depends in part on how comfortable you are when you talk about the subject and how you approach it. The sooner you start explaining the menstrual cycle to her, the better prepared she will be to care for herself when her cycle starts. Avoiding the subject until she begins to menstruate is not a good idea because at first she won't understand what is happening to her.

You may find these suggestions helpful to explain the menstrual cycle to your daughter before it begins:

• Tell her that all girls menstruate, and it is a sign of growing up.
• If you haven't found the "right" occasion to bring the subject up, try placing a box of sanitary pads in a conspicuous place so she will notice them. If she raises questions about them, take this opportunity to

begin teaching her what they are, why they are needed, and how they are used.

• Let her know she may have cramps or backaches when she begins to menstruate, but that those pains will go away.

When your daughter begins to menstruate you may want to try these suggestions:

• Assure her that she isn't sick or in any danger.

• Be sure she lets you know if there is severe pain so you can give her relief with an over-the-counter pain reliever or a prescription from your doctor.

• Explain—and this is important—that she should feel proud that she is growing up.

• Keep a special calendar and teach her to circle the days that her period begins and ends.

• Help her remember to change her sanitary pads. If she has learned to keep herself clean and wear clean undergarments, she will be more likely to remember to do this on her own. And she will probably need several demonstrations before she accomplishes changing pads by herself.

• Remember that routine health checks are very important when your daughter begins to menstruate.

If you are concerned that your daughter won't understand your explanation about her menstrual cycle, bear in mind that Down's children almost always understand more than we give them credit for. However, repeated explanations are usually necessary.

STERILIZATION

Some parents have chosen to have their daughters undergo hysterectomies in an effort to ease the difficulties and pain of menstruation, and to eliminate the risk of unplanned pregnancies. Such surgery does not prevent a young woman from being sexually exploited—nor will it help her behave in a manner that is sexually or socially appropriate in public.

If you are convinced that your daughter cannot tolerate the physical and psychological effects of menstruation, and you believe she is not able to learn to use birth control methods, the choice of sterilization may be valid. Before you take such drastic and irreversible action, you should investigate the sterilization laws in your state. Many areas now have quite rigid laws that protect mentally retarded people from unnecessary or unwarranted sterilization methods and practices.

MASTURBATION

Like all children, your child may engage in masturbation, and like other parents, you may be upset when it happens. Touching and handling one's genitals begins naturally during infancy. You probably saw your baby touch the genital area when lying undressed on the bath table waiting to be bathed. That touching may not have been purposeful, but children do learn at a very early age that it feels good to touch or handle their genitals, so they continue to masturbate as they grow older. At the time of puberty you may notice an increase in your child's masturbation, which is a way of responding to body and glandular changes that accompany the age of puberty.

It is difficult to prevent masturbation. A better approach is to teach your child to do it in the privacy of his or her room. Relate the idea that masturbation is an acceptable form of sexual expression, but that it is not necessary to do it too often and that it is inappropriate to do it in public.

If your child masturbates excessively, it may be a sign of boredom, loneliness, or unhappiness. If you see any of these signs, try to make sure your child has plenty of other things to do that give him or her satisfaction. And do what you can to see that he or she has friends and playmates, and has a good time with them. Encourage your child as well to seek out friends and activities without your help.

Many adults have been taught that masturbation is wrong and sinful, something to avoid and feel guilty about. Most of us who have been taught this still believe it, either consciously or unconsciously, and as a result we convey these beliefs to our own children, often unwittingly. It is important, therefore, to do your best to guard against passing this message on. It is most likely to be passed on not through what you tell your child but by how you react to his or her actual masturbatory behavior. Remember that masturbation doesn't have the same meanings for a child as it does for adults. So if you can treat it wisely and calmly, both you and your child will be better off.

BUILDING GOOD HABITS

You can help your child form good habits in quite simple ways. All you need to do is let your child know what behavior you expect, then give positive reinforcement for the desired behavior.

For example, if you want your child to form the habit of hanging up his or her coat as soon as it is taken off, you begin by saying, "Hang up your coat." At the same time you show how this is done. Then remove the coat from the hanger, hand it to your child, and repeat, "Hang up your coat." Give help at first if it is needed. As soon as the coat is hung up, give your child positive reinforcement such as verbal praise, a compliment, or a smile. When this behavior is repeated so often that your child does it without any reminders or reinforcements, the behavior has become a habit.

Behavior that is immediately rewarded by a positive reinforcer will occur more frequently in the future. In other words, if you praise your child each time he or she hangs up the coat, it is more likely that he or she will do it the next time. However, you can expect to have to reward your child many times before hanging up a coat becomes a habit.

The key to helping your child form good habits is remembering to be consistent. This means that each time your child takes off his or her coat, you must communicate that you expect the coat to be hung up. It is important to continue reinforcing the desired behavior until it is learned and becomes a habit.

Even then you should continue to give your child occasional positive reinforcement. If you don't, the habit is likely to weaken. Positive reinforcers not only teach your child good habits, they also help him or her to retain those habits.

The positive reinforcement method can be used to help your child form any habit that is desirable. These are some of the habits he or she should be acquiring during the preteen years:

GOOD GROOMING

- Dressing without assistance and beginning to tie shoes.
- Learning to comb, brush, and part hair.

• Selecting clothes to wear that fit properly, are appropriate for their size and age, and go together in style, color, and design.

• Developing pride in personal appearance.

• Assuming the care of clothing, including folding and storing them in drawers, hanging them up in closets, and putting soiled clothes in the laundry.

• Caring for personal possessions, such as storing books or games on shelves, keeping jewelry in a case or container, and so on.

PERSONAL HYGIENE

• Learning to floss teeth.
• Taking baths or showers without being reminded to do so.
• Learning to regulate bath or shower water without assistance.
• Managing to shampoo hair without assistance and without reminders.

As you teach your child new habits or help refine those habits already acquired, always remember to break each activity into small steps. Teach one step at a time, and use positive reinforcement to encourage and strengthen the habit.

KICKING BAD HABITS

Your child can learn to form bad habits just as easily as good ones. In fact, many parents inadvertently encourage the formation of bad habits by reinforcing them. For example, if you picked your baby up every time he or she cried, you were, for all practical purposes, teaching your baby to cry to get attention. Another example often occurs at mealtime. Suppose your two year old smears food all over and everyone at the table laughs. The laughter reinforces your child for being messy and encourages him or her to continue to be messy. Still another common example happens when you have overslept and you must hurry to get your child ready for school. To speed things up, you dress your child even though he or she is capable of dressing without assistance. If you do this several times, you are reinforcing the undesirable behavior of helplessness. Even though you may have unwittingly encouraged your child to form bad habits such as these, you can help break them.

If you spank, slap, or threaten your child, he or she will, for the moment, stop the behavior that is annoying you. While punishment is one way to break a habit, it doesn't seem to have any long-term effects, and it can be upsetting for you both. A more effective, longer-lasting, and simpler technique is the use of reinforcers. When your two year old smears food, everyone should refuse to laugh. Instead, you and other family members should remember to reward your child's *good* table manners positively with praise, a hug, or a smile.

Remember, many children with Down's syndrome have an uncanny talent to mimic the habits of other people, both children and adults. The chances of your child imitating bad habits are probably just as high, if not higher, as they are for imitating good habits. This means that you and other family members can have a major effect on your Down's syndrome child by simply developing and exhibiting good habits yourselves, and keeping your own bad habits to a minimum. Your child is likely to pick up whatever habits you all have—whether they are good *or* bad ones. And if you say one thing and do another, your child is more likely to mimic what you do than to obey what you say.

Then again, there are other reasons besides mimicry for your child to develop bad habits. If there are times when his or her behavior leaves you wishing you could resign from parenthood, look behind the action for probable causes. Some things to consider are:

- Physical well-being. Is your child fatigued, hungry, or on the brink of an illness?
- General environment. Is your child completely hemmed in by "Don't do that"? Is there too much competition from other siblings? Are you expecting too much of your child?
- Lack of attention. A "good" child is sometimes overlooked; being "bad" is a sure way to get attention.

Whatever the reasons behind your child's bad habits, remember that you must help break them if he or she is to become socially accepted in the community.

COMMON BAD HABITS

Aggressiveness

If your child consistently bites, scratches, hits, throws temper tantrums, or breaks and destroys things, the following suggestions may be of help:

• Don't lose your temper. It's easier to handle the situation if you have your emotions under control.

• If it is necessary to restrain your child, do it in a kind but *firm* manner.

• Try redirecting your child's aggressive behavior into more constructive activities. For example, if your child is throwing a wooden block at a window, substitute something softer, like a ball stuffed with acrylic fabric.

• Distract your child's attention with a startling statement like, "See this?" and follow it up with a constructive suggestion like, "Let's bake a cake."

• Try to prevent aggressive behavior by avoiding situations that you know provokes such behavior.

Hyperactivity

If your child is fidgety, restless, or in constant motion, these suggestions may help:

• Consult with your child's doctor for physical causes. Such behavior may be caused by disturbances to one of these endocrine glands— thyroid, adrenal, or pituitary.

• Loud talk, blasting music, or other types of noise can aggravate a hyperactive child.

• Soft music and/or a gentle massage will help relax your child.

• Keep your child's environment simple and nonconfusing. Too much activity or excitement in the household can contribute to your child's hyperactivity.

• Examine your child's environment for things that might overstimulate him or her and remove them if possible.

• Arguments between parents, frequently expressed anger, and other strong emotions expressed by parents or siblings on a regular basis can also contribute to hyperactivity.

• If you see your child becoming fidgety, you may want to calm him or her before the situation gets worse. Read a story, or encourage your child to engage in some other quiet activity.

• Overtiredness can sometimes cause fidgeting and anxiety in children. Make sure your child gets enough sleep at night, and if he or she seems tired during the day, see that a nap is taken.

• Boredom and frustration can sometimes lead to hyperactivity. Do what you can to help your child have enough stimulating activities and enough friends.

• Hyperactivity can reinforce itself. In other words, if your child is running furiously around the house, the longer he or she is allowed to run, the more furious the running will become.

• It's possible that your child's overactivity is one way of getting your attention.

Nervous habits

A child may develop thumb-sucking or nail-biting to reduce tension, anxiety, frustration, restlessness, or overexcitement. These in turn may be caused by a lack of engaging activities, a lack of friends, too much activity or excitement, too much change in your child's life or environment, or your asking too much of your child. Doing what you can to provide fun and worthwhile activities for your child, to help him or her make friends, and to give a safe, secure, and loving home can all help to obviate these nervous habits.

If either (or both) of these problems do develop, it is not advisable to use restraints, or to put bad-tasting medicine on your child's thumb or fingers. These could do more harm to your child emotionally than the nervous habits themselves. Instead, ask your child to take the thumb or fingers out of his or her mouth, then you provide something else to do, such as playing a game. Use positive reinforcement: reward the behavior with praise, a smile, a hug, or even (on occasion) a special treat when your child goes without sucking his or her thumb or biting nails for a certain period of time. Keeping your child's fingernails short and smooth will also help reduce nail-biting.

Other nervous habits, such as twisting of hair, nose picking, or twisting or wringing the hands, often have the same causes and solutions as nail-biting and thumb-sucking. Keeping your child's hands and attention occupied in more constructive activities will help. Again, use positive reinforcement.

Negativity

Certain negative actions, such as resisting suggestions or refusing to comply with a request, begin when your child matures enough to recognize himself or herself as an individual. Such behavior, if it is not habitual, should be interpreted as a sign of growth because it is your child's way of asserting his or her independence. However, if negative behavior is prolonged over a number of years, or if it becomes habitual or obsessive, it is a sign that your child is not growing out of this stage of development. Here is what you can do to help your child overcome his or her negative habits:

• When your child starts showing independence through negative behavior, find situations that allow him or her to exercise independent actions, such as deciding what clothes to wear to school or choosing between a hamburger and a hot dog when eating out.

• Don't place too many demands on your child. This only encourages negative behavior.

• Be sure your child understands your requests. If he or she doesn't, you are likely to receive a negative response.

• Give your child just one direction at a time to reduce negative responses. For example, if you want your child to put on his or her coat and go out to the car, your first direction should be, "Put on your coat." When this has been done, then say, "Now go out to the car." This is preferable to "Put on your coat and go out to the car," simply because Down's syndrome children often have difficulty understanding directions that require them to perform two distinct and separate actions.

MANNERS

Every skill and every habit that you teach your child should be aimed at helping the child fit into society with as much ease and comfort as possible. You may find the following suggestions helpful:

• Polite language—Your child should become familiar with polite words and phrases long before beginning to talk. At a very early age he or she should have heard phrases like "Please" and "Thank you" repeated again and again. Such repetition is the key to helping your child acquire new skills.

Other polite words your child should learn are: "Excuse me," "Hello," "I'm sorry," "Good morning," "Good evening," "You're welcome," "How do you do," "No thank you," "Goodbye," and "Yes, thank you."

Your child must also learn when to use polite language, or else he or she could use the wrong phrase at the wrong time. You should explain why a certain expression is used. For example, if you gave your son a piece of candy, you should say to him, "I gave you candy. Now you say

'Thank you.' " Or if he walks in front of someone, tell him to say "Excuse me."

At first you will have to remind your child many times when to use polite language, but eventually he or she will learn to give the right response.

If your child forgets what to say out in public or if you have guests at home, avoid making a scene or calling attention to him or her with a loud reminder. Instead, take the child to one side and correct the mistake, or explain about it in low tones. If he or she doesn't respond correctly, drop the issue. Give your child more help when you are alone or when only the family is present.

• Table manners—Good eating habits are just as important for your child's social acceptability as is the use of polite language. An occasional error of not saying "Thank you" is much easier to accept than throwing food on the floor or smearing it in the hair. Here are some manners your child should acquire:

• Covering the mouth and turning the head away when sneezing or coughing.

• Carrying a tissue or handkerchief at all times.

• Eating slowly, one fork or spoonful at a time, and keeping the mouth closed while chewing.

• Taking small amounts of food and avoiding talking when chewing.

• Asking for food to be passed and using polite phrases such as "Bread, please."

• Learning to sit quietly at the table rather than jumping up and down.

• Saying "Excuse me" if he or she has to leave the table during a meal.

• Learning good posture at the table. Slumping in the chair or propping the elbows on the table are not appealing manners.

• Playing with food is an unpleasant habit. When this happens, assume your child is no longer hungry and remove the plate. Be sure to explain why you are taking the plate away and he or she will soon learn that food is to be eaten, not toyed with.

• Learning to use napkins and eating utensils properly.

It's a good idea for someone to sit beside your child at the table to help with difficult feeding tasks like cutting meat. However, your child should learn to perform these tasks alone as soon as possible. The longer you delay teaching these skills, the more the child will expect you to do it. Far too often I have seen parents cutting meat and vegetables for their grown sons and daughters, when clearly there was no physical reason for the children not to do this for themselves.

• Social situations—One set of habits that is *absolutely necessary* for your child's survival as an adult is knowing how to greet people and how to respond to greetings in an appropriate way. For instance, if your three year old hugs and kisses all the visitors that come to your house, everyone thinks it is cute. But the same behavior at age eight and beyond is not at all suitable and should be discouraged. And of course, the longer your child is allowed to display such behavior, the more difficult it will be to change that behavior. If you are faced with this problem, you can explain to your child that he or she should kiss and hug only close friends or family members. You can emphasize your point when your child is watching a romantic story on television: the pretty girls or handsome men don't kiss everyone.

Your child should acquire good habits of consideration for other people such as offering visitors a chair and not interrupting a conversation or using objectionable language. You probably can't protect the child from hearing such language, but you can help him or her learn that you object to the use of it.

Other situations that require courtesy and consideration of others are answering the telephone and doorbell, eating out in public, shopping trips, traveling, and so on. The best way to teach your child good manners is by setting a good example at all times and in all places. He or she will learn to be polite when surrounded by a family that is polite.

Although good manners are nothing more than habits of courtesy, gentleness, consideration, and kindness, learning them is a slow process. If you consistently help your son or daughter acquire these social graces, there will come a day when both of you will be complimented on your child's good manners.

INCREASING RESPONSIBILITIES

The preteen years are a good time to start preparing your child for greater independence as an adult by giving the youngster more responsibilities that promote habits and attitudes of independence. Now is the time to put significant emphasis on concepts such as the value of money, spending money wisely, and the concept of work.

You can teach your son or daughter the concepts of work by assigning specific tasks to do around the house, such as taking a turn at doing dishes, taking out the garbage, or collecting the mail. These jobs will also help your child learn to contribute to the family's well-being, and it will help him or her see how important it is for each member to make a contribution.

Your own attitude toward chores, and your spouse's, will have an effect on your child's attitude and willingness to complete his or her assigned tasks. If you moan and groan about your own responsibilities, your child is likely to do the same. But if you undertake your chores at home with enthusiasm, you can expect a similar response from your son or daughter.

It is also very important to help your child learn about money. A very expedient method of helping your child acquire money concepts is to make sure that these concepts are included in his or her individual education plan at school. Ask your child's teacher what concepts are taught in the classroom, and how they are taught. Is your child learning to recognize different coins and bills, to make change, and to understand that five cents is the same as a nickel or five pennies? If money concepts are not being taught, ask your child's teacher to begin teaching them.

Whatever is being taught in school, see if you can duplicate those same activities at home and while shopping. Take advantage of all the opportunities that occur in everyday life—paying bus fares, tipping waiters, making purchases, and so on. These opportunities should be real and practical, and real money should be used. For example, allow your child to select and pay for a treat when he or she accompanies you to the grocery store. You can expect to spend a great deal of time teaching these concepts, so a wide variety of methods, situations, and techniques will be needed.

Shopping for clothes offers you another practical opportunity to teach your child money concepts. Once the clothing items are selected, give your child the money to pay for them. Naturally, you will be close by to resolve any difficulties that may arise between your child and the cashier. Allowing your son or daughter to "purchase" clothes in this manner may be just the encouragement needed to make clothes shopping a pleasant experience for you both. (Boys seem to need more encouragement and motivation to shop for clothes than girls do.) "Clothes sense" is one skill that will really make a difference in the way your child will be accepted in the community, so these kinds of outings are very important.

When you are teaching your child clothes sense, you will want to emphasize these points: appropriate size, flattering colors, becoming styles, mixing and matching items that go well together and, of course, price. Again, you should be prepared to spend a great deal of time helping your child acquire this clothes sense.

A prerequisite to acquiring clothes sense is color discrimination. You will need to teach your child which colors complement one another and which ones clash. You can recruit your older children to take their Down's syndrome brother or sister along when they go shopping for clothes. Try to create a variety of opportunities that will help your child attain clothes sense. And don't forget, the youngster will imitate the examples and standards set by you and other members of your family.

Remember, too, that your child may go through a stage when little pride is taken in his or her outer appearance. But like all the other stages, this one will also pass.

RUNNING ERRANDS

You can give your child a big boost toward becoming as independent as possible by the time of adulthood when you give him or her the responsibility of running errands. You may have some apprehensions at first, but remember, this responsibility is for your child's benefit. The more responsibility handled now, the more responsible the child is likely to become as an adult—and the more accepted he or she will be.

Furthermore, if your child's siblings are allowed to run errands for you, sooner or later your Down's syndrome child will want the same privilege. It is in everyone's best interest to grant your child this privilege as soon as possible—certainly by the age of ten or eleven.

Use the show-and-tell method to teach your child how to run errands. Break the task into small steps and teach one step at a time. For example, to borrow a stick of butter from a neighbor down the street, show your child how to get to the neighbor's, what to ask for, how to ask politely, and how to get back home again. When you first begin sending your child on errands, go along through some of the errands, explaining each part of the process as you go through it. For instance, if you are showing your child how to buy rye bread, you point to the bread at the bakery and say, "These round loaves are rye bread. You say to the person behind the counter, 'One loaf of rye bread, please.'"

After you have accompanied your child on a few errands, you can gradually withdraw your assistance. For example, on trips to the bakery you might go along as far as the bakery but let your child go in alone. Then you might go halfway to the bakery, and finally you would let your child perform the task alone.

Teaching your child to run errands also means teaching safety precautions. Especially important is learning to cross streets. A child can probably learn to cross streets with traffic lights much faster than those without lights, because the lights give clear directions what to do. Crossing streets without lights requires the ability to make certain judgments which may take your child a long time to learn. Learning this skill will also require adult supervision at all times.

As with any other skill your child learns, there will be some setbacks while learning. But be patient and persistent, and the day will come when your youngster can be trusted to go on an errand several blocks away from home.

EDUCATION

In all of the preceding chapters, I have stressed how important it is for your child to learn a variety of skills that will help him or her gain social acceptance and independence. These skills—self-care, daily living, and social skills—are just as important to prepare your child for vocational education. For it is through vocational education that your child will learn the additional skills necessary to enter the world of work after graduating from high school.

You have already given your child a head start on this goal by helping him or her develop social and self-care skills. Now, during these preteen years, you can help your child maintain that head start by helping him or her become aware of the responsibilities of holding a job.

Before your child enters junior high school, emphasis should be placed on self-care skills that your child hasn't yet learned or mastered, and on refining those skills already acquired. During these preteen years, you should also be explaining to your child the importance of work, proper attitudes for getting and holding a job, and the relation of work to society as a whole. Don't get too complicated, but don't skirt the real issues either. Answer any questions your child may have about work openly and honestly. Stress the fact that he or she, like most other people, will need to work as an adult. These discussions are quite important, as they are laying the foundation for the vocational training your child will begin receiving at age eleven or twelve.

THINGS TO DO FOR YOUR CHILD

First, find out if your child's school, or other schools in the system, will be able to provide vocational training for your child. Check with your child's teacher, the principal, and the superintendent of schools in your area. If a complete vocational training program exists for handicapped people, this is ideal. If no such program does exist, you may want to try to have as much employment training as possible included in your child's educational program. See what can be arranged. Don't expect the impossible, but do stick up for your child's rights. It also can't hurt to strongly urge administrators to begin such a program for all handicapped children as soon as possible.

Keep in mind that your child may need to change schools to begin receiving vocational training.

If the school system offers no appropriate vocational training for your child, you may wish to write to your state and federal legislators, urging them to support education legislation that mandates vocational training. You will also need to seek other programs that might provide the right vocational training for your child. Some agencies to check with include the state Department of Education, and the local branches of The Association for Retarded Citizens, the National Down Syndrome Congress, and the United Way. Also check in the yellow pages under "Vocational Rehabilitation Services."

When you contact these organizations, be sure to describe your child and to explain exactly what skills and limitations he or she has. Some questions you might want to ask include:

How old must the child be to attend?

When and where is the program held? Is transportation available?

What kinds of training are provided? What skills are taught, and what careers does it prepare students for?

How does the child register and when?

What is the cost? Is financial assistance available?

THINGS TO DO WITH YOUR CHILD

When your child successfully completes an errand or an assigned task, consider a small payment in exchange for the work completed. This is one way to reinforce the money concepts that you have been teaching. It is also a way for your child to learn how wages are earned. If you allow your child to spend at least a portion of the allowance as he or she wishes, the youngster will eventually learn the importance of earning money.

Be sure to teach your child money management skills and help him or her to make appropriate decisions about the amount spent and the amount put into a savings account. When your child has had some experience making these decisions with your help, encourage independent decisions on saving or spending his or her allowance, and to accept the consequence of those decisions. For example, if you regularly give your child an allowance on Saturday and the entire amount is spent by Sunday, he or she must learn to wait until the following Saturday for more money.

Help your child become familiar with the concept of work by discussing the jobs held by you, your spouse, and other family members. Some facts to talk about are the kind of work you do, how you get to work, the hours you work, and the pay you receive. You may also want to discuss how banks, saving accounts, and checking accounts work, and how the money you and your partner earn gets spent (so much for food, rent, and so on).

You must be realistic about the kind of employment your child can eventually do, and you must encourage this same realism in your child. Don't be misleading in your discussions. If you are a TV producer, don't give your youngster the impression that he or she can become a TV producer too. Explain the kinds of jobs the child will likely be able to choose from, the kind of pay he or she will likely earn, and the kind of lifestyle he or she will be able to afford. The most important things for your child to understand are that most people do have to work for a living, that there are a great many different kinds of jobs, that when grown-up he or she will need to take a job, and that the training for the job needs to begin soon.

PERSONAL APPEARANCE AND OTHER TRAITS

Now, more than ever before, your child should learn the importance of personal appearance, and of social and self-care skills. Give every opportunity for your child to practice and refine dressing, eating, and grooming skills, and insist that he or she do these things without your help. The youngster will still need an occasional reminder to perform these tasks, as well as some supervision. But try to let him or her do them with as little help from you as possible.

While good self-care habits will improve your child's personal appearance, it can be enhanced even more through regular exercise. Exercise and physical fitness activities will not only help your child feel good and look good, they also help to develop coordination, stamina, dexterity, and strength. All of these skills will be most helpful when he or she is old enough to seek a job.

You should give equal attention to reinforcing and refining your child's social skills. Again, you should try and give your son or daughter every opportunity possible to interact and socialize with many nonhandicapped people, which is an excellent method to help your child learn how to get along with a variety of people.

The following resources should be helpful to preparing your child's sex education program.

The Rights of Mentally Retarded Persons A handbook by Paul R. Friedman that includes chapters on the right to sexual expression, and sexual and marital rights. Published by Avon Books, 250 West 55 St., New York, N.Y. 10019.

Who Am I? Teaches sex information and identity for the handicapped. Available at the Center for the Advancement of the Human Sexuality Potential, 2134 Chapel Ave., Cherry Hill, N.J. 08002.

Let's Make Sex a Household Word A book by Sol Gordon, Ph.D., for parents to explain sex education to their children.

Facts About Sex for Today's Youth A book by Sol Gordon, Ph.D., on sex education for teenagers.

Girls Are Girls and Boys Are Boys—So What's the Difference? A book by Sol Gordon, Ph.D., on sex education for children ages six to ten.

Did the Sun Shine Before You Were Born? A sex education primer by Sol Gordon, Ph.D. for children ages three to seven.

All of the books by Sol Gordon are available from The Exceptional Parent Bookstore, P.O. Box 902, Manchester, N.H. 03105.

Film Strips

Sexuality and the Mentally Retarded Two hundred and fifty slides available from The Standfield House, 900 Euclid St., P.O. Box 3208, Santa Monica, Calif. 90403.

Birth Control Methods: A Simplified Presentation for the Mentally Retarded A filmstrip with script, twenty-five-panel flip chart, and one-hundred-forty-page monograph developed by Planned Parenthood of Northern New York. Available at Perennial Education, Inc., 1825 Willow Rd., P.O. Box 236, Northfield, Ill. 60093.

CHAPTER 9

From Teenager to Adult

The onset of puberty and adolescence will probably be accompanied by conflicts and stresses between you and your child. During this age of transition from childhood to adulthood, various forces will be tugging at your child wanting to shed the childhood role but not quite knowing how. He or she yearns to be more independent but doesn't always have the ability to cope with that freedom. This is the age when you are apt to hear your child talk about dating, getting married, driving a car, or going to college. Such talk is not idle chatter. He or she sees other people doing these things and wants to do the same. You will need to make clear to your child which of these are real possibilities and which ones (college, driving a car) simply aren't going to happen.

Your child is also faced with new responsibilities—preparing for the world of work and developing social traits that will allow living and working in the community.

If you are having difficulty dealing with the concept of independence for your child, perhaps it's because you are seeing only the retardation —not his or her abilities or existence as an individual. Or perhaps you are still thinking of your teenager as a child, rather than as the adult he or she soon will be.

A child who is constantly told what to do, or when and how to do it, has no chance to develop judgment, no chance to become independent. Such a child will remain immature, even when he or she physically becomes an adult.

As parents, you are faced with the reality that your child is growing up. Your challenge now is one of allowing your teenager all the freedom and responsibility he or she can handle, and at the same time providing the necessary supervision and guidance he or she needs.

Nevertheless, you may be reluctant to help your child achieve the freedom and independence he or she desires because you're not sure of the child's ability to cope with the risks and responsibilities associated with that freedom. But if you really want your child to achieve independence, you *must* allow him or her to make decisions and take actions to carry out those decisions.

It's the risk of failure involved with those actions and decisions that may concern you. You are not sure your son or daughter can handle failure. Yet you must remember that there are times when learning can come through failure, and that it is through failure as well as success that your child will grow and will learn to become an adult. Learning to take risks is an important part of growing up for all children. You must therefore allow your child the freedom to take these risks.

Not only must your child be allowed to make decisions and take actions to carry out those decisions, he or she must also be capable of assuming the responsibility of those decisions and actions. For example, if your child immediately spends an entire allowance on candy, he or she must understand that additional money won't be available until the next allowance payday.

There may be times when your concerns for your child will outweigh your attempts to help him or her achieve independence. Yet, in all fairness to your child, *you must overcome this concern*. You will need to maintain a delicate balance between allowing your child to be independent and providing the necessary support while that independence is acquired. This is not always easy, but it is not impossible.

INDEPENDENT LIVING SKILLS

Everything you do to encourage your teenager's growth and development brings him or her one step closer to a smooth transition into adulthood. You are in fact laying the groundwork for the time when he or she will eventually move away from home. Even though this move may not occur for several years yet, it is important that your child is well prepared for that move when it does happen. And the best preparation you can give your son or daughter is the necessary encouragement to learn the daily living skills that will help him or her become as independent as possible.

MEAL PREPARATION AND GROCERY SHOPPING

Among the daily living skills your child should learn are how to shop for groceries and how to prepare meals. If you are reluctant to teach your child these skills because he or she is a nonreader, don't let that become a barrier. Your child can learn to cook and buy groceries successfully without reading. All that is needed are some visual aids, such as pictures of food and utensils clipped from women's magazines and mounted in scrapbooks. Rather than you doing all the clipping and mounting, encourage your child to do it while you watch. Provide as little assistance as possible. While your child clips pictures, repeat the name of the particular item shown in the picture. For instance, if your child is clipping a picture of a potato, have your child repeat the word "potato"; then talk about how potatoes can be cooked.

When this scrapbook is started, have your child make a separate section for each of the five food groups: fruits; vegetables; grains and starches; dairy products and eggs; and meat, poultry, and fish. Begin each section on a new page or new group of pages. It will be helpful to use a different color paper for each food group, for example, the fruit pages might be yellow, the vegetable pages green, and so on.

Another section (or even another scrapbook) should feature pictures of cooking and eating utensils: knives, forks, spoons, pots, pans, and so on. Be sure to keep eating utensils on pages separate from those used for cooking.

Once this scrapbook is completed, you can use it to help teach the art of shopping for groceries. As you prepare to go to the grocery store, give your child the responsibility of selecting one or two pages from the food section of the scrapbook and taking it along. At the store, have your child look at the picture on one page, then ask him or her to locate that section of food illustrated in the picture. For example, if your child has selected a page with fruit on it, ask him or her to find the fresh fruit section. At first it's helpful if the two of you are near the section to be found. When the section is located, have your child repeat the names of each fruit as he or she points at the actual fruit and at the picture. You can repeat this process for all the food and utensil pages in the scrapbook.

Once your child can recognize and locate different food sections in the store, he or she should begin to locate specific items in those sections. For instance, ask your child to go to the fruit section of the store and select two apples and an orange for purchase. At the checkout counter, let your child pay for the fruit, giving whatever assistance is needed.

Be sure your child has many opportunities to practice selecting and purchasing all the foods pictured in the scrapbook. Eventually he or she will perform the task of food shopping with ease and confidence.

The picture book method can also be used to teach your teenager how to prepare meals. Help your child assemble a scrapbook of pictures of different dishes, fully prepared and ready to eat. Here again women's magazines can provide usable pictures. You may also use illustrations from food labels and packages.

Divide the book into sections for breakfast, lunch, dinner, snacks, and beverages. Each dish should be on a separate page or group of pages. At the top of each page should be a picture of the fully prepared dish. Beneath it, have your child mount pictures of all the foods needed to make that dish. Beneath the foods, have your child paste up pictures of all the utensils needed to prepare that dish. Finally, have your child mount pictures showing each step in the preparation of the dish. Make sure these are pasted up in the proper order. These step-by-step pictures are not always easy to find, so you may want to take photographs for your teenager to use in the scrapbook. Remember that you will need to tell your child *exactly* what foods and utensils are used for each particular dish. If slicing is involved, you must include both a knife and a cutting board; if a sharp knife is necessary, make sure the picture is of a cutting knife, not a table knife. If paper towels are necessary to blot meat or vegetables dry, include a picture of them. If a recipe calls for a dash of salt, include a picture of a saltshaker. Your child will learn whatever you teach, so be sure the pictures are both thorough and correct from the start. It is a good idea to go through the process of cooking the dish yourself—at least mentally, and preferably for real— and listing exactly what foods and utensils you use. Then, after the visual recipe is pasted up, double-check it to make sure that nothing is left out.

The dishes you teach your child to cook should be very simple ones at first. When your teenager masters these, you can move on to more difficult ones. By the way, there is no reason why your teenager can't learn to cook a few gourmet dishes, providing they're not too difficult to prepare. You don't have to stick to the basics only, though of course you should teach the basics first.

Let's say, for example, that you want to teach your teenager how to make a lettuce and tomato salad. Begin by having your child paste a colorful picture of that salad at the top of the page. This helps your child visualize the finished product. Beneath this picture, have your child mount pictures of all the necessary ingredients—a head of lettuce, a tomato, and a bottle of salad dressing. Beneath these pictures, have your teenager paste up pictures of the necessary utensils—a cutting board, a sharp knife, a measuring cup, a salad bowl, and a large fork and spoon for tossing the salad.

Next, have your child mount pictures illustrating the following:

- Washing the lettuce and tomato
- Breaking up the lettuce into a bowl
- Slicing the tomato on the cutting board
- Scattering tomato slices over the lettuce
- Putting a measured amount of dressing in the measuring cup
- Pouring the dressing over the salad
- Tossing all the ingredients together

When directions include cooking, be sure to include a picture of a stove or oven (whichever is appropriate) and a large picture of the stove or oven dial showing exactly how much heat to use.

Although having your child prepare a scrapbook of recipes like this is ideal, if it is not possible you can buy a commercially published cookbook for nonreaders. It's called *101 Picture Recipes* and is published by the Ottowa County Association for Retarded Citizens, 246 S. River, Holland, Mich. 49423.

With cooking, as with shopping, your teenager will need a great many opportunities to practice preparing a variety of dishes. You should of course provide supervision at first, and as much assistance as necessary—but *absolutely no more* than necessary. As your child becomes more and more adept at preparing a certain dish, gradually withdraw your assistance until he or she can handle doing it alone. The first time your child can make the salad or entrée for your family's dinner will be a moment of unforgettable pride for both you and your child.

If possible, it is also helpful to have training in grocery shopping and meal preparation included in your child's educational plan at school. Some schools do offer such training on a regular basis. However, even if your child learns these skills in school, you should still allow and encourage cooking at home and shopping with you. This extra practice reinforces the learning process and helps your teenager master cooking and shopping skills at a faster pace.

MAINTAINING A CLEAN HOUSE

Among the habits your child should have developed by now are keeping the bedroom clean, making the bed, tidying up other areas of the house, folding or hanging up clothes, and completing specific chores, such as setting the table for dinner. Now you should encourage your child to expand on these habits. The degree of this expansion will, of course, depend on your child's readiness to learn, as well as on his or her capabilities for learning.

The new chores he or she should be acquiring include doing laundry, dusting and polishing furniture, using a vacuum cleaner, scrubbing and waxing floors, and cleaning the stove, refrigerator, and cupboards. These chores will increase your child's sense of responsibility, help him or her become more independent, and prepare for the day when he or she moves away from home. Knowing that your child can perform a variety of household tasks should be comforting to you.

The best way to teach your child these new chores is to break each task into small steps and then demonstrate and explain each step in sequence. For example, the following steps must be accomplished when your child learns to launder his or her own clothes: sorting the clothes into piles according to color and fabric; checking and cleaning out all the pockets; selecting the proper wash cycle and/or water temperature; loading the clothes into the machine; measuring the soap, bleach, and fabric softener; adding these items to the washer; starting the washer; and unloading the clean clothes. You will want to teach your child as well how to rearrange a load if it becomes unbalanced; how to check to be sure the machine is not overloaded; what to do if the machine is overloaded; and how to treat stains. Then you will want to teach your teenager how to use a dryer and/or a clothesline and clothespins.

Be sure your child masters the first step before you start to teach the second. When you do teach a new step, be sure to have your child continue to practice all the previously learned steps as well. You should follow this procedure for each household task that you expect your child to learn, and for each appliance he or she will use to complete the task.

If you want to include household tasks in your child's individual education plan, by all means do so. Then you can encourage practice of these at home. This extra practice will reinforce the skills your child learns at school and help him or her transfer those skills from a school to a home environment.

USING PUBLIC TRANSPORTATION

By allowing your child to learn to use public transportation, you are helping him or her take a significant step toward independence. You are also providing your child the opportunity to move about in the community just as nonhandicapped people do. Deciding the right time for this may be more difficult than actually teaching your child how to use public transportation. All the parents I've talked to say it depends on both your child's abilities and desire to learn.

Once you have decided your child is ready to use public transportation, you will want to develop a travel training plan. Here are some points to consider as part of that plan.

Learning the area. Teach your child the details of the area between home and the bus, train, or subway stop. Point out landmarks that must be passed on the way. Encourage your child to draw pictures or maps to help him or her remember the area and the route to the stop.

Arriving at the stop or station. Are there steps, escalators, or ramps leading to the boarding area that your child must learn to use? Will your child need to buy a ticket from a person or a machine? You will need to teach your child how to purchase a ticket.

Waiting. If your child must wait for a bus or train, are there benches or enclosures available? How far are they from the boarding area? Is there a turnstile to be passed through? Will the bus or train be announced?

Taking the right bus or train. Your child must learn to recognize which bus or train goes to his or her destination. If reading skills are limited, teach the child the letters, colors, or numbers that appear on the proper vehicle. Be sure to instruct your child how to ask conductors, drivers, ticket sellers, and other passengers for help when necessary.

Getting on the bus or train. Your child must learn how to get from the waiting area to the train or bus, how the doors open and close, and about the signal for opening or closing doors.

Paying the fare. Your child must know how much the fare is, and when and how it is collected, and to hold the safety rail, if there is one, while paying the fare. If he or she has difficulty handling money, put the fare in an envelope so it can be handed to the conductor or driver. You may want to seal the envelope and indicate on it the amount of money enclosed.

Seating. You and your child should study the kinds of seats used in the bus or train. If the seat can be raised and lowered, teach your child how to accomplish this. You must also teach your child what to do if there are no seats available. He or she too should learn what to do when the bus or train makes a sudden start or stop.

Arriving at the destination. To help your child learn when and where to get off the bus or train, have him or her memorize landmarks along the route to a particular destination. He or she must learn when and how to use the signal for leaving the bus or train and also how to ask the driver or conductor for help if he or she misses the destination point.

You should separate your child's travel training program into three parts. First, you, your spouse, or an older sibling must accompany your child through the entire process of getting to the bus or train stop, getting on, paying the fare, selecting a seat, and getting off at the right destination. Call attention to landmarks, numbers or colors on the bus or train, and anything else that helps mark the route from home to destination. It's a good idea to do these trial runs during off-peak times when drivers and other personnel have time to be helpful. Be prepared to repeat this first part again and again. At first, tell your child what to do each step of the way. Then gradually withdraw your instructions until your child can make the trip without any verbal instructions.

The second part of your child's travel training program should be separated into three steps:

1. Select a familiar destination, one that your child has learned and practiced frequently during part one. Accompany him or her from home to the destination and back again, reviewing all the processes along the way.

2. When you and your child are ready, repeat the trip, but this time you play the role of a passenger instead of your child's companion. He or she should go through the entire process of what has been learned, from getting to the bus or train stop to getting off at the appointed destination. You should stay within calling distance of your child in case your assistance is needed, but otherwise you should act just like

another passenger. For all intents and purposes, your child will be traveling alone.

3. When your child has mastered step 2, he or she is ready to try taking the rehearsed trip alone. Both of you go to the station or stop and review all the things your child must do to arrive at his or her destination. Explain that he or she will make the trip alone, and that you will be there at the destination point by taking the next bus or train or driving your car there. Then let your child make the trip alone.

After much repetition, both of you will gain confidence in your child's ability to travel alone to this prearranged meeting site. Once he or she can manage this trip alone, you can begin practice reaching other destinations in your community.

If there are reasons you cannot develop a travel training program for your child, then you may want to include such a program in his or her individual educational plan. The classroom teacher would then have the major responsibility for developing and teaching the program while you could help practice and reinforce the skills your child is learning in school.

If you have encouraged your child to become as independent as possible, he or she may be able to take an airplane trip alone, as several of my teenage Down's syndrome friends have done. One, a fifteen year old, recently flew unaccompanied from Minnesota to California to visit his grandparents. There were no problems.

If you do have your child take a plane trip, or some other long-distance journey, be sure to have friends or relatives waiting there when he or she arrives at the destination.

USING COMMUNITY SERVICES

When your child learns to travel by bus, train, or subway, whole new worlds begin to open up—places to visit, things to do, and people to see. Among the new worlds your child should become familiar with and learn to use are the services that are available in your community. These services include health programs (going to the doctor's office, health clinic, or hospital), recreation facilities (parks, the zoo, and the local pool), restaurants, museums, and movies.

Learning to use community services helps your child satisfy his or her desire to participate in activities, just as nondisabled people do. At the same time, your child learns more about the community, which in turn broadens the horizons beyond home, school, and church. And the more your child is involved in community services, the more aware the community becomes of people with Down's syndrome. This will gradually lead to more community acceptance and concern for all disabled people.

As your child learns how and when to use community services, he or she also gains more independence and takes a significant step toward a smoother transition into adulthood. For example, if your teenager learns when he or she should see a doctor, knows how to get to the doctor's office, and what to do while at the office, you will feel confident that he or she will retain this ability as an adult.

To teach your child how to use community services will again depend on his or her readiness to learn and your readiness to act as a teacher. You can help yourself and your child reach this readiness stage by going to various places in the community such as the library, park, and swimming pool. Point out landmarks on the route. It is very likely you will spend a great deal of time on these prereadiness activities.

Once you and your child reach the readiness stage, you should develop a training plan similar to the one suggested for traveling alone. Begin your plan by listing every step or phase of a particular activity you plan to teach your child—how to get to the activity, what to do upon arrival, how to complete or end the activity, and how to return home again.

For instance, a trip to the museum would be divided into these phases: getting there, locating the ticket office, purchasing a ticket, exploring the museum, leaving the museum, and returning home. Each of these phases should be divided into smaller tasks that your child can learn. Be sure to teach the tasks in sequence, and to give your teenager the necessary assistance for as long as it is needed. Then gradually reduce your help until he or she can complete the task alone.

You do have the option of including in your child's individual educational plan at school a program that will teach using community services. If you choose this option, be sure you monitor what is being taught and how the material is presented so you can help your child practice and reinforce outside of school the skills learned there.

Keep in mind when teaching your child all these independent living skills—shopping, meal preparation, housekeeping, using public transportation, and using community services—that positive reinforcement works wonders. Be sure to reward your child for each task completed and everything learned or mastered with a smile, a hug, or words of praise.

SOCIAL GROWTH

During this adolescent phase of your child's development, it is necessary for you to put special emphasis on the improvement of his or her social competence. Now is the time for the refinement of the ability to get along with people outside the family circle. The degree to which your child can master this phase of social competence will determine his or her ability to succeed or fail in the world of work.

The teen years are also the time in which your child must learn to behave appropriately in mixed-company social activities such as school dances. Of particular concern to many parents is their children's ability to refrain from inappropriate affectionate behavior and to control their sexual drives and sexual expression.

SEGREGATED VS. MAINSTREAMED SCHOOL AND ACTIVITIES

Your child's teenage years are not only a time for social growth, they are also a time for *you* to be prepared for that social growth. You must understand that your teenager, like all teenagers, has an especially strong desire to be with peers, and to be accepted by them. These peers will have a powerful influence on your child's behavior. You can expect insistence on wearing "in" clothes, using the latest fad language, and adopting fad gestures.

If this behavior becomes a problem, you may have to take some disciplinary action. An effective technique in this case is the reward system. When your child uses language or gestures that you disapprove of, explain why you disapprove and follow it up with taking away a cherished privilege. However, when your child avoids the behavior you find inappropriate, *be sure* to reward him or her either with a new privilege or by restoring a lost one.

If your child is integrated (or mainstreamed) into regular classes and attends class dances, parties, or field trips, you may wonder what effect these school functions will have on your child's behavior. You can't help assuming that the teen behavior he or she is suddenly exhibiting is the result of attending those classes and functions. Your assumptions are indeed correct, at least in part, but it's not so much the school functions in and of themselves that affect your child's behavior. Rather, it is the behavior of the other students that your child observes and imitates, because he or she wants to act like the peer group.

It is quite possible that the students your child chooses as behavior models may not meet with your approval. In this case, integrated school functions are not advantageous for the improvement of your child's social competence. The possibility exists, too, that your child may be teased, ridiculed, or subjected to teenage pranks at these functions. This can be a real disadvantage, especially if this engenders feelings of being inferior and unwanted.

Yet these integrated school functions can have a favorable effect on your child's behavior, as they will help him or her deal with the nondisabled world. And the better your child learns to cope with the nondisabled world, the smoother his or her transition into that world will be as an adult. Good coping skills also help your child succeed in the world of employment with nondisabled peers.

In addition to coping skills, your child learns through integrated classes that he or she can survive and get along in the nondisabled world. This knowledge helps improve your teenager's self-esteem and self-worth at a time when such reinforcement is badly needed.

You must carefully consider whether the favorable effects that integrated classes and activities have on your teenager outweigh the unfavorable ones. If you decide that the unfavorable effects are too great, you do have some alternatives.

• You can remove your child to segregated classes where he or she will associate only with other handicapped children.

• You can help your child to avoid questionable behavior with positive explanations like "Teenage girls and boys dress neatly" or "Teenagers try to control their anger."

• If there is a behavior you wish to reinforce in your child, you must demonstrate that behavior yourself, and you should strongly encourage your spouse to do the same. Remember, your child is more inclined to do what you do rather than what you say. If you want your child to keep his or her hair combed, your child is not going to learn unless you set a good example of this behavior.

If you decide that segregated classes are more appropriate for your child, you should be aware of the disadvantages these classes pose for your child's social growth.

• He or she will be exposed only to other disabled children. While this exposure reduces your child's chances of imitating unwanted teen behavior, it also reduces his or her chances of learning to cope with people who are not handicapped.

• Attending a segregated school can also reduce your child's chances of interacting with neighborhood children. If these children don't get to know your child, they may be unfriendly toward him or her.

• Your child, because of limited contact with nondisabled children, may actually learn to fear them. When kids who are not disabled sense this fear, they are likely to respond by teasing and harassing your child, which in turn may stimulate your child's fears even more. And so a vicious cycle begins which is likely to continue as long as the segregation of your child does.

It is when people interact and associate with one another that social competence is learned and developed. If you expect your child to survive in the nondisabled world, he or she must start dealing with it sooner or later. Integrated school functions can give this an early start.

HELPING YOUR CHILD FEEL GOOD

Feeling good about oneself and being attractive to other people involve more than physical appearance, no matter what the cosmetic and fitness industries claim. People can also gain a good feeling from making decisions, developing a hobby, taking pride in a job, or enjoying a social activity.

The teen years are, for most people, a time to search for their identities. It's a time of confusion as they shed childhood roles to take on adolescent ones. And in this search and confusion they may not find many things that help them feel good about themselves. Your teenager may experience similar feelings, but you can do a great deal to counteract them.

If your child hasn't developed a hobby, now is the time to help find one. It may take some experimenting before something is found that is both enjoyable and achievable but when that happens, your child will glow with pride. One young man I know keeps a scrapbook of scenes from a favorite television show that he reproduces using crayons. He developed this hobby as a result of attending art class. Whenever I compliment him about the book, he radiates with pleasure.

If your child can't participate in social activities at school, church, or community centers, you may want to have social gatherings at your home and invite his or her friends. This will ease the danger of social isolation. Be sure the guests include both disabled and nondisabled teen-agers to enhance your child's opportunities to interact with able-bodied peers.

You may discover that your son or daughter does one particular chore or task better than you expected. Letting him or her know how pleased you are with the performance is an excellent way to help him or her feel good. When your child does do something well or exhibits ability in a certain area, see if you can find a way to turn that skill into a hobby, a class, or a regular activity.

COSMETIC SURGERY

Some parents and professionals believe that surgical intervention also helps a child with Down's syndrome develop better feelings about himself or herself.

The facial features of most Down's syndrome children are different from those of the general population. This difference tends to create a barrier to their integration into society, simply because of the emphasis we put on being handsome or beautiful. In an attempt to overcome this societal barrier, plastic surgery has been performed on 250 Down's syndrome children in West Germany and Israel since the late seventies. Initial results of this surgical intervention, known as *cranio-facial surgery* in medical terms, show that the facial appearance of people with Down's syndrome can be improved, which in turn can promote a better self-image. Hospitalization is usually brief for this surgical technique, and costs *may* be covered by insurance. While such surgery is not un-common in the United States, parents who are contemplating this type of intervention for their child should discuss with their family doctor the risks and costs that are involved.

The characteristic features of Down's syndrome people who are most responsive to plastic surgery include flat nasal bridge, flat cheek bones, hanging lower lip, protruding ears, enlarged tongue, flat chin and epi-canthic folds (the extra tissue at the side of the nasal bridge).

Surgical intervention to improve the facial features of Down's syndrome people is not without controversy. The arguments against the technique are:

• It is society that needs changing, not the child.

• Society will expect too much of people who look bright but who are in fact mentally retarded.

• Most Down's syndrome children or adults cannot give informed consent to the surgery.

• It is likely to raise unrealistic expectations for parents, which can be dangerous.

• The surgery doesn't improve the child's intelligence.

• To change a child's facial features, thereby changing his or her individual identity, is not morally correct.

Proponents of plastic surgery techniques for Down's syndrome people respond to the arguments against it as follows:

• Changing society—Numerous studies show the importance society attaches to physical attractiveness in our daily lives. It is almost impossible to prevent the general population from seeing people with Down's syndrome as different, and unless this difference is minimized, society is not likely to fully accept these people.

• Society's expectations—The potential of people with Down's syndrome is often *underestimated* simply because of their physical appearance. Cosmetic surgery can help counter this.

• Informed consent—Plastic surgery is commonly performed and accepted as proper treatment for children who cannot specifically give informed consent. As your child's legal guardians you have not only the right, but the duty to improve the quality of life for your child. If you and your spouse believe that cosmetic surgery is appropriate and beneficial for your child, then you should feel free to go ahead with that surgery without guilt. However, it is a good idea to discuss with your child as many facts about the surgery as possible, presenting both sides, and let your child decide whether or not the surgery should be performed.

• Parents' unrealistic expectation—The rapid and innovative advances in educational techniques for people with Down's syndrome indicate more than ever before the significant strides these people can make. Therefore, if it is proper to invest in their intellectual well-being, isn't it also proper to invest in their emotional well-being?

• Intellectual improvement—Although improvement in a child's physical appearance does not directly affect his or her intellectual ability, it should stimulate improvement in self-image, and thus in speech, communication, and social functioning, all of which can lead to greater fulfillment and better acceptance.

• Changing individual identity—Nonhandicapped people routinely undergo cosmetic surgery without any worries or questions about changing their identity. There is no reason why such moral questions should apply to people with Down's syndrome. At the very least, any moral questions should apply equally to both handicapped and non-handicapped people. If you feel that such surgery is morally wrong, simply don't consider having it done.

If you are considering plastic surgery for your child, you should carefully consider the following questions before making a decision.

What are the health risks?

Will there be permanent scars?

Will there be psychological and/or emotional trauma?

What is the reason for the change? Who really wants this change— you or your child?

Will coping with society be easier for your child?

Will it be more frustrating for your child to be treated as "normal" and not be able to respond in a nonhandicapped way?

If you are considering corrective surgery for your child, it is extremely important that you both discuss this surgery, and that you take his or her feelings, reactions, and wishes into account when making your decision. Explain as best you can why you are considering the possibility of surgery and present both the reasons for surgery and the reasons against it. Be sure you discuss all the questions listed above. Also be sure your child understands that surgery will mean going to the hospital, and that healing from it may be painful. You will need to explain about the surgery again and again. When you feel your child understands about the surgery as much as he or she can, find out whether or not he or she wants to have it done.

Throughout these discussions, it is important that you let your child know that his or her present appearance is not wrong or bad in any way. You must let your child know that you are not displeased with how he or she looks and that it's the attitudes of *strangers* that make surgery useful.

It is also extremely important to discuss all of these issues thoroughly with your spouse. You should not proceed with the surgery unless you, your spouse, *and* your child all agree to it. However, if your child is severely retarded and unable to understand, you and your spouse will need to make the best judgment that you can.

SEXUALITY AND HUMAN RELATIONS

Far too often I've met parents of Down's syndrome children who see their sons or daughters as sexless human beings who have no interest in or curiosity about the opposite sex. When I've asked these parents the reason for their opinion, they all gave the same answer, "Because my son or daughter is mentally retarded."

The truth is that sexuality is a part of your child regardless of the fact that he or she is mentally retarded. Your teenager needs your guidance in developing healthy attitudes about sexuality and the opposite sex. Your help is also needed to form standards of appropriate sexual behavior. And your child needs the opportunity to know other teenage boys and girls and to learn how to get along with them.

Like many parents of Down's syndrome children, you may wrestle with the question of whether or not your son or daughter should be allowed to go on dates. Some parents believe dating is vital to their children's social and emotional growth. Others are especially concerned about their daughters being taken advantage of. The question of dating particularly becomes an issue if there are older siblings at home who have that privilege. Your child will certainly notice and very likely will want to do the same.

Here are some actions you can take to help your child develop an appropriate attitude toward dating:

• Allow your child to take part in supervised social activities such as school dances, parties, and picnics at which boys and girls learn how to relate to each other.

• Provide similar opportunities at home.

• Enroll your child in supervised social-recreational activities sponsored by local churches or by social services agencies such as The Association for Retarded Citizens. If these programs aren't available in your community, you may want to join forces with other parents and start one of your own.

Be sure you explain the standards of behavior you expect from your son or daughter while he or she is attending these activities. Let him or her know that a breach in that behavior will result in some form of disciplinary measure. As always, when situations arise that require discipline, remember to be consistent. Don't just threaten with the loss of a privilege, carry out your threat.

As your child participates in these social activities, you will soon recognize if he or she is socially and emotionally mature enough to go on individual dates. Then and only then should that privilege be granted.

SEXUAL ABUSE

Information about sexual abuse should be an integral part of every child's safety education. It is particularly important for your child's safety because he or she may be more vulnerable to abuse simply because of being handicapped. The abuser may assume that your child because of the handicap won't resist being abused or won't talk about being assaulted.

MYTHS AND FACTS ABOUT SEXUAL ABUSE

There are several myths about sexual abuse that can cloud parents' perspectives on the issue. These in turn make it difficult to stop or prevent such abuse. When parents recognize these myths for what they are, they can begin to deal with the reality of child sexual abuse.

MYTH: The incidence of child sexual abuse is too low to warrant concern.

FACT: Recent studies estimate that one in every four or five girls and one in every nine or ten boys are sexually abused before they reach age eighteen.

MYTH: Children are most often assaulted by strangers.

FACT: In almost 98 percent of known cases, the child is abused in the home by close relatives, family friends, or neighbors. The single largest group of abusers (77 percent) is parents.

MYTH: A discussion of sexual abuse will frighten children.

FACT: Inaccurate information is more frightening than ignoring the issue. Informing children about sexual abuse alerts them to possible dangers and how to avoid those dangers.

MYTH: Sex offenders are lustful old men.

FACT: Sex abusers come from all socioeconomic backgrounds, and as many as 75 percent were sexually abused as children.

PREVENTING SEXUAL ABUSE

You simply cannot protect your child from sexual abuse by restricting his or her activities with other people. This may keep your child safe from strangers, but not from someone he or she knows, such as a friend, a caretaker, or even a family member. Furthermore, by restricting your child in this way, you are running the risk of lowering his or her self-confidence and fostering an attitude of dependence. A far wiser course of action is to teach your child how to avoid unwanted sexual contact, and how to get out of the situation when such contact seems likely or has begun to occur.

Here are some positive steps you can take to help your child avoid sexual abuse:

• Make sure that he or she receives positive information about sex appropriate for his or her age and intellectual ability. If your child has a positive understanding of sexuality, he or she will be able to identify abusive behavior. This should also enable your child to talk about abuse if it happens, especially if you have given him or her the appropriate words relating to sex and sexuality.

• Talk to your child about different kinds of touch. That holding hands, petting animals, and similar actions are positive kinds of touch. That a confusing touch is one that is not really good or bad, but feels uncomfortable. That any unwanted touch, like hitting, or biting, or sexual abuse, is a negative touch.

• Talk to your child about sexual abuse. Be sure you give specific information about sexual abuse so that he or she will recognize it if it happens. Tell your child that sexual abuse can start out as a confusing touch and then can turn into an unwanted sexual touch.

• Teach your child to be assertive, that no one has the right to touch him or her without permission. If your child feels uncomfortable when being touched, he or she must learn that it's all right to say "Stop" or "No"—and that if this doesn't work, it's all right to try to leave or get away.

• Teach your child personal safety techniques such as never let a stranger in the house; don't give out phone numbers, names, or addresses to strangers; don't go anywhere with a stranger.

• Encourage your child to tell you if he or she has been sexually abused. You must make your child feel comfortable when talking about sexual matters. If you can, it will help your child be more willing to tell you about an abuse, even if he or she was warned not to tell anyone by the abuser.

BEHAVIORS AND SYMPTOMS OF SEXUAL ABUSE

If your child is not able to talk about sexual abuse, you can suspect he or she has been a victim if there are any of the following symptoms or behaviors:
• a reluctance to be alone with certain people
• knowledge of sexual activities that you don't know how he or she acquired
• nightmares or disturbances in sleep patterns
• sudden reversion to more childish behavior
• withdrawal or depression
• genital infections, rash, tenderness, or soreness
• sudden and drastic change in appetite, school performance, or social behavior
• sudden reversion to bed-wetting

If your child exhibits any of these unusual symptoms or behaviors, ask what is wrong. If your child says something about sexual assault, believe what he or she tells you. Children rarely lie about such things. If your child isn't able to talk about what happened, use dolls or pictures to help explain what he or she is trying to tell you. Report the abuse to your local police and child protection agency. (If you don't know how to contact the child protection agency, ask the police for assistance, or call your county attorney or your personal lawyer.) It is important that the offender be prosecuted so that other children will not be harmed.

Contact your local social service office to get counseling for both you and your child, and to find out how you can help your child deal with the incident. Remember, your child isn't at fault and neither are you. You are both victims of a serious crime.

Some communities have a Parents Anonymous chapter that provides personal assistance for parents and their abused children. To find out if there is a chapter in your area you can write to Parents Anonymous, 2230 Hawthorne Blvd., Torrance, Calif. 90595 or call toll free 1-800-421-0353.

To find out what laws exist in your community and state about sexual abuse of children, criminal sexual conduct, mistreatment of vulnerable adults, and intrafamilial sexual abuse, call your local law enforcement office, social service agency, or county attorney.

RESOURCES FOR DEALING WITH SEXUAL ABUSE

The following resources, aimed for general use, contain suggestions that can be adapted to meet the needs of disabled children.

He Told Me Not to Tell A parent's guide for talking to your child about sexual assault. Available from King County Rape Relief, 305 South 43 St., Renton, Wash. 98055. ($2.00)

Top Secret Sexual assault information for teenagers only. Available from King County Rape Relief, 305 South 43 St., Renton, Wash. 98055. ($4.00)

Private Zone A book by Frances Dayee teaching children sexual assault prevention. Available from The Chas. Franklin Press, 18409 90 Avenue West, Edmonds, Wash. 98020. ($3.00 plus $1.00 shipping)

No More Secrets A book by Caren Adems and Jennifer Fay about protecting your child from sexual assaults. Available from Impact Publishers, Order Code NMA, P.O. Box 1094, San Luis Obispo, Calif. 93406. ($3.95 plus $1.00 shipping)

What If . . I Say No! A pamphlet by Jill Loustalot Haddad and Lloyd Martin. Available from M. H. Cap & Co., P.O. Box 3584, Bakersfield, Calif. 93385. ($3.50)

Red Flag, Green Flag People A coloring book available from Rape and Abuse Crisis Center of Fargo/Moorehead, P.O. Box 1655, Fargo, N. Dak. 58107. ($3.00)

Child Sexual Abuse Prevention: Tips for parents. Available from NCCAN Clearinghouse, P.O. Box 1182, Washington, D.C. 20013. (Free)

PREPARING YOUR CHILD FOR THE WORLD OF WORK

Now that your child is growing up, one of the responsibilities you must deal with is helping your teenager move from the home and school environments into the world of work. Whether or not you realized it, everything you have done thus far on your child's behalf has actually been preparation for an eventual move into employment. The self-care, the social, educational, and recreational skills your child has learned all are aids to succeeding in the world of work. During this stage of development, your child must be helped to develop realistic expectations about future employment. You and your child need to seriously consider these questions:

- What kinds of jobs are available in your community?
- Which jobs can your child handle?
- What skills or training does your child need to be employed in those jobs?
- Can your child get the training that is needed for those jobs?
- Where can he or she get that training?
- What jobs or activities does your child enjoy? (Asking your child directly for any likes and dislikes is important here. Don't simply assume your child likes something—and *never* decide for him or her or try to put your own likes or dislikes in his or her head. Also be careful to avoid thinking that your child likes a certain activity merely because you would.)
- What jobs or activities is your child especially good or adept at? It would be tragic if your child, like so many Down's syndrome people, is seen as being capable of performing custodial or factory work only. He or she should have opportunities to explore other job alternatives.

By now, your child should have acquired other assets that are necessary before successfully entering the world of work. These assets include personal hygiene, social competence, telling time, safety habits, money concepts, physical fitness, and emotional stability. While all of these assets are important, most employers place the greatest importance on social competence, particularly the ability to get along with other people. Research has demonstrated that most job failure is due to social incompetence rather than inadequate job performance or skills.

During these teen years, your child should spend the greatest portion of the school day learning specific vocational skills that will lead to employment after graduation from high school.

The key to your child's vocational success depends on his or her abilities rather than on his or her limitations. Far too often both parents and educators look at a child's disability and assume that he or she cannot hold certain types of jobs. Such assumptions are unfair because *you are letting the disability determine your child's future.* Instead, you should look beyond the disability and ask yourself, "What abilities does my child have that he or she can use in a vocation?"

To help answer that question, you should insist that vocational training be a vital part of your child's education plan as soon as junior high or middle school. You should also insist that that vocational training plan take into consideration your child's abilities, not just his or her limitations.

VOCATIONAL EDUCATION JARGON

Just as you had to learn special education jargon when your child started school, now you should become familiar with vocational education jargon. Here are some of the more common terms.

Community-based training—learning to perform a job at a site within the community. For example, if your child is going to learn retail sales skills, he or she should acquire those skills in a retail shop.

School to work transition—a program designed for high school students to determine vocational abilities and employment goals, and to provide the services they need to meet those goals.

DVR—Department of Vocational Rehabilitation.

DRS—Department of Rehabilitation Services.

Job shadowing—the working together of a rehabilitation training specialist and a trainee at the job site to help the trainee learn job responsibilities and meet employer expectations.

Customized job training—a program that provides specialized training in "job skills clusters," which enables trainees to qualify for related community employment. Job skills clusters in a food service training program, for example, include setting tables, preparing food, busing dishes, dishwashing, and maintaining food preparation equipment.

Sheltered employment—employment for handicapped people provided at a workshop that has a controlled working environment and where workers are constantly supervised. Employees acquire skills in production work such as packaging, collating, or assembling, and each person works at his individual rate of speed. The wages are based on productivity and employees may later progress out of the sheltered workshop into mainstreamed employment.

Adult services—vocational training and employment programs provided by rehabilitative agencies (DVR or DRS) for disabled people after they graduate from high school.

Competitive employment—a mainstreamed workplace as opposed to a sheltered workshop. Here a handicapped worker works at a job in the community with or alongside nonhandicapped workers. He or she is expected to meet accepted standards of performance and rate of production that are comparable to those expected of nondisabled workers.

In addition to understanding vocational jargon, you should also understand the similarities and difference between vocational education and vocational rehabilitation programs.

Vocational education is a program for high school graduates that prepares students for a specific occupation in business or industry. Classes are taught by certified vocational education teachers and are offered in such areas as industrial art, automotive maintenance and repair, health services, business technology, and food services. Course work can be completed in six to twenty-four months. In some states vocational education is available for high school students.

Vocational education programs are open to anyone, both handicapped and nonhandicapped students, who can keep up with the course work.

Vocational rehabilitation is instruction designed specifically for people who because of a permanent or long-term disability have limited employment potential, but whose skills can, through rehabilitation, be improved or increased. These services are available:

• Medical diagnosis to determine physical conditions that might limit the kinds of work your child can do.

• Counseling and testing to help your child aim for the right kind of job in keeping with his or her interests, capabilities, and limitations.

• Medical and hospital care to attend to physical problems that may interfere with the preparation for work.

• Prosthetic appliances for a physical disability.

• Job training that will lead toward a definite job goal and employment.

• Maintenance and transportation during rehabilitation, if needed.

• Tools and equipment for the job, if needed.

• Job placement in a position most suitable for your child's training and abilities.

• Job follow-up to make certain that your child and his or her employer are both satisfied, to provide any other adjustments that are needed, and to help your child get off to a proper start.

THINGS TO DO FOR YOUR THIRTEEN TO FIFTEEN YEAR OLD

When your child is in junior high or middle school, you should:

• Support the efforts of your child's teachers to provide job training in community-based sites. If need be, you can help locate sites that can provide potential jobs your child could hold in the community, such as in restaurants, hotels, banks, or offices. (The potential jobs in these sites would include food service, housekeeping, bell hop, janitor, and messenger.) Or perhaps training sites can be found within your child's school —in grounds or building maintenance, as a messenger in the principal's office, in food services in the cafeteria, and so on. On-site training is more desirable than training in the classroom because it offers your child the opportunity to interact with other employees rather than just his or her classmates. Furthermore, the best way your child can learn job skills is to practice those skills in a real job setting.

• Make sure your child's educational plan includes specific vocational training in a *variety* of potential jobs. This varied training will help identify your child's vocational likes and dislikes, abilities, and potential for acquiring work skills.

• Begin to inquire about the job-training programs that will be available when your child reaches high school. Several programs should exist, and your child should have the opportunity to gain experience in all of them. These programs are described later in this chapter.

• Contact your state rehabilitation service agency and ask about the training services and job possibilities that are available in your community for your child. Agencies are listed in the yellow pages under "Rehabilitative Services." If there are few or limited vocational programs in your area, insist that improvements be made. There are federal laws that require that vocational services be available to people with disabilities.

• Help your child find work away from home during summer vacation or on weekends. The job may pay a wage, or it may be on a volunteer basis. The idea is to get your child accustomed to working with people other than the family, getting to work on time, and following a schedule.

THINGS TO DO WITH YOUR THIRTEEN TO FIFTEEN YEAR OLD

• Continue to help your child improve his or her appearance and physical fitness. A sloppy, unkempt appearance is a major reason for not securing a job, or for losing one.

• You should insist that your child always maintain good grooming habits.

• Be sure that your child exercises regularly to build up strength and to control weight.

• Assign regular household chores to your child. If you pay an allowance, make sure he or she gets paid only when these chores are completed satisfactorily and within the allotted time. This teaches responsibility.

• Accelerate the opportunities for leisure activities in your community—take your child to restaurants, movies, and other community events.

• When it's time for new clothes, let your child choose them with as little help or advice from you as possible.

THINGS TO DO FOR YOUR SIXTEEN TO EIGHTEEN YEAR OLD

By this time your child should be spending a major portion (at least half) of the school day in vocational training. A vocational guidance counselor should be assigned to your child. This counselor has the responsibility to inform you and your child about the various training and employment options that are available. With the counselor's help, you and your child can determine which options are the best. Once these options are decided upon, the counselor will develop an employment training program for your child which should be written into his or her educational plan.

Your child's employment plan should list, in writing, the specific skills to be acquired before graduation from high school. These skills include work habits—punctuality, personal hygiene, and quality performance; social skills—getting along with others and controlling emotions; dexterity skills—handling equipment; and job skills—learning to do a specific job.

In addition to these skills, your child's employment plan should include clear directions for the transition from school to the workplace. This transition is discussed later in this chapter and in Chapter 10.

Be certain that your child's employment education plan includes vocational training in specific jobs. Teachers should know what jobs are available in the community in both competitive and sheltered sites. You should insist that your child's training for these jobs take place in community settings if at all possible. This too should be written into his or her educational plan.

Make sure a transition-planning team is formed to design your child's employment program after graduation. This team, consisting of you, your spouse, your child, teachers, and a vocational guidance counselor, should be meeting and planning as early as two years before your child graduates. Remember, the school is not normally required to provide services for your child after he or she graduates. However, if an employment program is written into your child's educational plan before graduation, the school is responsible for implementing that program. In this way you can make sure your child receives services after finishing school.

You should encourage teachers to find, place, and train your child in a part-time job while he or she is still in school. Be sure your child is paid for the work to help him or her understand the relationship between working and earning money. If volunteer work is all that is available, try to pay your child a small salary yourself in exchange for work that is completed satisfactorily. A part-time job has another advantage for your child: the experience gained on the job helps to ensure a smoother transition into sheltered or competitive employment after graduation.

Learn all you can about available services for handicapped adults in your community. Make sure before your child graduates that he or she is enrolled in those services, especially if they offer employment referrals and opportunities.

The ideal option for your child is to move into competitive employment immediately after graduation from high school, within two to four weeks at the latest. If your son or daughter can't move into competitive employment, be sure he or she moves into sheltered employment.

While your son or daughter is in high school, you should continue to help him or her improve the necessary skills to succeed throughout adulthood. High on this list are daily exercise, good grooming, learning to handle money, and completing household chores. In addition to helping your son or daughter improve these skills, you should provide many opportunities for him or her to get out into the community and be as independent as possible.

WORK PROGRAMS

For many years the most common work preparation programs that existed for Down's syndrome people were sheltered workshops and day activity centers. People having high potential achievement attended sheltered workshops, while those with lesser abilities were enrolled at activity centers.

Today new work preparation programs are constantly developing, due to a new philosophical attitude toward people with Down's syndrome. This attitude is based on the concept of the "least restrictive alternative," as set forth in Public Law 94–142, the Education for All Handicapped Children Act. This concept is now used as the major guideline in the development of *all* programs for people with Down's syndrome. This means that many programs are designed to offer your child the greatest opportunities to acquire the skills he or she needs to become an independent, self-sufficient member of the community. The more opportunities that are offered, the less restrictive are the alternatives. Although new work preparation programs are continually developing, the rate of their development varies among communities. Not all programs are available in each community.

The following list describes the different work preparation programs that now exist. To find out what is available in your community, contact the department of vocational rehabilitation in your state. The programs are listed in order from *most* to least restrictive.

DAY ACTIVITY CENTERS

These programs are sometimes called Developmental Achievement Centers. They offer training for acquiring more skills in communication, the use of leisure time, appropriate behavior, and community awareness. Also offered are vocational activities to help people reach entrance-level standards for sheltered workshops.

WORK ADJUSTMENT TRAINING

This is a program of services that is designed to modify vocational and personal behavior based on a person's identified potential and deficits. The program uses a work setting supplemented by supervision and counseling. The areas covered in a work adjustment training program include developing work habits, developing a physical capacity for work, and orientating to the job market.

WORK ACTIVITY

In this program, manufacturing activities and other production work is utilized for the primary purpose of providing vocational skills development for people who are handicapped.

SHELTERED WORK

This program offers employment which is (a) a step in the rehabilitation process for those who cannot be readily absorbed in the competitive labor market, or (b) available during such time as employment opportunities for those in the competitive labor market do not exist.

Among the newest and least restrictive programs to be developed are:

SCHOOL-TO-WORK TRANSITION

This program helps junior and senior high school students prepare a vocational plan that will lead to employment immediately after graduation. Vocational counseling, evaluation, and job placement services are provided. In counseling sessions, a vocational counselor discusses employment options with students and their parents. At the conclusion of the counseling sessions, students take a variety of aptitude tests and are evaluated in actual work situations to determine job skills, job interests, and potential for different kinds of work. After completing the evaluation phase, a vocational plan is developed and the student begins training at the job site of his or her chosen vocation. For instance, if the counseling and evaluation phases show that your child has the potential for clerical work, this is written into the vocational plan. During the training phase, your child will learn clerical job skills in an office in the community. His or her work will be supervised by a job-training specialist during the entire training period. Once training is completed and your son or daughter finishes high school, the job-training specialist will help in finding employment. The length of the training phase will depend on your child's ability.

COMMUNITY-BASED TRAINING AND EMPLOYMENT

This service is designed for adults. It provides work experience in community businesses or industrial settings to help trainees master job skills and work behavior required to qualify for community employment. The services provided in this program are:

• Vocational evaluation. Trainees participate in actual work situations to determine what kinds of job skills and abilities they already have, what kinds of work they are interested in, any special needs they have, and their ability to perform different kinds of work.

• Job evaluation. Trainees explore vocational choices by observing various workers at their jobs.

• Planning. The trainee, his or her parents or guardian, a case manager, and a vocational counselor discuss the trainee's vocational skills and potential, and together they develop employment goals for the trainee.

• Work experience. The trainee works at a variety of jobs in the community to acquire appropriate work behavior and social competency, and to improve work performance. He or she is consistently supervised by a job-training specialist.

• Job placement. A placement specialist works with the trainee on an individual basis to prepare him or her for the job search process, such as filling out job applications, being interviewed, and so on. The specialist also places the trainee in an appropriate job in the community. Follow-up counseling services are provided for at least one year to help the trainees integrate themselves into the workplace successfully.

The trend in work preparation programs is toward increased use of community resources for training and preparation. As this trend continues, people with Down's syndrome will have wider and wider choices for employment.

FROM GRADUATION TO EMPLOYMENT

Since the early eighties, significant emphasis has been placed on the transition of handicapped students from school to work. This emphasis has stimulated the development of vocational education programs that provide training in a variety of jobs once considered beyond the capability of most disabled students.

Rather than ask the question, "What jobs are available for my child?" you should ask, "What jobs are my child capable of doing, if he or she receives the appropriate training?"

If you use job *availability* as the measuring stick for your child's employment future, you are limiting his or her choices. By pressuring for a job that is available at the moment, you may trap your child in a job he or she may not like, that is boring, or that offers very limited opportunity for job advancement or self-improvement.

But using job *possibility* as a guideline for your child's occupational career, you are opening up entirely new vistas. You are allowing your child to make choices among a variety of occupations. You are giving him or her the opportunity to secure job training and employment in a variety of work settings.

Thinking in terms of job *possibilities* means your son or daughter will first have the opportunity to observe a variety of people—messenger clerks, filing clerks, grill cooks, and so on at work. Then, depending on his or her interests and abilities, your child should be given the opportunity to learn the job skills of the occupation he or she chooses by actually working at that job in a community setting such as an office or cafeteria.

An exemplary program of this type is the Vocational Educational Alternatives (VEA) program in Madison, Wisconsin. VEA was begun in April 1980 and is funded by the United Service Board of Dane County. Its graduates have high job placement and job retention. As of January 1983, VEA clients were working as messengers, laundry workers, grill cooks, warehouse laborers, unit clerks, waitresses, cashiers, and personal attendants.

In addition to job training and placement services for disabled people, VEA also teaches parents how to work for improved employment training for their children.

Programs such as VEA that provide community-based training are rapidly replacing the traditional sheltered workshop.

GUARDIANSHIP AND CONSERVATORSHIP

As a parent, you are your child's legal guardian until he or she turns eighteen. At that time, most children then become legally independent, able, and required by law to make their own personal and financial decisions. They are also eligible to vote, marry, own property, and enter into contracts on their own behalf. Eighteen-year-old men must also register for the draft.

In *theory,* all this holds true for your Down's syndrome child. In practice, however, things are sometimes quite different. Although federal law provides certain rights for mentally handicapped people, they are not always upheld and protected. Many states have laws that prohibit mentally retarded people from exercising the same rights and privileges as nonhandicapped people exercise.

One thing that is *not* different from state to state is draft registration. If you have a son with Down's syndrome, he must register for the draft on or before his eighteenth birthday. This is true regardless of the degree of his handicap, and regardless of his inability to perform military service of any kind. He can register at any post office, just as any other eighteen-year-old man can. If your son cannot manage this on his own, then you must accompany him. If you have concerns about his registration, then you and he should go explain them to your local draft board office.

The rights of a handicapped adult do vary from state to state. To find out exactly what rights your child upon turning eighteen will or will not have in your state, contact your attorney. If your attorney cannot help you, ask for a referral to someone who is familiar with this area of law. (See Chapter 12 for information on locating such an attorney.) The nearest offices of the Protection and Advocacy Agency, The Association for Retarded Citizens, or the Down Syndrome Congress should also be helpful.

Whatever rights your child does have you will want protected as completely as possible. Unless your child is capable of handling all of his or her own personal and financial affairs—and chances are very good that this will not be the case—you will want to retain guardianship or conservatorship after he or she turns eighteen.

A guardian has the legal authority *and duty* to protect the rights and liberties of another person, to see that that person's needs are met, to act on behalf of that person, and to be legally responsible for that person's legal, personal, and financial affairs. The rights and obligations of a guardian of a Down's syndrome adult are exactly the same as the rights and obligations a parent has for his or her child until that child turns eighteen. If your son or daughter is incapable of making routine decisions or of caring for himself or herself, then you will want to continue to be your child's guardian. This means that you will continue to be responsible for seeing that your child's financial and personal needs are met.

Conservatorship is a limited form of guardianship for people who require some, but not complete, supervision and protection. Suppose, for example, your child is mildly retarded and can handle his or her personal affairs adequately but cannot sufficiently comprehend money matters such as checking and savings accounts. You will then want to appoint a conservator to handle your child's financial affairs. In this case, your child would have legal authority over everything in his or her personal life, but the conservator would have legal authority over the financial affairs.

Or, if your child is moderately retarded, needing both financial and personal affairs managed by other people, you may still want to put his or her financial affairs in the hands of someone, such as an investment broker, who is well informed about money matters and investments. However, you could appoint yourself as conservator or guardian of your child's personal affairs.

Since these protection laws vary among states, you should seek the help of an attorney who is knowledgeable about them.

Most parents appoint themselves as guardians or conservators. However, you may wish to appoint a friend, relative, or an agency such as The Association for Retarded Citizens as a guardian or conservator for your child—provided, of course, that the person or organization is willing and able to accept this responsibility and agrees to accept it in writing. When your child is placed under the guardianship or conservatorship of someone other than yourselves, he or she becomes a ward of that person(s).

You may also name your state government as guardian or conservator of your child, although this should be considered *only* if you have no other options simply because of the restrictions state guardianship or conservatorship can have on the legal rights of the child. If you do appoint the state as your child's guardian or conservator, be sure to find out what legal implications such an appointment has. In some states, anyone placed under state protection cannot

• marry or be adopted without approval.

• enter into contracts for purchases except for such necessities such as food and clothing.

• exercise the right to vote.

Establishing guardianship or conservatorship is a legal process. It requires the preparation and signing of legal documents, and it requires the assistance of an attorney. If your attorney cannot prepare these documents for you, check with your state protection and advocacy agency, attorney general's office, or with the nearest office of The Association for Retarded Citizens or the Down Syndrome Congress.

Because guardianship or conservatorship normally takes effect on your child's eighteenth birthday, and all the necessary legal arrangements will need to be completely worked out by then, you should begin considering this issue shortly afer he or she turns seventeen.

In your legal preparation, you must also decide and specify who will act as guardian(s) or conservator(s) for your child when you and your spouse cannot care for him or her due to illness or death. This is not a pleasant thing to think about but is extremely important for your child's continued well-being. If a guardian or conservator dies, or for some other reason is no longer able to fulfill the appointed duties, and no other person or organization has been legally appointed to succeed that person as guardian or conservator, then your child could become a ward of the state. This means that your child's personal and/or financial well-being become the responsibility of the state government. In certain cases, it can also mean that all your child's assets may be taken over by the state.

The selection of a guardian or conservator should be made wtih great care and concern. First of all, you need someone who is both willing and able to shoulder what could be a very large responsibility. This means you need to discuss the matter carefully with whomever you wish to name as successor. It must be a person(s) or organization that you trust, and that will always put your child's best interests first.

Most parents ask one of their other children to assume this responsibility. However, do not try to force or coerce a child—or anyone else— into doing this. Only someone who cares enough about your Down's syndrome child to voluntarily take on this role should be trusted with it. Indeed, only someone who voluntarily accepts such a role will continue to keep your child's best interests in mind at all times.

You will also want to explain to your successor how to appoint his or her *own* successor. Once guardianship or conservatorship passes into the hands of an individual or couple, a new successor should be found and appointed as soon as possible. In this uncertain world, death or debilitating illness can come at any time, and unless this eventuality is prepared for, your child could find no one but the state to turn to for protection and support.

Most parents who appoint a person or couple as their successor choose people who are younger than they are for the simple reason that these people are likely to be around after the parents die. For example, if you are forty years old now and appoint someone who is forty-six to succeed you as guardian of your Down's syndrome child, chances are that your "successor" will die before you do. If you do appoint a successor who is not significantly younger than you are, then I strongly suggest that you also select a *second* successor, one who will take over once both you and your first successor no longer can. This second successor should be considerably younger than you are, and his or her right (and responsibility) of succession should be included in all legal documents concerning conservatorship or guardianship of your child.

If your child lives or will be living in a foster home, group home, or some other type of residential facility, you may still retain guardianship or conservatorship. If you prefer, however, you can have that responsibility assigned to someone else. Generally, how or where your child lives does not affect your (or anyone else's) rights or responsibilities as conservator or guardian. But it is a good idea to appoint someone who lives relatively near to your child because it is more convenient when fulfilling guardianship or conservatorship responsibilities.

As your child approaches the age of eighteen, it is a good idea to discuss with a qualified attorney these different matters: your child's legal rights as an adult; the setting up of guardianships or conservatorships; your own obligations as guardian or conservator; your and your spouse's wills; your child's legal right of inheritance; and the establishment of a trust for your child.

CHAPTER 10

Into Adulthood

Your child's transition from adolescent to adult doesn't happen overnight. Yet it may seem that way to you simply because you have been so busy dealing with everyday concerns. The day your child graduates from high school is the day you'll realize that all those years of struggling and all the effort you spent on behalf of your child were worthwhile. All the concepts your child has learned and all the skills he or she has acquired will continue to serve well into adulthood.

Now that your son or daughter has graduated or is approaching graduation, you must give serious consideration to his or her future as an adult.

MOVING AWAY FROM HOME

Not so very long ago, the options available to parents who needed an alternative to family care for their retarded children were extremely limited. Many large, state-run institutions existed, and only a few small, privately operated programs were available. Community-based programs were practically nonexistent. And whatever option parents chose, it was considered to be a permanent solution for the needs of their disabled child. There were very few opportunities for change, adjustment, or mobility among programs. And in almost all cases, only the most basic needs of the residents—food, clothing, and shelter—were met.

Since the late sixties, parents have insisted that their mentally retarded sons and daughters should have the right to the same living opportunities as nonhandicapped children do. This insistence led to a number of important changes. First, many of the large institutions were closed; at others, the number of residents was sharply reduced. Second, many people were moved back into the communities from which they came. Third, smaller living programs called group homes were developed within communities.

Since then, still other programs and arrangements have evolved. New ones continue to spring up all over the country. Each of the programs currently available will be discussed later in this chapter.

Dealing with the idea of your son or daughter moving away from home can be difficult. This difficulty can be eased, however, if you consider the move as part of your plan to protect his or her future and to ensure that all needs are met when you and your spouse no longer can do this.

At first you'll probably want to discuss the plan in private with your spouse. This helps you to get comfortable with the idea of your son or daughter moving away from home. As soon as you have accepted this idea, other members of your family, including your Down's syndrome child, should take part in the discussion.

There are several reasons for such discussions. First, this move is a family affair. Each of you will be affected in one way or another, and these discussions should give everyone a chance to express his or her feelings and adjust to the idea. Second, you need to discuss the benefits of moving away from home for your Down's syndrome child. Third, moving away from home should be a natural event in the life of your Down's syndrome child, just as it is for any grown-up son or daughter. And the more naturally you treat the move, the easier it will be for everyone to accept.

This natural, accepting approach to your child's move away from home will help any resistance he or she may have toward the move. If your child shows resistance to the idea, the best course of action is to discontinue any reference or discussion about it for a short time and reintroduce the subject again. You may have to repeat this several times before your son or daughter is comfortable with the thought of moving away from home.

There are some issues, both pro and con, that you the parents must consider when you decide whether or not your son or daughter should move away from home.

These are the issues that favor such a move:

• Since neither of you is blessed with immortality, you certainly should consider your ages. How much longer can you care for your child?

• If there are younger children at home, how much time can you devote to their needs while still tending to the needs of your adult Down's syndrome son or daughter?

• You, your spouse, and other family members must learn to accept the fact that you are not the only ones who can care for your child.

• Has the care of your child placed significant stress on you and other family members? If so, it can be relieved by this move.

• The separation that results from your child leaving home is an important part of his or her development as an adult.

These issues may not favor your child leaving home:

• Does the distance from your home to the facility prohibit frequent visits between you and your child?

• In case of an emergency, is there someone available to care for your son or daughter?

• If the care of your child is not producing any stress on you and your family, and you and your spouse are young enough and healthy enough to provide the care needed, then you can probably afford to put off making a decision about your child living away from home.

The amount of freedom you give your child to help decide whether or not to move away from home will certainly depend on his or her level of intellectual functioning. It is not likely that your child could make such a decision alone, but you should provide every opportunity for the expression of his or her feelings about the idea. This can be done through the family discussions you should have before a final decision is made.

When you take your child for preliminary visits to the facilities in your area, observe his or her interactions with the staff and other residents. Does it happen easily and readily or is your child reluctant and resistant? These interactions are another way for your child to express feelings about moving away from home. They are also clues to help you determine whether or not your son or daughter can adjust to other people as potential housemates and supervisors, and be happy living with them.

Ultimately, of course, the decision to have your child move away from home should be one that is mutually agreed upon by *all* the members in your family. And helping your child choose the best living program is very important. So is deciding exactly *when* your child should move away from home. Here are some clues to help you decide what time is right:

• The separation should be made while your son or daughter is young enough to make a good adjustment. The older the child, the more difficult and painful his or her adjustment will be. This is particularly true if your son or daughter is thirty or older.

• The separation should be planned and prepared for well in advance. Both you and your child should know exactly when it will occur —and, barring any emergency, the separation should take place on schedule. This will make the separation easier for everyone, particularly for your child.

• A planned and deliberate break is always better, and always goes more smoothly, than one that is the result of a crisis or a sudden decision.

Choosing the right out-of-home living situation for your child will depend on his or her needs and skills, and on what is available in your community. If several options exist for you to choose from, be sure to visit and inspect *all* of them before making a decision. Visiting some or all of them more than once is a good idea. Appendix IV will provide information to help you to make your choice wisely.

The following section describes the most common alternative living arrangements. To find out which ones are available in your area, call your local or state departments of health and human services, your state department of mental retardation, or a social service agency such as the Down Syndrome Congress, The Association for Retarded Citizens, or the United Way.

GROUP HOMES

As the name suggests, group homes usually accommodate fifteen to thirty people and are licensed and operated according to state regulations that determine the number of people to be served and their types of disability and age levels. For example, a group home may be licensed to serve only multihandicapped adults aged eighteen and over.

Group homes provide health and rehabilitative services for each resident according to an individual living plan which is agreed upon in writing by parents and group home staff. To the degree possible, these needs must be met through programs provided within the larger community, rather than just within the group home.

These facilities consist of shared sleeping quarters (two residents per bedroom) and communal dining and recreation areas. Staff are on duty twenty-four hours a day on a rotating basis. They assume total responsibility for meeting all the needs of the residents, from dispersing medications to helping them fulfill religious obligations. In fact, group home staff become, in a sense, surrogate parents.

The advantage of these group homes is that your son or daughter has the opportunity to interact not only with staff and residents, but with the community at large. Although these facilities attempt to achieve a homelike atmosphere, the fairly large number of residents can be a disadvantage.

A recent trend in group home development limits the number of residents to a minimum of six and a maximum of fifteen.

RESIDENCES

Of the various living options, residences serve the largest numbers of people, usually fifty or more. Residents in any one facility can (and often do) range from very young children to senior citizens.

Whatever the resident needs are—education, recreation, self-help, personal improvement, and so on—they are met within the confines of the facility, which is made up of several buildings clustered together in a campus-style arrangement. Residents are housed in these buildings according to age, sex, and social ability. Each building contains classrooms, activity rooms, meeting rooms for staff and parents, and sleeping, dining, and kitchen areas. Each building is self-contained and may house as many as thirty-six people. The needs of each resident are provided for in accordance with his or her individual living plan.

These residences draw much criticism from proponents of the mainstream concept because of their size, and because the people served are isolated from mainstream society. These facilities do, however, offer an alternative for the retarded person whose needs cannot be met within the community.

SEMI-INDEPENDENT LIVING SERVICES

These programs, semi-independent living services (SILS), are an intermediate option that prepare adult (age eighteen or older) mentally retarded people for living independently. In these programs, two to four people share an apartment, duplex, or a house. They are supervised by staff from an agency licensed specifically to provide SILS programs. Services provided are based on individual needs. These services could include learning to cook, to shop, to use public transportation, or to improve personal hygiene and physical appearance. Whatever the resident needs to help to function independently in the community is provided in his or her independent living plan. Residents are responsible for paying rent and utilities, buying food, preparing their own meals, and maintaining their own households. This means they must each have a source of income—a job, financial assistance from relatives or government, or income from an investment, trust, or bank account. The amount of staff supervision is significantly smaller than that in group homes or residences and normally is provided only during evening hours and on weekends. However, staff is available in between these times if the residents need or request extra help.

In most cases, residents who demonstrate that they no longer need round-the-clock supervision will advance to the more independent living style offered by SILS. It is possible for some people to move from their family homes directly into a SILS facility.

The advantages of SILS programs are that the support system provided by staff helps the residents make good decisions, and the residents assume total responsibility for themselves and their daily lives.

SILS programs are a fairly new development for Down's syndrome and other mentally handicapped adults. Because these programs come closer to the concept of mainstreaming and normalization than do group homes or residences, they are in great demand. Unfortunately, the demand exceeds the supply in most communities.

FOSTER CARE

If your daughter or son can't benefit from any of the living arrangements I have just described, you may want to consider foster care. This provides the benefit of a family setting, which is an advantage over group homes and residences. Many parents, however, tell me they are reluctant to choose a foster care program for their children because they believe it would be a negative reflection on their parenting skills. This concern is entirely unfounded. Do not let this fear sway you. If foster care appears to be a good option for your child, don't hesitate to make use of it.

LIVING INDEPENDENTLY

Whether or not your son or daughter is capable of assuming total responsibility for all of his or her needs is a decision only you, your spouse, and your adult child can make. Ideally, this decision should be made by the three of you together.

When you are deciding whether your son or daughter can live on his or her own, here are some questions you need to consider. Can your son or daughter

- prepare well-balanced meals in an adequate manner?
- buy groceries, clothes, and other necessities?
- pay bills and cash checks?
- do laundry and other housekeeping chores adequately?
- get to and from work without difficulty?
- participate in appropriate recreational opportunities and get out and about? (Even if your child can take care of all the basic needs, living independently is not an acceptable option if your child simply sits at home each night and every weekend.)

For most adults with Down's syndrome, living independently of any supervision or program still means sharing living quarters with one or more other retarded (or nonhandicapped) adults.

This is almost always preferable to living completely alone—it is less stressful and less expensive, for starters. Furthermore, sharing a home gives your child regular opportunities to interact with housemates and the chance to share household chores and responsibilities. Living completely alone is a far more difficult task, and it is not generally recommended.

UNDERSTANDING THE REGULATIONS FOR LIVING PROGRAMS

Some of the laws regulating the various living programs vary from state to state. However, there are some regulations that are common to *all* such programs regardless of where they are located.

COSTS

The daily costs (or per diem rates) of each program are regulated by state government. Foster care is the least expensive. Per diem rates are usually based on the kind and amount of care that must be provided in a particular program. For example, it costs more to provide twenty-four-hour-a-day skilled nursing care for a medically fragile person than it does for someone who is less handicapped.

Because of your child's disability, he or she may be eligible for federal and/or state financial assistance such as Social Security or Medicaid. Often one of these assistance programs, or two or more programs in combination, will pay for most or all of the per diem costs. See Chapter 11 for detailed information on securing financial assistance for your child.

To find out what the costs are for each type of program in your state, call your state or county department of health and social services. (In some states this agency may be called the Department of Mental Retardation Services or the Department of Human Services.)

ADMISSIONS POLICIES

Admission to any program is based on most or all of the following factors: your child's age, the degree of disability, the appropriateness of the program in meeting your child's needs, and the space available in the program. All of these factors are stated in the operational license issued to the facility. For instance, a person or organization that operates a group home may apply for a license to serve only adults age eighteen and over who are mildly retarded and who have no other complications or disabilities.

The program you choose for your child may have no current openings, and you may have to put your child on a waiting list. Depending on the program, the wait may be only a few weeks, or it could be a year or more. If there isn't room for your child in the program that is best for him or her, find out exactly how long the wait is likely to be. You may want to consider other living options for your child, at least temporarily.

In areas where the demand for certain programs far exceeds the available resources and facilities, some parents apply for their child's admission to two or more programs. If you find yourself in this situation, and your son or daughter finally gets admitted to a program that is your second or third choice, you will need to consider carefully whether to keep your child at home and wait until a better choice presents itself to enroll your child in that program indefinitely, or to enroll your child temporarily until a place opens up in a program better suited to his or her needs.

HOUSE RULES FOR RESIDENTS

Each facility has house rules that residents are expected to follow. These include specific times for rising and going to bed; rules regarding leaving the premises; prohibitions against borrowing the personal possessions of other residents without their permission; requirements for doing personal laundry and helping with meal preparation; and rules for keeping sleeping areas clean.

These house rules apply to all residents, and conforming to them may be difficult for your son or daughter at first because a subtle double standard may have existed in your home. For instance, you may have accepted some inappropriate behavior from your Down's syndrome child, but not from his or her siblings.

Be sure to inquire what the house rules are regarding visiting rights for you, other relatives, and your child's friends. Also ask about your child's right to come home for regular visits.

INDIVIDUAL LIVING PLANS

State regulations specify that each resident in a living facility must have a written individual living plan that will help the resident acquire new skills or maintain the skills he or she has already achieved.

Before your child begins living at the facility, you, your child, and facility staff will together draw up such an individual living plan. And in making up this plan, it will be helpful if you make a list of your child's likes, dislikes, habits, skills, abilities, and limitations. Write or type this list out, and give it to staff members at the facility to which your child will move. Typically, an individual living plan will include services such as education, social skills, self-improvement skills, vocational training and support, health care, recreation, religious activities (if desired), behavior control, self-care skills, and so on. Such a plan is normally drawn up before your child enters any living program, including SILS programs and foster homes.

CHANGING PROGRAMS

Once your son or daughter has moved into a residential facility you should make every effort to keep in close contact with your child and with the staff. There are good reasons for this. You can determine how well your son or daughter is adjusting to the new living arrangements and whether or not his or her needs are being met. Keeping in close contact with your child also is an assurance that you have not abandoned him or her, that your love is as strong as ever, and that you are deeply concerned about his or her well-being.

Even though you keep in close touch with your son or daughter, you may not be able to really determine if he or she is really getting along in the new environment. This is a good reason to maintain close contact with the facility staff as well. You should have no qualms whatever about checking with the staff on a regular basis about your child. Raise the questions that you may have about his or her adjustment such as eating properly, getting enough sleep, and participating in activities.

Remember though, that while you should feel free to communicate regularly with the staff, don't overdo it. They just might interpret the constant communication as a sign of mistrust on your part. Another reason for not overdoing the communication is that it probably interferes with the staff's responsibilities of carrying out the daily program for your child and the other residents.

In most cases, group homes, foster homes, and other living facilities admit new residents on a trial basis to determine whether or not they can adjust to their new environment and whether or not their needs can be met. This trial period will vary among facilities, but generally lasts for one or two months. At the end of the trial period, a staff evaluation is completed on the overall performance of the new resident to determine whether the placement should continue. As parents, you have the right to participate in this evaluation or, at the very least, have the staff explain to you the methods they used to do the evaluation. This helps you to understand whether or not the process was a fair one.

When the results of the evaluation are gathered, you, your spouse, your son or daughter, and the staff should discuss them to decide if your child should continue living at the facility. If the decision is no, then the staff should be prepared to help you find another program. If they can't assist you, they should refer you to a source that can, such as the local health and human service agency, welfare department, or another social service agency.

If the results of your child's evaluation indicate that he or she should become a permanent resident, you should know that there must be at least a yearly performance evaluation for as long as he or she resides at the facility. These annual evaluations are done to determine how well your child's needs are being met, whether he or she should continue with the program, or if he or she has gained enough skills to move into a program that provides more independent living opportunities. Whatever decision is made at these annual evaluations (sometimes called reviews), it must be mutually agreed upon by you, your spouse, your child, and the staff.

You don't have to wait for these annual evaluations, however, to request a change in your child's program. There may be reasons such as acquiring independent living skills faster than expected, or not adjusting to the new environment as anticipated, that warrant a change. In such cases, you should ask for an evaluation, and if the *results confirm that a change is needed,* then it should be made. Be sure you prepare your son or daughter for this change.

Although the end result of a group home or other type of living program is to prepare the resident to move into a more independent situation, it's a good idea to make that move only when the evaluation indicates that such a move will benefit your child. Changing programs for the sake of change or based on a whimsical excuse is not a good idea because uprooting your child could cause him or her psychological harm.

THE STRESS OF LIVING AWAY FROM HOME

The time when your son or daughter moves away from home can be a time of considerable stress for your entire family. *Everyone* will be affected, just because it is so hard to let go. Your child must let go of familiar surroundings and a caring family. The rest of you must let go of this beloved person whom all of you have nurtured through good times and bad over the years. Few, if any, families escape the emotional turmoil that accompanies a Down's syndrome person's moving away from home. There are some things you can do, however, to ease this stress and turmoil.

PREPARING YOUR CHILD

You can help your son or daughter become accustomed to the idea of being away from home by doing the following:

• Allow him or her to spend a weekend with grandparents or with a brother or sister who has moved away from home.

• Enroll your child in overnight, weekend, or week-long camping programs on a regular basis.

• If a brother or sister is attending college and staying in a dorm, take your child to visit and tour the dorm while you explain that someday he or she will move away from home too.

• Have your son or daughter visit the different facilities that are available in your area. Perhaps you can make arrangements for him or her to stay overnight occasionally while you and your partner enjoy an evening out. Try expanding the overnight stays to a weekend visit. After each visit, ask your child to tell you what happened, and what was and wasn't good about the stay.

• Use the above activities to help explain to your son or daughter that young people do move away from their parents' homes and into places of their own. Also explain that young adults need to be around others their age, and that it is enjoyable to live with other people one's own age. It may seem that your child doesn't understand your explanations, especially at first, but chances are that he or she does and that at some point will say or do something that will tell you he or she comprehends what you are saying.

• Set a specific day on which your child will leave home. As the day approaches, let your child know exactly how far away that day is. Then make the move on schedule.

PREPARING YOURSELVES

Moving away from home will probably be difficult for your son or daughter. It is likely to be much more difficult for you though. In fact, you and your spouse may need more preparation than does your child. You'll discover—to your amazement, perhaps—that he or she will adjust to the idea of moving away much faster than you will. So don't be surprised if, once your child understands and accepts that idea, he or she becomes impatient to make the move.

Here are some tips that can help you prepare yourselves for your child's move away from home.

• Be sure the decision is a mutual one between you and your spouse.
• Have regular family conferences about the move. Include your other children in those conferences, both those still at home *and* those who have already left.
• Talk to other parents of Down's syndrome children who have grown up and left home.
• Prepare a list of all the things you have wanted to do (both alone and with your spouse) that for one reason or other always got postponed. After your son or daughter has left, do them!
• Once you and your spouse have decided that your child will move away from home, don't change your minds. The temptation for altering plans is a strong one, and it will surface again and again, especially between the time that you apply for your child's admission to a living program and the day of the actual move.

MAKING THE MOVE

The closer you get to the day that your son or daughter moves out, the more fears and doubts you are likely to have about your decision. This is the time when you will experience the greatest temptation to reverse your decision, especially on the day you help with the packing. But don't give in to this temptation. Stick to your decision.

If your son or daughter has had a room alone, chances are he or she has collected quite an array of personal possessions. Since your child will probably share a room with another person at the facility (or share a house with one or more other people in a SILS program) you will need to make some decisions about the number and the kinds of personal possessions to be taken along.

Perhaps the most difficult moment will occur when you have helped your son or daughter move in and it is time to say goodbye. If you are like most parents, you will have more difficulty with this than your child does. If at all possible, try to hold back your tears until you are out of your child's sight. He or she may not understand the reason for them, and this in turn can upset your child.

If the move has been to a foster home, group home, or residence, it is quite likely that the facility staff will get your child involved immediately in some activity like meeting the other residents, watching television, or going for a walk. This is to help ease the difficulty of saying goodbye. Knowing that someone else can and will care for your child and that you have made the best decision you possibly can should also help ease the pain of separation.

MAINTAINING CONTACT WITH YOUR CHILD

Letting go of your son or daughter means that you have relinquished the care to someone else. It also means that you have taken one more significant step toward helping your child achieve his or her independence. You have chosen to let your child lead a life apart from your family—a life that is his or her own.

But letting go doesn't mean that you have given up your parental rights or your concern for your son or daughter. Nor does letting go mean you no longer love your child. It's because you love him or her so deeply that you can let go regardless of the pain it may cause you.

Don't be surprised if, for the first few days after your child has moved away, you find yourself experiencing overwhelming concerns or worries. It is quite likely that your child is doing fine and probably isn't so lonesome, being too busy adjusting to the new lifestyle.

To ease your concerns during those first few days, call the residence staff once for reassurance. You won't be the first parents to do this, and the staff members should understand the difficulty you are having. If your child is living in a SILS program or independently, call your child *once* during the first few days of separation to see how he or she is getting along.

Depending on the house rules regarding parental visits, you may want to visit your son or daughter within a few days after the move and the settling into the new routine.

It is extremely important for you to maintain consistent contact with your child no matter how old he or she grows. Once you are assured that your son or daughter is comfortable and happy in the new surroundings, it is important that you keep in touch either by phone or in person, and preferably both. The same is true for other members of your family—brothers, sisters, grandparents, and other relatives. After all, you are still a family—only your lifestyle, and that of your son or daughter, has changed.

You can maintain this contact in another way by having your son or daughter come home on weekends and/or holidays. Reinforce your family ties by occasionally taking your child to a movie or to some other form of entertainment he or she enjoys.

Even with this change in your son's or daughter's lifestyle, you may have difficulty recognizing or accepting the fact that your child is indeed an adult and should be treated that way. On home visits you may want to do things that you know he or she is quite capable of doing. The urge to treat your son or daughter as a child can be a strong one, but you *must* resist that urge for the simple reason that he or she is no longer a child and deserves and *needs* to be treated and respected as an adult. That is the way he or she will be treated by the staff at the facility or by roommates in a SILS program or independent living situation. If you treat your son or daughter in childlike ways and other people do the opposite, you will only cause confusion. And the more childish your approach, the more childishly he or she is likely to behave.

Your challenge now is to establish and maintain an adult relationship with your grown-up son or daughter and, without being overprotective, to provide help when it is needed. Give him or her a chance to experience the dignity and pride that comes from being as independent as possible.

SOCIAL ACTIVITIES

Now that your son or daughter is an adult, chances are he or she is more socially involved than ever before. In whatever type of facility you have chosen for that adult to live, it is the responsibility of the staff at that facility to provide social activities for all the residents. These activities must be written into your child's individual living plan developed by you and the facility staff. This plan should describe what kind of activities will be provided for your child, the reason for them, how often they'll be provided, and where they will take place. To the degree possible, these activities should be provided within various community settings, which gives your child the chance to be out in the community, just like nonhandicapped people.

One activity that I particularly recommend for inclusion in your son or daughter's individual living plan is adult education. Many public schools have community education departments that offer evening adult education classes for people with Down's syndrome or other disabilities. These classes include subjects like reading, money concepts, health, nutrition, good grooming, and music.

If your child moves into a SILS program, that staff also has the responsibility of helping residents maintain a social life. However, there is a difference between the responsibilities of SILS staff and those of group home staff. In a group home, all social activities are planned by staff and the residents are free to choose the activity in which they want to participate. In a SILS program, *residents* plan their activities with the help of staff. This encourages residents to choose activities that interest them and it helps them understand the importance of social activities as part of daily living. Planning one's social activities and participating in them are necessary and important skills that SILS residents must acquire before they move into complete independent living.

If your child is capable of living alone, he or she should have access to various social activities that are appropriate for young adults. Many communities offer such activities through community education or community recreation programs that are especially designed for people with Down's syndrome. To find out what is offered in your area, call your local public school administration office or the city government office.

Remember, though, that having access to activities is not enough. Your child, if he or she is capable of living alone, must also be capable of choosing appropriate activities and knowing how to get to and from them.

When your son or daughter is home for a visit, the social activities he or she engages in should always be age-appropriate. Dances, spectator sports, active sports such as bowling, and trips to the museum or zoo are a few examples.

MARRIAGE

Whether or not your son or daughter should marry, and who makes this decision, are matters that can be answered only after you have carefully considered several important issues:

- His or her age
- Whether or not there is a guardian or a conservator for his or her personal affairs
- The consent of that guardian or conservator

If marriage is a possibility under consideration, I strongly recommend that you consult an attorney to discuss your son's or daughter's rights, restrictions, and options.

Depending on the legality of, or restrictions to, marriage for your son or daughter in your state, the following stipulations normally apply:

- If your child is under eighteen, he or she cannot marry without the consent of the legal guardian(s). Normally, this means his or her parents.
- If your child is eighteen or older and is responsible for his or her own personal decisions, your consent is not required. "Responsible for his or her own personal decisions" means that your child is capable of making such decisions and therefore has no need for a guardian or conservator for his or her personal affairs. If your child has a conservator who supervises financial affairs, that conservator has no authority regarding child's personal affairs, and his or her consent is not required.
- If your child is eighteen or older and you have retained guardianship, he or she may not marry without your permission. If another person has assumed guardianship, your son or daughter may not marry without the permission of that person.
- If your child is eighteen or older and you have retained conservatorship of the *personal affairs,* he or she may not marry without your permission. The same is true if someone else has assumed the conservatorship of your child's personal affairs.

If your son or daughter wishes to marry, the right to do so is not the only issue. Below are some other issues you need to consider carefully. If your consent is required, then these questions will help you decide whether or not to give that consent. Even if your consent is not required, it may be helpful for you to consider these questions carefully, then discuss them with your child, giving the best advice you can.

You should, of course, discuss each of these questions with your spouse as well. If you are divorced or separated from your child's other parent, it is still a good idea to discuss these concerns. Whatever decisions you make, or whatever advice you offer to your child, they should be arrived at jointly by you and the child's other parent.

Here are some of the issues you need to consider carefully:

• Will your child and his or her spouse have a sufficient income to pay for all their needs? If they both work, they may be able to. If either or both receive social security, supplemental security, or welfare, this may be sufficient, particularly if one member of the couple works full- or part-time. If the two of them will need financial assistance from you and/or the other parents, you need to consider carefully how much you are willing and able to contribute both now and in the future. You may want to discuss this issue with the parents of your child's spouse. If you do offer financial assistance, you also need to consider who will assume that financial responsibility after your death or if you are no longer able to provide that assistance. You need to discuss this issue with your other children, other relatives, or with anyone else who may be interested in providing financial support in your absence.

• The question of where your married son or daughter and spouse will live must be considered. Since this issue is closely tied with finances, can they afford an apartment? If not, what choices do they have? Some communities provide a SILS program especially designed for mentally handicapped people who are married. In these programs, the couple reside in their own apartment, rather than sharing living quarters with other handicapped people. Your son or daughter and spouse may also qualify for subsidized housing. This means they pay only a small percent of the total rent for an apartment, and the remainder is paid by the federal government under Section 8 of the Housing and Urban Development Act. You and your partner will need to investigate the housing options that are available for your child in your state. You can contact the local offices for Community Action Program, County Health and Social Services, or the city council for information on subsidized housing.

• Does your son or daughter have the ability to handle parenthood and its accompanying responsibilities? (Not every married couple may want or plan to have children, of course, but the issue still needs to be considered carefully, and in advance.) It is important that you explain these responsibilities fully and carefully to your child. You should also explain the possibility of Down's syndrome being hereditary. (There is no known instance of a Down's syndrome man fathering a child. However, Down's syndrome women are capable of conceiving if the father has another form of retardation or no handicap at all. In such cases, chances are 50 percent that the child will have Down's syndrome.) Keep in mind that you may need to repeat your explanation a number of times. As always, answer your child's questions fully and honestly.

Your explanation should not be an effort to convince your child not to have children. A better approach would be a frank discussion of pregnancy, the birth of a child and its accompanying pain, the care that a baby needs, and the necessity of caring for a child until he or she grows up.

• Is your child socially and emotionally capable of dealing with the day-to-day decisions of married life, and with the conflicts and misunderstandings that can arise between two people?

• Is your child capable of understanding and properly using birth control? A complete explanation of birth control methods is extremely important; however, explaining birth control to your child has little value unless he or she is intellectually capable of using those methods appropriately. Of equal concern is whether your son or daughter is socially, emotionally, and physically mature enough to deal with sex. (If you are uncomfortable talking to your son or daughter about birth control and sex, or if you lack complete information on birth control, seek help from the Planned Parenthood office in your community, or from your family doctor.)

• You should also help your son or daughter understand that not everyone gets married. Many people prefer to stay single. What is important is leading a life that is rewarding and satisfying. Your child should choose whatever lifestyle will be most appropriate and rewarding. It is very likely that he or she will need a great deal of help from you to make this choice.

• All of these questions also apply to your child's future spouse whether or not his or her intellectual functioning is similar to or above that of your child's.

Because your child's life is so closely interwoven with the lives of other family members, the question of his or her marrying cannot be considered without taking into account its effect on you the parents, and your other children.

Now that your child with Down's syndrome is an adult and has begun to assume adult responsibilities, you and your spouse can find pleasure in both looking back and looking ahead—back at all your child's accomplishments and years of growth, and forward to the years ahead when you can continue to enrich your own lives while staying in touch with your grown-up child.

Chances are you built some fences along the way that were intended to help and protect your child, just as other parents have done. Chances are, too, that you would have preferred to keep those fences in place, but you were strong enough to bring them down and allow your child to become his or her own person.

The decisions you have had to make over the years, on behalf of your child, were no doubt difficult ones. And perhaps they were shadowed at times by thoughts of whether or not they were the best ones you could have made. Yet you forged ahead, making other decisions and taking other actions. Now looking back, you will realize that you have done your best.

There's a wonderful feeling of comfort and accomplishment that comes from a job well done. Let that feeling surround you now. Yes, you should even bask in it as you take time to sit back and relax. Not only do you deserve that rest—you've earned it.

CHAPTER 11

Receiving Financial Assistance

Families with a Down's syndrome child may be eligible for certain types of financial assistance from the state and federal governments. Your child with Down's syndrome may also be eligible for direct state and/or federal aid.

What follows is a list of the most common benefit programs. Some cover living expenses, others cover medical expenses. Some may cover both. Benefits may vary in some programs from state to state.

Your state or community may have other financial aid programs in addition to the ones described here. To learn exactly what is available in your area, contact your state department of welfare or your state protection and advocacy agency. It is possible to receive benefits from two or more programs simultaneously; however, some limitations do apply.

AID TO FAMILIES WITH DEPENDENT CHILDREN

Aid to Families with Dependent Children is a federally funded, state-administered program that provides income to eligible needy families with children up to eighteen years old. The age is extended to nineteen if the child is in school and finishes the school program before his or her nineteenth birthday. Families with one of the following problems may be eligible:

• Absent parent—One parent is not physically present in the home to provide support.

• Incapacitated parent—One parent has been or is expected to be disabled or ill for at least ninety days. Medical proof must be provided.

• Unemployed parents—The primary wage earner has been unemployed during the past twenty-four months.

In addition to these requirements, applicants must also meet specific income eligibility guidelines. This program normally makes payments for living expenses. In certain instances, however, payments for medical care are also available through this program.

GENERAL ASSISTANCE

General assistance is a state-funded program for single adults under the age of sixty-five, for couples without children, and for families not eligible for Aid to Families with Dependent Children. Eligibility is determined by the following categories:

1. A person unable to work because of illness, injury, age, or some other incapacity

2. Someone who must stay in the home to care for a member of a household who is ill, injured, disabled, or of preschool age

3. A person unable to find a job due to a lack of marketable skills

4. A person who lives in a licensed or certified health care facility, such as a nursing home or a group home for the mentally retarded

To receive assistance under this program, applicants must meet asset and personal property guidelines.

MEDICAID

Medicaid provides medical care to certain eligible individuals and families with low income. It is funded by state and federal government but run by the states.

The following are eligible:

• People eligible for Aid to Families with Dependent Children

- Needy people over sixty-five years old
- Needy children under twenty-one
- People between the ages of twenty-one and sixty-five who are disabled or blind (Generally speaking, as applied to mentally retarded people, the criteria of disability mean that moderately, severely, or profoundly retarded persons are likely to be found disabled, whereas in people with mild mental retardation, a finding of disability will usually depend on the presence of complicating conditions such as secondary handicaps. In most cases, Down's syndrome people are considered to be moderately retarded and therefore eligible. However, all cases are examined on their individual merits.)
- Families with children who are not receiving Aid to Families with Dependent Children but who meet the child and parental status requirements and the income and resource criteria of Medicaid (The resource criteria refer to real and personal property limitations.)
- Any pregnant woman who would be eligible for Aid to Families with Dependent Children if her child were already born and living with her

Almost everything is covered if it is medically necessary—hospital, doctors' services, dental care—but there are limits on costs. Many services must be approved before being performed or Medicaid will not pay. Medicaid will not fund abortions except in certain cases where there has been rape or incest, or to save the mother's life.

SOCIAL SECURITY

Social Security is an insurance program for people who have worked a certain amount of time and have regularly paid a part of their wages or income in Social Security taxes. It is a federal program and is administered by the Social Security Administration. Social Security benefits are *not* distributed on the basis of financial need.

Social Security benefits are generally paid to people who are retired, aged, disabled, or members of the immediate family of an adult who has died. This list, however, is not 100 percent complete. (For example, if you are the mother of a child, and the father of that child dies, you may be eligible to receive benefits even if you were never married to your child's father.) Check with your Social Security office to see if you and/ or your child qualify for benefits.

Developmentally disabled people, including Down's syndrome people, usually receive Social Security on the basis of their disability, provided that they meet certain eligibility requirements.

Generally, any person over the age of eighteen is eligible for Social Security disability benefits if (1) he or she is unable to engage in substantial gainful activity, and (2) his or her disability is expected to last for at least one year.

The evaluation of the individual's ability to engage in gainful work will be based on medical evidence from a licensed physician. You or your child must submit (1) a physician's report describing the existence of the disability throughout the time in question, (2) copies of medical records of time spent in a hospital or other institution, and (3) any other significant medical evidence.

Monthly disability benefits can be paid to (1) disabled workers under sixty-five and their families; (2) people disabled before age twenty-two who continue to be disabled and who are the dependents of eligible, insured workers; and (3) disabled widows, disabled widowers, or disabled divorced wives over fifty whose spouses were insured at the time of death.

SUPPLEMENTAL SECURITY INCOME

Supplemental Security Income is a rather new avenue of financial help for mentally retarded people. It is a federal program that makes monthly cash payments to disabled people who don't own much in the way of property or other assets, and who have no or limited incomes.

It makes no difference how young a person is; children (including infants) as well as adults can receive Supplemental Security payments as disabled people.

Income payments will vary based on what other income and assets the recipient has. The amount of aid varies from state to state. It is possible to receive both Social Security and Supplemental Security payments simultaneously or either one alone.

People can have some income and/or assets and still get Supplemental Security payments. People who work while they are getting Supplemental Security income payments can earn as much as sixty-five dollars a month without reducing their aid. The payment is reduced one dollar for each two dollars in earnings over sixty-five dollars.

In determining the eligibility of a child under the age of eighteen (or under twenty-two if the child is in school), part of the parents' income and assets are considered to be the child's. Allowances are made for work and living expenses, and for other children living in the home.

You cannot receive both Supplemental Security payments for your child and Aid to Families with Dependent Children payments. But if your child is eligible under both programs, you can choose whichever program best suits your family.

MEDICARE

Medicare is a federal health insurance program for people age sixty-five or older and for certain disabled people including those who are mentally retarded. It is managed by the Health Care Financing Administration. Your local Social Security office takes applications for Medicare and provides information about the program.

Medicare is a related benefit of the Social Security and Supplemental Security Income programs. For example, when your child has received Social Security benefits for two years, he or she becomes eligible for Medicare assistance.

Medicare has two parts—hospital insurance and medical insurance. The hospital insurance can help pay for inpatient hospital care, inpatient care in a skilled nursing facility, and home health care. Medical insurance can help pay for medically necessary doctors' services, outpatient hospital services, and a number of other medical services and supplies that are not covered by the hospital insurance part of Medicare.

Medicare does not pay the full cost of some covered services. For people with very low incomes, the Medicaid program in their state may pay the amounts Medicare does not pay and some health care expenses not covered by Medicare. To find out exactly what is covered in your state, contact your local Social Security office.

Medicare payments are handled by private insurance organizations under contract with the government. Organizations handling claims from hospitals, skilled nursing facilities, and home health agencies are called intermediaries. Organizations handling claims from doctors and other suppliers of services covered under the medical insurance part of Medicare are called carriers.

Your Social Security office can answer any questions you may have about Medicare, how to get it, situations that can end your Medicare payments, and what is and isn't covered.

You also have the right to appeal if you disagree with a decision on the amount Medicare will pay on a claim or whether services you received are covered by Medicare. For more information on the right of appeal and how to request this appeal, call any Social Security office or the Medicare intermediary or carrier that made the decision. There is also a handbook entitled *Your Medicare Handbook* that is available from the United States Department of Health, Education and Welfare, Social Security Administration, DHEW Publication No. (SSA) 74–100, Baltimore, Md. 21235. Single copies are free.

HOW YOUR CHILD'S DISABILITY WILL BE EVALUATED

The term "disabled" does not, unfortunately, mean the same thing in all financial assistance programs. Some programs use the same definition as others, some use different ones. This means that your child might be considered disabled by one program and nondisabled by another.

The manner in which your child's abilities are evaluated to determine whether or not he or she is disabled may also vary from program to program. Social Security, for example, normally works with a state agency, usually the vocational rehabilitation agency, to decide whether or not your child counts as disabled. This state agency, in turn, evaluates reports from psychologists, psychiatrists, and/or other professionals. You may also submit additional evidence. If an additional test is required, the Social Security Administration will pay for it.

Other agencies may accept Social Security's determination of whether or not your child is officially disabled—or they may set criteria or make a determination of their own. Again, this means that your child could be considered disabled by one program and not disabled by another.

In addition, each program has its own set of guidelines as to which disabled people qualify for benefits and under what circumstances they qualify.

All of this is confusing, and sometimes it can be exasperating. But it is the reality of seeking financial assistance.

TO RECEIVE BENEFITS OR INFORMATION

To apply for benefits for yourself and/or your child, to find out more about a particular assistance program, or to find out if you and/or your child are eligible for a particular program, contact these offices.

Social Security and/or Supplemental Security. Contact any Social Security office. Look in your phone book under "United States Government Offices," under the sublisting "Social Security Administration." (Note: Social Security and Supplemental Security payments will not be made until at least six months after an application has been filed.)

You will be required to bring when you apply: written records of you and your child's social security numbers, if available; you and your child's birth certificates (or the oldest proofs of age available); and medical records or other evidence of your child's disability. If medical records or reports are not available, you should provide the names and addresses of doctors, hospitals, and clinics that have provided treatment for your child, and if appropriate, the names and addresses of social workers, school principals, and/or institution superintendents.

All other forms of assistance. Contact your local welfare or public assistance office. By law, staff members in either office must give you eligibility information for each program, explain how to apply, and tell you of your right to apply and your right to appeal if your application is denied.

You will be required to bring *proof* of your total current family income; birth certificates of all family members; social security numbers of all family members; records showing all the real and personal property of family members; copies of all insurance policies held by members of your family; your address; a statement from your child's doctor explaining his or her disability; and any employment and financial records for all members of your family.

If birth certificates are not available, you can submit a religious record of births or baptisms recorded before the age of five. Other records might be acceptable. If you're not sure just what is best, call any Social Security office. The people there can tell you what kind of documents are acceptable.

CHAPTER 12

Legal Rights of Down's Syndrome Children and Adults

Theoretically, any person with Down's syndrome has the same civil rights as any nonhandicapped person does, unless he or she is under the guardianship or conservatorship of a person, couple, organization, or institution. In practice, however, this is not always the case.

In practice, many states have enacted statutes that specifically and categorically limit and/or deny all mentally retarded people the right to vote, the right to marry, and/or the right to enter into contracts. In some states retarded people have even been legally denied the right to an education, to due process, to employment, and to humane treatment.

Fortunately, much of this has changed, beginning in the early 1970s. As a result of class action suits and the enactment of federal legislation, all disabled people, including those who are mentally retarded, are beginning to gain the rights and privileges that all other citizens are granted by the United States Constitution. Full equality has not yet been reached—for example, zoning laws prohibit or restrict the establishment of group homes in many communities in the United States—but each year our country inches closer to equality for people who are mentally retarded.

Two landmark laws passed in the mid-seventies have greatly enlarged the opportunities of all handicapped people. PL 94–142, the Education for All Handicapped Children Act, is discussed in detail in Chapter 5. This law provides for and requires free public education for all handicapped individuals through the age of twenty-one.

Section 504 of the Rehabilitation Act of 1973 will also play a very important part in your child's life. This law, considered to be the Civil Rights Act for handicapped people, was implemented in 1977. It states that no person shall, solely by reason of his or her handicap, be excluded from the participation in, be denied the benefits of, or be subjected to discrimination under any program or activity receiving federal financial assistance.

Section 504 addresses the areas of education, employment, social services, transportation, and housing. The provisions of Section 504 relating to education are similar to those contained in PL 94–142. Other provisions included under Section 504 are:

EMPLOYMENT

1. No qualified handicapped person shall be subjected to discrimination on the basis of his or her handicap.

2. Discrimination is prohibited in

   a. recruitment, advertising, and the processing of applications;

   b. hiring, alterations in job status, and rehiring;

   c. job assignments and classifications, lines of progression and seniority;

   d. rates of pay and other forms of compensation;

   e. leaves of absence, sick leave, fringe benefits;

   f. selection and financial support for training, conferences, and other job-related activities;

   g. employer-sponsored activities, including social or recreational programs.

3. Employers must make reasonable accommodation to the known physical or mental limitations of an otherwise qualified handicapped applicant or employee. This may include

   a. modification of work schedules or job restructuring;

   b. physical modifications or office relocation so that facilities are accessible to and usable by handicapped persons;

   c. the provision of readers or interpreters.

HEALTH, WELFARE, AND OTHER SOCIAL SERVICES

1. Providers of health, welfare, and other social services may not deny a qualified disabled person benefits or services, or limit his or her participation in programs available to the public.

2. Services must be equal to those provided to the nonhandicapped.

3. Hospitals and other facilities employing fifteen or more people must provide appropriate auxiliary aids to people with impaired sight, hearing, mobility, or speaking skills. Such aids may include brailled and taped materials, or interpreters.

4. Programs must be accessible to the handicapped.

TRANSPORTATION

1. Railway, bus, and airline stations must be designed with efficient and convenient routes for handicapped people to major areas such as ticket counters, baggage areas, and boarding areas.

2. Carriers cannot deny transportation to handicapped individuals and must provide certain services to assure accessibility, such as storing wheelchairs or delivering of food when dining is inaccessible.

3. All parking areas must have designated parking for the handicapped only, which should be as convenient to major service areas as possible.

HOUSING

1. Government-funded housing shall be available in sufficient quantities and variety to provide eligible handicapped people with a choice of living arrangements comparable to that of eligible nonhandicapped people.

2. Sites for housing development should be chosen so that they do not exclude the handicapped.

These regulations and laws apply to all recipients of federal financial assistance. Examples of these recipients include

• all public and most private elementary schools, secondary schools, colleges, and universities.

• all public and most private hospitals.

• all social welfare agencies.

• many state agencies, departments, and programs.

• federally subsidized public transportation systems.

• federally subsidized housing projects.

Human rights commissions at local and state levels are encouraging private and independent businesses and organizations to adopt similar measures to ensure equal opportunities for all handicapped persons.

PROTECTION AND ADVOCACY SERVICES

As a direct result of class action suits, and of federal laws that grant certain rights to disabled people, many states now provide protection and advocacy services to ensure that those rights are protected.

Advocacy is the representation of the interests of one person or a group of people. An advocate can provide assistance to your child when his or her rights are threatened or denied.

An advocate can be any one of the following:

• Case manager. This person, trained in advocacy techniques, is the primary advocate for someone (your child, for example) within a service system such as education. A case manager has the responsibility of securing appropriate services for your child such as job training. A case manager is an employee of the service system he or she represents, and is required to monitor your child's programs to determine if all the needs are being met.

• Guardians and conservators. These people are advocates in the sense that their major responsibility is to protect the rights and interests of the ward for whom they are responsible. While advocacy training is not necessarily a requirement for guardians and conservators, it is a helpful technique for them to acquire. At the very least, they should be aware of advocacy resources if a situation occurs that requires the advocacy process on behalf of their ward.

• Ombudsperson. This is a public official whose job it is to serve and protect the rights of a particular group of people, for example, all mentally retarded people or all hearing-impaired people. An ombudsperson usually serves as an advocate within a state, city, or county government. However, he or she can also be someone serving a particular group within an agency or organization, for example, within a group home or sheltered workshop. An ombudsperson is normally considered a link between the larger organization and the people he or she represents, with the job of communicating with both sides and acting as a go-between.

• Groups or associations. The Down Syndrome Congress and The Association for Retarded Citizens are examples.

• Legal advocate. This is any person with a legal background (attorneys and paralegals) who provides civil legal representation to people with developmental disabilities. This may be someone who specializes in advocacy for the handicapped or it may be your own lawyer.

• Parents. Many organizations like The Association for Retarded Citizens provide advocacy training for parents of children who are mentally retarded. This is an effort to help parents acquire the skills they need to advocate on behalf of their children.

Advocates should meet the following basic requirements: a thorough knowledge of the rights of people with disabilities, the ability to analyze a situation to determine if someone's rights are being denied or abused, and adequate knowledge of the advocacy resources that are available to help resolve problems that are beyond the capabilities of the advocate. The advocate who does not have a legal background should also have significant training in both the basic principles of paralegal advocacy and the legal rights of people who are disabled.

Here's an example of how a paralegal advocate would represent the interests of a mentally retarded person.

SITUATION Assume that your son's individual education plan includes (in writing) a school-to-work transition program that was to have started on his eighteenth birthday. It is now six months past that date and the program has not begun. You are getting concerned. Assume also that you have had paralegal advocacy training and want to advocate on your son's behalf.

SOLUTION Step 1. You should first contact both your son's classroom teacher and vocational counselor, if he has these. This can be done in writing or by phone. If you write, be sure to keep a copy for your records—keeping accurate records is extremely important in all advocacy cases. Whatever contact method you use, identify yourself, express your concern about your son's program, and request a meeting to discuss your concerns. This meeting should be arranged at a time and place that is convenient for you.

Step 2. Be sure to take your son's individual education plan with you to the meeting to verify that he should be receiving a school-to-work transition program. When everyone is assembled, explain your concern and ask when your son's program will begin. If you receive an answer such as next week, or in two weeks, ask for a precise date. If the teacher or counselor agrees to your request, insist that the date be inserted into your son's individual education plan. If his program begins on the agreed date, your case is settled. If there is a delay in the starting date, you can take further action.

Step 3. Contact in writing or by phone, the director of special education in your school district. Explain the previous meeting you had with your son's teacher and counselor, that the program didn't begin on the agreed date, and request a meeting with the special education director, yourself, and the teacher and counselor. At this meeting you'll want to ask why the program didn't start and when will it begin. If you don't receive satisfaction at this level, you have the right to ask for a due process hearing.

Step 4. The due process hearing can be conducted before the school board, an individual designated by the school board, a person mutually agreed to by the school board and yourself, or a person appointed by the department of education. The hearing officer (the person who conducts the hearing) is selected by the school board and takes testimony from you and the representative of the school. After all the testimony has been presented, the hearing officer must issue a decision in writing within five days after the hearing.

Step 5. If you object to the hearing officer's decision, you have the right to appeal that decision to the commissioner of education. However, you must do so within a specified time. In Minnesota, for example, such an appeal must be filed within fifteen days. (At this point it is a good idea to seek the help of your protection and advocacy agency to help you file this appeal.) The commissioner will review the testimony from the hearing and then make a decision which is final, subject only to an appeal to the district court of the county in which the school is located.

You have the right to seek assistance from your local protection and advocacy agency at any of the steps listed above. It's a very good idea to obtain this assistance at the due process and/or the appeal level.

The advocacy process may vary from state to state, so you should contact your protection and advocacy agency for the appropriate process.

Advocates of handicapped persons have gone to court more and more often in recent years because legislative and governmental action often give people their rights and opportunities only on paper. There will always be some people who will not receive the services to which they are entitled unless an advocate is involved. And there are times when normal advocacy fails, and a lawsuit is the only valid alternative.

A directory listing over 725 organizations, agencies, projects, and individuals that provide advocacy services to people with mental and other developmental disabilities is now available. This volume is entitled *Legal Resources for the Mentally Disabled: A Directory of Lawyers*

and Other Specialists. Single copies of this twenty-nine-page directory
are available for five dollars from the American Bar Association's Commission on the Mentally Disabled, 1800 M Street NW, Washington,
D.C. 20036.

Your local Association for Retarded Citizens or Down Syndrome
Congress chapters should also have information that will help you locate other advocates in your area.

If your child is denied a benefit or service to which he or she is
entitled under PL 94–142, Section 504, Social Security, and so on, you
have the right to complain on behalf of your child and to have your
complaint investigated and reviewed by the agency denying the service
or benefit, or your local and/or state human rights department, or you
may, in some instances, file a complaint in your federal district court,
without having to first complain to the agency or human rights office.

Because each type of benefit or service involves a slightly different
procedure for resolving complaints, it is wise to check with your attorney or a protection and advocacy agency about the best way to proceed
with your complaint.

The following examples show the differences between the process for
filing a complaint in a discrimination case and a case where benefits
have been denied.

DISCRIMINATION UNDER SECTION 504

Suppose your daughter attempts to board a local public bus and, for
some reason, the driver refuses to let her on. You have the right to file a
complaint against both the bus driver and the bus company. This complaint can be filed with your local human rights agency and/or federal
district court.

Because of stringent time requirements for filing claims with both
human rights agencies and federal district courts, it is *very* important to
seek the advice of an attorney who practices in the area of human rights
litigation. If your own attorney does not engage in such practice, perhaps he or she can refer you to someone who does. Or you can seek the
help of your local protection and advocacy agency.

To file a complaint with your local human rights department, you or
your attorney should send a letter to the supervisor of that department
explaining who was discriminated against, in what way, by whom or by
what organization, when the discrimination took place, and who can be

contacted for more information, your name, telephone number, and address. Your letter should include a clear account of exactly what happened. You should also explain why you believe the events that occurred were discriminatory.

When a complaint is filed with the human rights office, the following procedure takes place: (1) the complaint is investigated; (2) the human rights office determines if there is enough evidence to proceed to a hearing; (3) if there isn't, the complaint is dismissed; or (4) if a hearing is held, you and the defendant(s) (the bus driver and the company) appear before a hearing officer from the human rights office and present your evidence. The hearing officer then decides what to do next—either proceed or dismiss. If procedure is warranted, the hearing officer may either try to resolve the problem between the defendant(s) and you, or call for another hearing. At this hearing a decision is made by the hearing officer. If this decision does not satisfy you, you may take your complaint to a federal district court.

DENIAL OF BENEFITS

Suppose your son is denied state medical assistance. The first thing you should do is seek the help of a lawyer or person experienced in social welfare advocacy.

The following process would then occur. You and your advocate should talk to the welfare supervisor and ask for restoration of service. If the service is still denied, be sure to get this denial in writing. You ask the welfare supervisor for an appeal request which you and your advocate complete and give to the supervisor. Be sure to keep a copy for yourself. The welfare department must send you a paper that summarizes the issues of fact and law upon which the decision to deny service was based. (This letter may sound complicated to you so it is very important to have the assistance of an experienced welfare advocate help you check the state welfare regulations and determine what those regulations say about your complaint.)

You have the right to see and examine your son's entire welfare record once the appeal is filed. You should ask for photocopies of *anything* in that record that has to do with your appeal. (In some cases there may be a charge for copying.)

You and your advocate should gather as much evidence as possible to support your case—income statements, notes from your doctor—anything that strengthens your position in the appeal.

Then you must prepare an outline of your case that includes (1) the decision in dispute, (2) the facts of the case as you see them, (3) a list of the evidence you'll present to support your case, (4) any previous legal decisions that lend support to your appeal, and (5) your best arguments as to why your child should receive the service that's been denied.

Now you should be ready to go to an appeal hearing, either at the county or state level, depending on where you live.

The hearing is a less formal process than a court trial. You, your advocate or attorney, a representative from the welfare agency, and a county or state hearing officer must be present. Each side presents its case and calls witnesses to testify on its behalf. At the completion of all testimony, the hearing is closed and the hearing officer makes a decision. This decision must be mailed to you within a specified time (usually ninety days) after the date of the appeal hearing. This decision is final. If you are dissatisfied with the decision, however, you can appeal to a court.

APPENDIX I

Physical Characteristics Common to People with Down's Syndrome

No one with Down's syndrome has all of the characteristics listed below, and there appears to be a significant variation in the number of characteristics found among people with this condition.

Head
Open soft spot (beyond one and a half years of age)
Flat back of head
Face
Red cheeks
Rough and scaly cheeks
Eyes
Slanting
Vertical fold of skin on eyelids near the nose
Inflammation of the eyelids
Crossed eyes
Ears
Prominent ("sticking out")
Malformed
Small or absent lobes
Nose
Flat

Small
Flat nasal bridge
Mouth
Constantly open
Small teeth, irregularly aligned
Large, protruding tongue, often furrowed
High-arched or narrow palate
Neck
Broad and short
Chest
Funnel chest (concave)
Pigeon breast (convex)
Heart murmur
Abdomen
Muscle separation in abdominal wall
Genitalia (male)
Small penis and scrotum

Undescended testes

Feet

Hands

Gap between first and second toes

Short and broad

Groove across foot sole

Horizontal creases across palms

General

Short fingers

Diminished muscle tone

Short, curved fifth finger

Raucous voice

APPENDIX II

Organizations and Government Agencies That Can Help

The organizations and government offices listed below can provide helpful information and services. Many of these have local and/or regional branches. Feel free to contact any of these national offices to learn if there are branch offices in your area that can be of help.

Organizations whose names are followed by "Pr" are primarily for professionals. They can often be helpful to parents, however, and you should feel free to contact them.

If an organization has moved by the time this book is published, you can obtain current phone numbers and addresses by contacting Closer Look, National Information Center for the Handicapped, Box 1492, Washington, D.C. 20013; 202 833–4160.

Private Organizations

American Alliance for Health, Physical Education, Recreation & Dance (Pr)
1900 Association Drive
Reston, VA 22091
703 476–3400

American Coalition of Citizens with Disabilities
Suite 1124
1346 Connecticut Avenue NW
Washington, DC 20035
202 785–4265

American Occupational Therapy Association (Pr)
1383 Piccard Drive
Rockville, MD 20583
301 948–9626

American Physical Therapy Association (Pr)
1111 Fairfax Street

Alexandria, VA 22314
703 684–2782

Association for Children with
Learning Disabilities
4156 Library Road
Pittsburgh, PA 15234
412 341–1515

Canadian Association for the
Mentally Retarded
Kinsmen NIMR Building
York University Campus
4700 Keele Street, Downsview
Toronto, Ontario, Canada M5R2K2
416 661–9611

Canadian Rehabilitation Council for
the Disabled
1 Yonge Street, Suite 2110
Toronto, Ontario, Canada M5E1A5
416 862–0340

Council for Exceptional Children
1920 Association Drive
Reston, VA 22091
703 620–3660

Down Syndrome Congress
1640 W. Roosevelt Road
Chicago, IL 60305
312 226–0416

Federation of the Handicapped
211 West 14 Street
New York, NY 10011
212 206–4200

Foundation for Children with
Learning Disabilities
Second Floor
99 Park Avenue
New York, NY 10011
212 687–7211

National Association for Down's
Syndrome

Box 63
Oak Park, IL 60303
312 534–6060

National Association of Private
Residential Facilities for the
Mentally Retarded
6269 Leesburg Pike
Falls Church, VA 22044
703 536–3311

National Association of Private
Schools for Exceptional Children
P.O. Box 34293
West Bethesda, MD 20817
301 299–3004

National Association for Retarded
Citizens (ARC/US)
2709 Avenue E East
P.O. Box 6109
Arlington, TX 76011
817 640–0204

National Committee Arts for the
Handicapped
Suite 418
1825 Connecticut Avenue NW
Washington, DC 20009
202 332–6960

National American Riding for the
Handicapped Association, Inc.
P.O. Box 100
Ashburn, VA 22011
703 777–3540

Quebec Association for Children
with Learning Disabilities
5003 Victoria Avenue
Montreal, Quebec, Canada
H3W2NZ
514 861–5518

Sex Information & Education
Council of the U.S. (SEICUS)
Room 407

80 Fifth Avenue
New York, NY 10001
212 929–2300

Western Law Center for the
Handicapped
Suite M-22
849 South Broadway
Los Angeles, CA 90014
213 736–1030

Government Agencies
Administration on Developmental
Disabilities
Office of Human Development
Services
Department of Health and Human
Services
Room 3194
330 Independence Avenue SW
Washington, DC 20201
202 245–2890

Office of Special Education
Department of Education
Donohoe Building
400 Maryland Avenue
Washington, DC 20202
202 732–1723

President's Committee on
Employment of the Handicapped
Department of Labor
1111 Twentieth Street NW
Washington, DC 20036
202 653–5044

Special Education and
Rehabilitative Services
Clearinghouse for the Handicapped
Department of Education
Switzer Building, Room 3106
400 Maryland Avenue SW
Washington, DC 20202
202 723–1723

APPENDIX III

United Nations Declaration on the Rights of Mentally Retarded Persons

On December 20, 1971, the United Nations issued a declaration setting forth the rights of retarded persons. This declaration includes the following seven principles:

1. The mentally retarded person has, to the maximum degree of feasibility, the same rights as other human beings.

2. The mentally retarded person has a right to proper medical care and to physical therapy, and to such education, training, rehabilitation, and guidance as will enable him to develop his ability and maximum potential.

3. The mentally retarded person has a right to economic security and to a decent standard of living. He has a right to perform productive work or to engage in any other meaningful occupation to the fullest possible extent of his capabilities.

4. Whenever possible, the mentally retarded person should live with his own family or with foster parents and participate in different forms of community life. The family with which he lives should receive assistance. If care in an institution becomes necessary, it should be provided in surroundings and other circumstances as close as possible to those of normal life.

5. The mentally retarded person has a right to a qualified guardian when this is required to protect his personal well-being and interests.

6. The mentally retarded person has a right to protection from exploitation, abuse, and degrading treatment. If prosecuted for any offense, he shall have a

right to due process of law with full recognition being given to his degree of mental responsibility.

7. Whenever mentally retarded persons are unable, because of the severity of their handicap, to exercise all their rights in a meaningful way, or it should become necessary to restrict or deny some or all of these rights, the procedure used for that restriction or denial of rights must contain proper legal safeguards against every form of abuse. This procedure must be based on an evaluation of the social capability of the mentally retarded person by qualified experts and must be subject to periodic review and to the right of appeal to higher authorities.

This declaration also called for national and international action to ensure that these seven principles will be used as a common basis and frame of reference for the protection of retarded people's rights worldwide.

APPENDIX IV

Advice for Parents Who Have Decided to Place the Care of Their Down's Syndrome Children in the Hands of Others

If you have chosen to place the care of your child in the hands of others, then you have another choice to make: Whose hands will you place that care in? Obviously you want the very best and most appropriate care for your child, and you want your child to live somewhere where he or she will be happy.

Your basic options will be adoption, foster homes, group homes, and institutional care. Foster homes are run by foster parents, who provide round-the-clock care in their own homes. A foster home may have one to several children.

Institutions may house anywhere from a few dozen to several hundred children; care there is provided by a staff of trained social workers and other professionals and paraprofessionals. The quality of institutional care, generally speaking, has improved in the past two decades. However, an institution always feels and looks like an institution.

Group homes vary from the aforementioned options in that the settings can range from a single-family-type dwelling that houses six people to a semi-institution-like building that can house fifteen or more people. Care is provided by professionals and paraprofessionals rather than by live-in foster parents. See Chapter 2 for more information on each of these options.

If your child is eighteen years old or more, he or she may also have the option of a semi-independent living arrangement. This option is described in detail in Chapter 10.

Your first step in seeking alternative care is to learn of all the different programs that are available in your area. To do this, check with the following people: your hospital social worker; your local social service agency; your nearby United Way; your pediatrician or family doctor; and the nearest office of The Association for Retarded Citizens or Down Syndrome Congress.

It's a good idea to visit all the programs in your community before making a decision. In fact, you really should visit all the programs more than once in order to give each one fair and thorough consideration. Every person, home, and organization has both good and bad days. Making two or more visits ensures that you have gotten the feel of a place. It will also help you feel that you have made your final choice wisely.

One basic consideration is money. Be sure to find out which options are available and at what cost. Find out what your financial responsibility is and whether or not your state or county has some financial responsibility as well. You can call your county or state welfare department or the department of human services for more information on financial responsibility in your area.

The following checklist should help you choose an alternative living arrangement for your son or daughter. You may want to add other questions to the list, especially after you've completed your first visit.

HOME APPEARANCE

• Does the facility blend in with its surroundings, or does its outward appearance set it off as "different"?

• Is it located near community resources such as shopping centers, libraries, churches, theaters, and schools?

GENERAL ENVIRONMENT

• Are the facility and yard clean, well maintained, and free of clutter?

• Is quiet space available for residents both within the facility and outside on its grounds?

HEALTH CARE

• Are physical and medical examinations given annually?
• Does a qualified person (a nurse or a doctor) disperse medications?
• Are medical and physical records kept up to date and easily accessible to all staff?
• Are parents notified in case of accident or injury to their children?

EDUCATION

• Is an infant stimulation and/or a preschool program available to infants and preschoolers?
• How much time do the children spend in these programs?
• Is the teacher-student ratio adequate to provide each child with necessary individual attention?
• Do parents have an opportunity to help plan and observe the infant stimulation and preschool program for their children?
• Do the school-age residents attend school? Is the program off-campus? Is it integrated into the mainstream or segregated?
• Do staff and parents have joint responsibility for developing programs?

VOCATIONAL PROGRAMS

• Do adult residents have jobs?
• How are they transported to and from their jobs?
• What assistance does the staff give to residents if they lose their jobs?
• Are residents expected to help with the overall maintenance of the facility? If so, are they paid for their work?

LEISURE ACTIVITIES

• Are social and recreational activities planned by staff?
• Do residents have a choice of participating in planned activities, or is participation mandatory? Are the activities age-appropriate? Are they well supervised by staff?
• Are there community resource opportunities available, such as concerts,

sports, or community recreation programs? How are the residents transported to these activities?

DAILY LIVING SKILLS

• Does the facility provide an interpersonal relations program for all the residents? Does that program include such topics as getting along with others, sex education, dating, birth control, and marriage preparation?

• Does the individual program plan for each resident provide opportunities to acquire skills in self-care, independent living, grooming, money and household management, hobbies, using public transportation and other community resources, appropriate social behavior during daily public interactions, and preparation to move from the facility to independent living within the community?

• Is there a follow-along policy for the residents who move into the community? How often is contact made? How is the contact made—by phone, a personal visit, or both?

RESIDENTS' RIGHTS

• What is the visiting policy for parents, other relatives, and residents' friends? Are there any restrictions? Are they reasonable?

• Are residents allowed to date? Are chaperones provided?

• Are personal possessions restricted? Is there a safe place to store possessions that are of value? Is an inventory of these possessions taken and is that inventory regularly checked?

• Are pets allowed?

• What are the privacy policies regarding a resident's room, guests, mail, and personal care? For example, if a resident needs help bathing, is the assistant of the same sex?

• Are residents restricted in their movement in or out of the facility?

• Are there curfews?

• Can residents sleep in on holidays and weekends?

• Are residents encouraged to visit friends and relatives?

• Does the facility have a human rights policy for the residents? Is it enforced? How?

• Are parents encouraged to visit their children on a regular basis? To take them home on weekends and holidays?

STAFF

- Does the staff appear interested and pleasant, or indifferent to their work and responsibilities?
- Do staff members respect residents' privacy and dignity?
- Is there a congenial rapport between staff and residents?
- Does the staff communicate regularly with parents?

CLOTHING

- Are residents allowed to be as independent as possible in their selection, purchasing, and maintenance of clothing, and in their coordination of outfits?

MEALS

- Does a dietician prepare the menus? Are the meals balanced?
- How are they served—family-style or cafeteria-style?
- Are the meals supervised?
- Are religious customs given consideration?
- Are snacks available?
- Are there opportunities to eat out?

The decision to seek out-of-home placement for your son or daughter will be difficult at best. Here are some additional suggestions that may help:

- Accept the fact that change can be beneficial.
- Don't rely too heavily on relatives for assistance in making your decision.
- Don't make your decision when you are angry or during a time of crisis.
- Once you've made your decision, don't feel as though you have to defend your action.
- Do what you think is best for you and your child.
- Don't adopt the attitude that you are the only one who can provide adequate care for your child.
- Some out-of-home living arrangements are better than others, but there probably isn't an ideal one.
- Be prepared to assume the responsibility of your decision. While you are relinquishing the day-to-day care of your child to someone else, you are not relinquishing your parental responsibility to your child.

APPENDIX V

Advice for Parents Who Have Learned Through Amniocentesis That Their Unborn Baby Has Down's Syndrome

The presence of birth defects in an unborn child can be detected by amniocentesis, which is usually performed between the sixteenth and twentieth week of pregnancy. This test is becoming a routine part of prenatal care, especially for women over the age of thirty-five and for women who have had a Down's syndrome child. These women are at a particularly high risk of conceiving a child with Down's syndrome.

Amniocentesis is a simple procedure that involves inserting a needle through the mother's abdomen and into the womb to collect a sample of amniotic fluid cells that surround the fetus.

Learning that your unborn child will not be perfect is likely to produce a chain reaction of emotions starting with shock, followed by disbelief, denial, and finally pain.

Just how long this emotional turmoil will last depends on you and how you deal with those emotions. Probably the best way to do this is to search for your own feelings toward your unborn child. As you do this searching let the religious, moral, and ethical values of you and your spouse be your guide. You may also want to consider other factual information to help you sort out your feelings toward this baby.

Like all babies, your yet unborn baby will be unique. He or she will have an individual capacity for growth and development that may at times surpass other children's growth. There will also be times when his or her progress is very slow.

Not too many years ago, there was a general attitude that nothing could be done for babies with Down's syndrome that would help them develop into social, competent adults. As a result, parents were given no hope, no encouragement and most important of all, no support or helpful advice.

Fortunately this trend has changed. We now know that every child can learn —at his or her own pace, in his or her own way. We also know that learning begins the day a baby is born. (In fact, there are studies that indicate learning takes place before a baby is born.)

Your baby will begin the learning process the moment you first hold him or her. Every time you touch or comfort your little one, every time you sing or talk to your infant, you are contributing toward his or her learning and development. A great deal of research has proven this to be true, which in turn has led to the development of infant education programs. These programs are available in most communities along with an impressive array of other services, such as parent support groups, family counseling, and early childhood development programs, to name a few. All of these will help you and your spouse help your baby become all that he or she can.

While all these new trends will surely help you and your child, they have done little toward changing society's negative attitude toward Down's syndrome people. You may have a difficult time coping with this attitude, but chances are you'll find a way just as other parents have.

When you balance these facts with your religious, moral, and ethical convictions, you will find the inner strength and courage to decide whether or not you should terminate this pregnancy. This same strength will help you through another decision you must make—how to tell your other children (if there are any), your relatives, and close friends why you did or did not choose abortion. It won't be an easy task, but this book contains a great deal of information that should be of help.

APPENDIX VI

Hints for Grandparents of Down's Syndrome Children

Under ordinary circumstances, a very special bond develops between grandparents and grandchildren. Perhaps it's because of the anticipation you experience while waiting for the birth of a grandchild. Maybe it's knowing that you have another opportunity to see the unfolding of a new personality. Or perhaps it is realizing that this grandchild is a connection between your past and your future.

Regardless of its cause, this bond is a strong one. But every once in a while its strength is really tested. This can happen when your eagerly awaited grandchild is born with the condition called Down's syndrome.

"Less than perfect," "always a burden," or "difficult to raise" were probably the first descriptive words you heard. Had you heard something like "black curly hair," "fat red cheeks," or "a tiny snub nose," the shock may not have been as severe, or the range of your emotions quite as large.

You'll probably ache deep down wondering what life has in store for this tiny newcomer and his or her parents. You may even feel some antagonism toward this wizened little person because he or she has let you down, deprived you of hope and joy.

These emotions are probably unavoidable. They are also destructive unless you find some way of venting them. If you don't, you may deprive yourself and your grandchild of a beautiful, special relationship in the future. So shed those tears, rage at God, yell to the heavens, or pray a lot—then settle down to the business of grandparenting.

Here are some hints that may help.

ACCEPTING THE SITUATION

It's hard to say how long you'll want to cry, rage, yell, or pray—but don't get stuck in this mire of emotions. Sooner or later you should try to get a handle on them. And don't get discouraged if, once you think those emotions have expended themselves, they break out all over again at the most unexpected times.

Although the birth of this grandchild may be the most shattering experience you've had, you must understand that seldom is one family member at fault. You'll probably want to point the finger of blame at someone, but this can create dissension at a time when cohesiveness is really needed. And only in a few cases can Down's syndrome be traced to hereditary causes.

You should understand that the baby's parents are also going through an emotional turmoil that far surpasses what you are experiencing. Knowing this may help you to accept the situation.

It may help to talk to other people like your priest, rabbi, or minister, or to the hospital social worker. Perhaps your local social service agency, the local branch of The Association for Retarded Citizens, or one of the organizations listed in Appendix II of this book can put you in touch with other grandparents who have been where you are now. Talk or visit with these people if at all possible.

Somehow you'll have to accept what is and stop wishing for what might have been. Learning to deal with the situation and accept it can be a slow, difficult process, but remember, time does heal. Until that healing starts, how you spend that time is critical to you, to your grandchild, and to his or her parents. If you can offer the love and support so badly needed by the baby's parents, you'll find that the healing takes place much faster.

RECOGNIZING THAT YOUR GRANDCHILD IS A PERSON

The first chance you get, try looking into your grandchild's eyes. Don't look *at* them, look *into* them. Look deep and take your time. The baby may give little sign of recognizing you, but you'll see something in those eyes, something that lets you know there is a real person behind them.

When you can look beyond the Down's syndrome label and see the child, you'll have taken a very important step. You'll realize that your grandchild will develop a unique personality, have his or her own likes and dislikes, and be naughty or good just like other children. He or she will go through the same developmental phases as all children do. The only difference will be the pace of development, which may be slow during some phases, faster in others, and right on target sometimes.

Like any other baby, this child is depending not only on his or her parents, but also on you for survival. His or her well-being, now and in the future, will be influenced and shaped by your acceptance or rejection.

This child needs to enjoy and profit from your experience and your knowledge. This child needs your love and support through good times and bad. If you can meet these needs for your grandchild, you will most certainly help him or her toward a rich and rewarding life.

GET INVOLVED WITH YOUR GRANDCHILD

A good way to learn more about your grandchild, and the kind of person he or she is, is through involvement. Talk to him or her as you would any child. Learn to do the infant stimulation exercises and practice them with the baby. Sing those songs from yesteryear to your grandchild. Spin those tales from the past that only you have knowledge of. Your past is part of your grandchild, so share it. It may seem that he or she doesn't understand, but don't give up. Eventually he will do or say something that lets you know he or she is listening and understanding—and enjoying it.

As your grandchild grows up, be sure to stay involved. Be sure, too, that this involvement is appropriate for his or her age. This is important to remember because if you're like most grandparents, you may have a tendency to spoil your grandchildren. That is a prerogative of grandparents, I suppose, but in this case you may be doing more harm than good. Children with Down's syndrome have an uncanny ability to recognize when they have a good thing going for themselves, and they will take full advantage of such situations. So if your ten-year-old grandson insists on a toy or game that is more appropriate for a five year old, don't give in.

The same is true of your grandchild's behavior. If you accept inappropriate behavior, that's exactly what you will get. Whatever ground rules the child's parents establish, you should follow them *with no exceptions;* otherwise, you'll just confuse the child.

Above all, don't play favorites with your grandchildren. Don't single out your Down's syndrome grandchild for more attention. It's just not fair to any of your other grandchildren. In addition, you could (and probably will) be misleading the Down's syndrome child into believing that he or she should have more attention and treatment from everyone he or she comes in contact with.

On the other hand, the child should not receive less attention than the other children. *At first* this may not be apparent to him or her. But as your grandchild grows older, surely the neglect and hurt will be felt. He or she may even blame himself or herself for your neglect or may come to feel undeserving of your love. Remember, mentally retarded people have the same feelings as everyone else.

Your involvement with your Down's syndrome grandchild will also help his or her parents at a time when they desperately need love, support, and understanding. Your acceptance of the child will ease some of the guilt and pain that all parents of Down's syndrome children experience at first.

Here are some other ways you can help the parents of your Down's syndrome grandchild:

• You know what sacrifices new parents must make with the arrival of a new baby. You know, too, the importance of a night out for the new parents and the economic crunch that accompanies raising children. So encourage the parents to go out and make it easier for them by offering to baby-sit if possible. And look for other practical ways in which you can lend a helping hand.

• The rich experience that most grandparents have often gives them a special view toward life. This view frequently enables grandparents to see right to the core of a problem, and to solve that problem very quickly and easily—often in ways that just never occur to new parents. So offer your experience and expertise to your son or daughter and to his or her spouse. (Never *force* it on them however; this only makes things worse.) By offering your special insight, everyone will benefit—your grandchild, his or her parents, and you.

• If you want to know more about Down's syndrome and how it will affect your grandchild and his or her parents, read the rest of this book. Although it's written primarily for parents, it can also be helpful to anyone else who cares about a special child.

Index

The abbreviation DS stands for Down's syndrome.